MW01201425

The Book of

528

Prosperity Key of

LOVE

by

Dr. Leonard G. Horowitz

Tetrahedron Publishing Group

OTHER BOOKS BY DR. LEONARD G. HOROWITZ

Healing Codes for the Biological Apocalypse

Death in the Air: Globalism, Terrorism & Toxic Warfare

Healing Celebrations: Miraculous Recoveries Through Ancient Scripture, Natural Medicine & Modern Science

Emerging Viruses: AIDS & Ebola—Nature, Accident or Intentional?

DNA: Pirates of the Sacred Spiral

Walk on Water

LOVE The Real da Vinci CODE

The Book of 528: Prosperity Key of LOVE
may be the most important book in history,
following the Holy Bible and Aristotle's *Physics*
that birthed modern religions and science.

The divided worlds of science and religion shall merge
from this knowledge of "528"—
the musical-mathematical frequency of spiritual energy
fundamental to space/time.

528 unites every field, illuminating LOVE
for the enlightenment of humankind.

528, "the universal LOVE constant,"
manifests miracles from LOVE, and makes LOVE miraculous.
528 is responsible for the constant flow of LOVE
that heals and sustains people spiritually.

The heart of this clear-channel of music,
528Hz on the universal dial, broadcasts you
into existence every nano-instant.

These revelations compel civilization to build
a new foundation in celebration of LOVE that is
sourcing, unifying, and guiding all creation.

May this 528 "key of the house of David" facilitate
civilization's salvation through spiritual evolution.

Tetrahedron, LLC

Cover design: Sherri Kane and Leonard Horowitz
Cover illustration: Perfect Circle of Sound™ by Leonard Horowitz
Manufactured in the United States of America
Signature Book Printing, www.sbpbooks.com

10 9 8 7 6 5 4 3 2 1

Library of Congress Cataloging Preassigned
Horowitz, Leonard G.
  The Book of 528: Prosperity Key of LOVE
  p.   cm.
  Includes bibliographical references.
  1. Popular Works;   2. Religion
    —Health science—Music therapy   —Intelligent design—Creationism
    —Alternative medicine—Physics
    —Energy medicine—Mathematics
    —Water science—Bioenergetics
  3. Health Education   4. Spiritual Healing
  5. Judeo-Christian Theology   6. Metaphysics

Card Number: Pending
Additional cataloging data pending.

ISBN: 0-923550-78-X

Additional copies of this book are available for bulk purchases.
For more information, please contact:
Tetrahedron, LLC • 5348 Vegas Dr., Suite #353 • Las Vegas, NV 89108;
1-888-508-4787; E-mail: tetra@tetrahedron.org,
URL web site: http://www.tetrahedron.org

Contents

Foreword by Sherri Kane   XI

Preface   XVII

1   Introduction to Musical Creationism   1
2   528, John Lennon and The Church of Satan   35
3   Pi, Phi and 528 by Showell and Horowitz   49
4   Musical Cult Control Through A=440Hz Tuning   85
5   The 528LOVERevolution   123
6   Revelations, Tranformation and Enlightment   141
7   528 and Musical History   155
8   528 and Space/Time Probabilities   171
9   Divine Music and the Key of 528   195
10   Healing with 528/LOVE   229
11   528 Physics and Consciousness   255
12   528 Genetics and Biocide   267

Appendix   291
An Essay on 528: The Key of the House of David   293
Sealed by 528: Fulfillling Prophesy and Revelation   303
Apocalypse and the Ark of the Covenant   313
528 in the *INCEPTION* Movie   325
Commercializing 528   335
Synthesizer Retuning to The Perfect Circle of Sound™   337
Commentary on Showell's and Walton's Findings   349
Musicians' 528 Discussion   353
i528Tunes.com: Spreading LOVE   375
About the Author   379

Resources   381
Notes   383

The Book of 528

Figures

1 Structure of the Standing Gravitational Wave of the Universe 10
2 Musical Notes and Nodes In the In(6)" Scale of Life 11
3 Cymatics of Hebrew Sounds and Respective Letter Shapes 29
4 "Pepperland" is a Metaphor for "Babylon" 37
5 Church of Satan Leaders in Entertainment 41
6 Bending of Light Through Pyramid Crystal 56
7 Electromagnetic Spectrum of Wave Frequencies 57
8 Sacred Geometry of Energy Carrying Pigments 58
9 528Hz Hydrosonic CymaGlyph by Reid 60
10 528Hz Links to 16 Point Star from Masonic Temple 64
11 Showell's Exercise in Pyramid Geometry 67
12 Giza Pyramid Energy Collector Theory 68
13 "Mass Hysteria" During Elvis Concert, 1954 87
14 Elvis's Intelligence Agent, "The Colonial" 93
15 Early U.S. Navy Recruiting Poster 99
16 Early Military Experiments in Cymatics 105
17 Manson, the CIA, LSD and "Helter Skelter" 114
18 Sound Waves Travel in Circles 138
19 Walton's Experimental Chakra Tuning System 139
20 Water Cluster from Solar Recording 176
21 Star Decahedron Showing 360 Degrees 180
22 5th Century Synagogue Zodiac Mosaic 181
23 Destiny Card System Birthdate Relationship Chart 184
24 Destiny Card System "Life Spread" Chart 185
25 Destiny Card System "Spiritual Spread" 186
26 U.S. Defense Intelligence Agency "Hit Cards" 189
27 Rodin's Mathematical Matrix Includes Ancient Solfeggio 198
28 Famous Companies Use "69" in Logos 199
29 Haramein's "Grand Unification Theory" Double Toroid 201
30 Rodin's Mathematical Infinity Pattern 204
31 Rodin's Mathematical Infinity Pattern Structurally Like DNA 205
32 The Packed Ball Hypothesis in Biophysics 206
33 The Perfect Circle of Sound™ 208
34 Proof of Water Throughout Space 209
35 Foundations of Mathematical Harmonics 213
36 The "Pythagorean Comma Crisis" 214
37 528 is at the Heart of the Pythagorean "Crisis" 215
38 McClain's Ancient Babylonian Sexagesimal System 217
39 Algebraic Yantras in Sacred Geometry 219

40 Crystals of Protein and Viruses Grown in Space   231
41 Hexagonal Structured Water Produced by Water Resonator   233
42 Difference Between Polluted and Structured Water is LOVE/528 235
43 Electromagnetic Functions of DNA & Clustered Water   236
44 Human Fetus "Ultrasound" Image in "Breath of the Earth™" 244
45 "Breath of the Earth™"Water Clusters of Heart & Yin/Yang Symbol 246
46 "LIVE H₂O" Concert Crop Circle Formed in Wiltshire, England 248
47   Decrypting a Crop Circle Message: Phi, 528 and Math   248
48 Computer Generated Fractal Art   257
49 Cross Section of Double Helix DNA with Double Pentagram   269
50 Spiraling Galaxy Photographed by NASA   273
51 Circular Formations of DNA Helices   275
52 Phase-Locking Instruments to the Universal Matrix   285
53 Shaman Performs "Baptism" in Ecuador   298
54 Traditional Concept of the Ark of the Covenant   315
55 Vitruvian Wo/Man Decryption by Horowitz   323
56 Room 528 Musical Extraction In *INCEPTION*   327
57   Vibrating Water From *INCEPTION* Movie   329
58 INCEPTION Movie Icon: Heart of the Universe   332
59   Proof 528 Is Instrumental to the Speed of Light   372
60 Solfeggio Frequencies' Relationships Chart   373

Tables

1 Derivation of English Letter Number Code   6
2 Column Showing Multiples of Eights (8)   7
3 Victor Showell's Analysis of 741 Numerology   50
4 Victor Showell's Analysis of 528 Numerology   52
5 Analysis of of 528 & 432 As Important Co-Factors   81
6 Solfeggio Keys for the 144,000 Vocalists Fulfilling Rev. 14:1 130
7 The Ancient Solfeggio Frequencies   133
8 Stable Intervals of Set 3, 6, 9 on the Logarithmic Line   202
9 Stable Intervals of Set 3, 6, 9 in Celestial Bodies   203
10 Perfect Circle of Sound Conversions by Walton   357

Foreword

by Sherri Kane

There is "a lot of sickness, sadness, and pain in the world," I was told as a child.

Witnessing close friends and relatives addicted to pharmaceuticals for managing pain from man-made diseases is a reminder of how true those words are.

As early as I can remember, when people would ask me, what my dream was, I would say, "I wish I could help save the world...save the children...for the future."

My spiritual path has taken me to the bottom and top of the world. I have lived in squalor with the poor, and in luxury with the wealthy. This incredible journey made me see that no matter what your social success level was, or is, to be optimally prosperous, we all need LOVE.

Little did I know what the future would hold... I would partner with Dr. Leonard Horowitz, a true hero and genius, to advance a revolution...the 528LOVERevolution in health and spirituality, changing the way people live their lives, and offering new hope for saving civilization from self-destruction.

For me the first step was realizing that we all come from ONE SOURCE, and are connected to our maker by LOVE. Now we learn from Dr. Horowitz that this metaphysical Super-Power thinks most highly of the number "528"—the sound, frequency, or vibration of LOVE.

I was saddened when I awakened to the knowledge that for centuries vicious wars were created by "banksters" to engage and terminate "true patriots" or nationalists most profitably. I realized that *We The People*, in our ignorance, arrogance, apathy, and silence, accept, and even encourage, the global elite's agendas, and our own demise.

In fact, researching the New World Order agenda by reading Dr. Horowitz's books, including *Emerging Viruses: AIDS & Ebola—Nature, Accident or Intentional?*, I learned the only hope for humanity is precisely what Dr. Horowitz prescribes—528— more LOVE in the world.

From *The Book of 528: Prosperity Key of LOVE*, I learned that this solution is in music we can sing and dance to.

When I first learned about the "528" frequency, I thought, What a concept! I imagined how much more beautiful the world would be with the 528 LOVE vibration permeating the air. I envisioned people healing physically, mentally, emotionally and spiritually, by listening to this music, and helping the planet by making and broadcasting it. This, Dr. Horowitz explains in this book, can bring us "into harmony with nature and our Creator."

So I began to listen to music composed in 528Hz by pioneers like guitarist Scott Huckabay, harpist Peter Sterling, and sound healing expert Jonathan Goldman. As Dr. Horowitz predicted, their 528 performances and recordings can really give listeners a warm fuzzy feeling in their hearts.

With this new monumental experience and understanding of how powerful the 528Hz frequency is, I was convinced I needed to get involved right away in helping Dr. Horowitz get this important message to the world.

So I volunteered to help publicize "LIVE H_2O—Concert for the Living Water," in honor of the Living Water in each of us. Then I partnered with Dr. Horowitz to form Healthy World Organization (HWO)—our answer to the corrupt World Health Organization (WHO).

We began producing educational news commentaries on video, wrote articles that were published nationally and internationally, and disseminated many newsletters and articles in *Medical Veritas* journal. We also produced a docu-comedy called *PharmaWhores: The Showtime Sting of Penn & Teller*, bringing to light a most serious neglected conspiracy—the control of the mainstream media by BigPharma in partnership with the Energy Cartel given license to kill humanity by poisoning and polluting people and environments internationally.

Dr. Horowitz and I furthered HealthyWorldAffiliates.com— a cooperative program in which your affiliation provides a way for you to partner with us. Together we can save lives by spreading knowledge about natural healing using some of the best alternatives to pharmaceuticals on the planet, many of them incorporating 528.

Then Dr. Horowitz accepted Dr. Gary Goldman's invitation to become Editor-in-Chief of the peer-reviewed journal, *Medical Veritas*. This online service publishes suppressed truths in medicine, and is the first periodical heralding facts about 528 that may eventually terminate people's sickening reliance on drugs. I am now honored to serve as Vice President of Medical Veritas International, Inc. the parent organization dedicated to securing natural health freedoms and discovering and disclosing medical truths.

Next, we started a record company like no other—528Records.com. Our goal is to "save the world" by broadcasting "The LOVE Vibration" through 528 music. We encourage musicians to tune their instruments from A=440Hz to A=444Hz (that includes C = 528Hz pitch) and record in this tuning. We then publish their 528 recordings online, and the artists receive a 60% royalty on all donations made for their works. 528Records.com can also transpose recordings performed in "standard tuning" to 528Hz frequency for everyone's benefit.

From my own experience, the more we all engage a *528LOVERevolution*, the more we will desire to learn about ourselves, in relation to this beautiful, mysterious, optimal state of health and well-being called LOVE.

I have taken many spiritual journeys and paths in my life to get closer to the true meaning and experience of unconditional LOVE. Personally it meant letting go of fear and opening my heart to embrace more LOVE.

Many of my friends are doing the same, as though we are called to condition our hearts with Divine LOVE, to gain protection, and even prosper, from what is befalling humanity regarding geopolitics, the economy, and healthcare.

In this book, Dr. Horowitz concludes that the most important "key" to opening people's hearts is LOVE, referenced in the Bible as the "key of the house of David." He encourages us to consider this cosmic energy wave of 528 is naturally opening our hearts like flowers blossoming to receive the sun's light.

Standing between us and unconditional LOVE is our fearful egos. Egos have always been involved in war-making between nations and persons.

So if we want peace, we need to understand what Dr. Horowitz is evidencing here. We must realize we can't get to peace and harmony using our egos that are tuned to 741 (A=440) Hz frequency. The Power of LOVE comes from within our hearts, in 528Hz. This LOVE/528 sources from the heart of our Creator.

Dr. Horowitz emphasizes here that *faith* is key in accessing and activating this prospering technology whether you pray and chant in Christian churches, Buddhist temples, Jewish synagogues, and Muslim mosques, on mountains, in the ocean, or at home.

Alternatively, disciplines and doctrines, religious or otherwise, neglecting LOVE and faith are empty and destructive.

Jesus modeled LOVE best when he claimed that the Divine law of the universe was most righteous. The path to enlightenment and eternal salvation, he said, involved loving God and each other like brothers and sisters.

I remember being asked by a pastor, the first time I read the New Testament completely through, what I understood from it. I replied, "I got that Yeshua was all about LOVE."

He replied, "Is that the only message you got?"

I said, "Yes, what else is there?" To me, Jesus' conviction that LOVE for the Father, achieved through faith is "The Way" to commune with God most optimally and consciously.

Here is Dr. Horowitz's labor of LOVE. Herein, I learned that LOVE, as a frequency of pure spiritual energy, resonates in God's heart, the heart of The Law of the universe, and the heart of nature.

LOVE/528 can turn a grinch into an angel, an ill person into a healthy one, and ultimately create lasting peace on earth.

In this "mission possible," Dr. Horowitz's practical solution of using Water to deliver LOVE/528 as a virtual baptism for global salvation, is fascinating. Take note of the connection between Water, its structure, and the 528Hz frequency of LOVE.

This book is based on more than a decade of tireless self-analysis in search of LOVE in his own heart. It is a compilation of research by a world class humanitarian, christened a "World Leading Intellectual" by peers in the World Organization for Natural Medicine. The blessings of revelation, knowledge, wisdom, and most importantly LOVE, that Dr. Horowitz brings in this monumental book, are the keys to prosperity that can set everyone free most completely and enduringly.

Sherri Kane,
Vice President,
Medical Veritas International, Inc.

Preface

LOVE has influenced the arts and people's lives more than any other emotion or motivation, yet its spiritual dynamics have been grossly neglected by modern scientists and religious scholars for millennia.

Aristotle wrote of "virtuous LOVE" in *Physics*—the book that launched scientific inquiry in the 3rd Century, B.C. The first letters of this title derived from *philia* (φιλία), Greek for LOVE. It used the symbol for Phi—"φ"—a mathematical constant characterizing nature and God as LOVE.

Lovingly, Aristotle promoted a theology of LOVE and foregiveness advanced by Jesus three hundred years later. He referred to humanity—the masses of ignorant people—as "forgivable anthropomorphism of the adolescent mind."

Aristotle's respect for God and LOVE, and affection for nature, math, and Phi, was shared by Plato, Vitruvius, da Vinci, and subsequent Pythagorean mystery school disciples. φ was known to all as a mathematical constant reflecting Divine design, expressing the Creator's LOVE. It was used routinely in physics and the arts to create ratios and proportions in music and architecture consistent with observations of nature.

During the past two thousand years, Phi's relationship to LOVE became trivial, even censored in modern times, in a world that celebrates science, music, and artistry, but neglects their foundation in simple vibrations; especially a *528Hz frequency* of resonance upon which Pi, Phi, and the Golden mean constants are based.

Yes, you read that right. Based on substantial evidence compiled in this book, the warm fuzzy feeling you have in your heart when you are in LOVE—the vibration of heart-felt adoration—is "528." It is a *key,* a musical note, like no other, fundamental to creation.

Pi, related to Phi by dividing a circle into 5 sections, would not exist if not for 528's participation in the musical-mathematical matrix of space/time.

528 cycles-per-second, like a wave of LOVE, has everything to do with prosperity too, considering the universe is so bountiful. The abundant energy and mathematical technology that creates everything, including you, is revealed here depending on 528Hz, a key available for beneficial uses by those who seek to honor this intelligence.

To manifest "prosperity in all ways," financial and otherwise, you can't maintain self-limiting beliefs. Among the beliefs you might need to extinguish is atheism, faithlessness, and paganism.

This book slam-dunks God's existence, demystifies LOVE, and explains Divine intervention, direction, and even "eternal salvation," all administered musically-mathematically according to the laws of physics.

Faith for Protection & Divine Interventions

This book contains amazing, even shocking, information that is prompting a 528LOVERevolution destined by Divine design to solve humanity's greatest problems. It is thereby threatening the status quo.

The Illuminati's investments in the world of music and managed chaos, waging spiritual warfare in the process is detailed in Chapter 4. This best explains why within days of launching i528Tunes.com, the first full-service music transposition site on the Internet, I was warned of an assassination plot against me.

The tip came from friends and angels who have been helping me write this book. The threat was confirmed by American intelligence agents.

The "religious murder" plot involved CIA/FBI operatives who had been promoting Leo Zagami, a religious fanatic with alleged ties to the Vatican. Zagami resembles Church of Satan founder Anton LaVey. He has claimed that music can save the human race from extinction, as I am theorizing here. Zagami was promoted to emulate me, to destroy my credibility, detract from this work heralding 528, and provide the religious murder motive.

These covert operatives claimed on the Internet that 528 was a favorite number of satanist Aleister Crowley; which is true, since Lucifer was given authority over music and light, according to Christian theology.

528, as you will soon learn, is among the most powerful creative sounds and light frequencies. So if Satan intended to outfox God, he would certainly abuse God's most miraculous frequency and creative technology to enslave humanity. This is precisely what has happened.

As this plot was unfolding, and I was launching i528Tunes.com, *INCEPTION*, the Hollywood blockbuster, was premiering. The psycho-thriller featured six references to the number 528. Most of the action during the film's climax happened in and around Room 528. Therein, special *music* was *urgently* required to "cue" espionage agents' return to reality from virtual nightmares—dreamlike states called "levels." The 528 code was used to "get back home" to where the heart is—where the LOVE for family, children, and relationships, is dearest.

Likewise, the marketing campaign for i528Tunes.com celebrated, "The Great Hollywood Ending." This positive affirmation was chosen to reflect two things: 1) The end of civilization's nightmarish enslavement to multi-national corporations, mass media mind-manipulators, and allied genocidalists who control populations for profit rather than permitting health, peace, freedom, and sustainability; and 2) the "happy ending" celebrating the 528LOVERevolution, or Spiritual Renaissance. i528Tunes.com, in support of this movement, encourages living our Divine destiny, rather than suppressing humanity's spirituality vibrationally, primarily through music.

Music and LOVE: A Cure for What Ails Us

The world desperately needs a cure for what ails us—a practical plan that brings people together for mutual benefit and sustainability. We do not need another fake fix. We have already had enough solutions that have created more problems. The various wars we have fought, or endorsed by our ambivalence and silence, have harmed masses to enrich a few. I have often said, "I can't wait till they give a war, and no one turns out to fight it."

That would take a *miracle*, and/or a universally accepted political ideology and religious theology, since all wars have been justified politically, economically, and/or religiously.

Ignorance encourages this mess. Our twenty-first century values and culture came courtesy of the Illuminati. And unless you are fully "enlightened," you are, like the rest of us, dumbed-down, spiritually-suppressed, and mind-controlled by the mainstream media that promotes barbarism, self-destruction, and pandemic biocide.

This book about 528—a number that best embodies *"the universal LOVE constant"*—prescribes a musical plan to generate more LOVE within each of us, inspiring every cell, around the world.

To cure depression, fear, greed and recession, you need joy, faith, LOVE and bravery to manifest prosperity in all ways. These feelings and emotions are *vibrations*. That is, they are "spirits" or energies. "E-motions" are just that, "e-" motions— electrons communicating vibrational energy characterizing

XX

numbers of cycles-per-second, called Hertz.

LOVE Hertz is what I am introducing here. 528 is felt in your heart as LOVE, faith, joy and bravery, based on the evidence compiled herein.

Previously, at LOVE528.com and elsewere, I reported on The Perfect Circle of Sound™—nine core creative frequencies fundamental to universal construction—and its 528 central triangle or triad that especially resonates the energy, or good vibrations, of LOVE, faith, joy and bravery.

Some Evidence 528 is the "Universal LOVE Constant"

528Hertz Frequency is:

1) Linked to the heart of everything.
2) Playing at the heart of the original Solfeggio musical scale.
3) Fundamental to Pi, Phi, the Golden Mean, and all sacred geometry including circles, squares, arches and architecture.
4) The greenish-yellow vibration of your heart chakra.
5) Required for space/time measurements.
6) Crucial to the mile with 5280 feet.
7) Needed to determine the speed of light; constructive to $E=mc^2$ since energy, mass, and light all depend on it.
8) Paramount to Water structuring in the form of a tetrahedron.
9) Key to the heart of God, reconciling the "Triune God"—Creator, Water and the Holy Spirit—as beneficent, life-giving, and constructive.
10) "Key of the house of David," reflecting the shape of "Solomons Seal" and Water, active as an amulet generating positive or protective power.
11) Central to *Genesis* in the command, "Let there be light."
12) Broadcast by the Sun and Jupiter.
13) Resonating the heart of rainbows and snowflakes.
14) Celebrated throughout the botanical world in the pigment chlorophyll—the reason the grass is green.
15) Structuring your hemoglobin and adding LOVE to prana, the "breath of life," oxygen.
16) Linked to positive heart-felt emotions: LOVE, faith, joy, and bravery—"e⁻motions" that are fundamentally vibrating electrons resonating 528.
17) Is the *MI*racle note of the universe, and much more. . . .

The 528LOVERevolution jibes with social psychologist Erich Fromm's quote that I found in my fortune cookie the other day:

**"LOVE is the only sane and satisfactory answer
to the question of human existence."**

The goal of this labor of LOVE/528 is peace on earth and healthy sustainability.

The "Miracle" Number of 528

The Book of 528: Prosperity Key of LOVE is about making miracles musically. This book reveals many compelling facts, including why the number 528, that reduces to the sacred number "6," is so special in manifesting miracles, including massive wealth.

528 digitally reduces to this sacred 6, by adding the numbers 5+2+8 = 15; and then 1 + 5 = <u>6</u>.

Route 66, for instance, was christened "America's Highway" to optimize commerce, thanks to the metaphysical attributes of the number "6."

66 is precisely the third octave below 528Hz/LOVE. Which means the Illuminati are "using LOVE to kill," and that is the punchline of the movie, *The Green Mile.*

This knowledge has been routinely used by the Illuminati to gain financial advantage over *We The People* who lack this knowledge. This secret sacred arcana is commonly used, for instance, by the Rockefeller family representing America's financial elite.

Also, Phillips 66 is one of the most profitable and successful petroleum companies thanks to the British Royal Family's affection for the 6s.

"X" is also "6" in the alphanumerics or Pythagorean mathematics underlying the English language. "F", "O", and "X", are 6s. So "FOX News" is actually "666 News," owned by the wealthiest media mogul, Rupert Murdoch.

This gift of secreted knowledge also explains why Jesus, in *Matthew* 6:33, urged all disciples to "Seek first the Kingdom of Heaven, and all else will come unto you." Included in this promise is *prosperity in all ways*.

In this book, I contend that study, knowledge, and applications of 528Hz, the "Miracle 6" musical note, engages the Kingdom of Heaven and unlimited prosperity "on earth as it is in Heaven."

I herald 528Hz as the "key" to musical creationism. All creation operates vibrationally, like language and music does most powerfully, to produce a physical result in space/time.

"Seek and ye shall find."

Dr. Joseph Puleo sought Divine guidance that came in 1997, through a vision of Jesus. The 528 code in the Bible was suddenly revealed after being hidden for millennia. This we detailed in *Healing Codes for the Biological Apocalypse* (Tetrahedron Publishing Group, 1998).

"Ask and you will receive."

Mathematician Victor Showell asked if 528 holds a key to sacred geometry. He was thrilled to learn the affirmative, and he shared his analyses, and conclusions herein. Based on solid mathematical determinations, 528 is fundamental to the laws of physics.

That is, the universe operates musically/mathematically, and 528 is its central "string" or tuning.

528 revelations can provide a peek into universal construction to help you reconstruct your life, enhance your health, co-create a better world, and celebrate peace and freedom. In other words, these revelations shall transform civilization.

In this book you will discover 528's relationship to life, and to the Kingdom of Heaven. When this "magic kingdom" is sought and found, it provides far more wealth than any other means of prospering.

"The Kingdom of Heaven is near," affirmed Jesus. It is right here, right now, and best experienced in your heart, vibrating in 528Hz.

528 is the *currency* of reality and spirituality. Reconsider that word, "Current-Sea:" The energy or movement of electrons happening NOW through a "Sea-of-Green."

Look at the greenish-yellow algae and phytoplankton enriching the oceans and atmosphere; mass producing chlorophyll to generate life-sustaining oxygen. This too depends on 528.

Chlorophyll is the optimal energy transducer and power carrier. It delivers electrons from sunlight to your blood, linked to the breath of life—oxygen, inspiring your blood. This energy of spirituality vibrates universally, eternally, and hydrosonically—vibrating reality into existence through electron resonance, through 528's presence.

Your DNA operates likewise, sending and receiving electronic (and bio-acoustic) vibrations anchored, like the sound of the sun, to 528Hz.

528Hz is helping to manifest you miraculously in this reality, right now! *You are the artistic rendering of mathematics and physics in a quantum field. You are dancing in a cosmic sound and light show.*

Ultimately, you are the result of "hydro-creationism." You manifest from sound on Water. This is the future of healing, through natural medicine, celebrating the math and music of LOVE in 528Hz.

Indeed, the music of the sun, and central sound of Jupiter, according to NASA recordings, vibrates in harmony with 528Hz.

This music, glorified by all life, is also the reason why aboriginal musicians and vocalists tune up or down from "standard" western world tuning. Intuitively, they realized, 528Hz, and its harmonics, is more appealing, healing, loving, and prophetically more fulfilling.

Welcome to the 528LOVERevolution.

Deep down, most people are called to follow a path to enlightenment. Seeking the Kingdom of Heaven first is wise. Alternatively, straying from this path leads to unhappiness, greed, corruption, emptiness, and eventual disillusionment.

To those with "no ears to hear," Jesus counseled: "Wake up! . . . But if you do not wake up, I will come like a thief [to steal your wealth], and you will not know at what time I will come to you."

Some people believe the time of Divine justice is upon us. A global economic collapse was prescribed for spoiled, unfaithful children. Humans are being disciplined, and your grasp of both physical and spiritual reality is being tested at this time.

Bible scholar Matthew Henry gave an excellent commentary relevant to *Matthew* 6:33 and this preface:

> God has given us life, and has given us the body. And what can he not do for us, who did that? If we take care about our souls and for eternity, which are more than the body and its life, we may leave it to God to provide for us food and raiment, which are less. . . . We must reconcile ourselves to our worldly estate, as we do to our stature. . . . Thoughtfulness for our souls is the best cure [for thoughtlessness in] the world. . . . Happy are those who take the Lord for their God, and make full proof of it by trusting themselves wholly to his wise disposal. Let thy Spirit . . . take away the worldliness of our hearts.

How do you take away "worldliness" from your heart? The task requires opening your heart to receive something different from what has already filled it up. A full measure of faith and LOVE is what this book suggests.

Is this an insurmountable task for "normal" humans operating in the physical world of psychological programming and mass media persuasion? Does population manipulation undermine or support this open-hearted transformation? Does fear and competition discourage LOVE and collaboration?

The fact is we need a miracle—a supernatural event to transmute ignorance, arrogance, and rampant stupidity.

This is the mission and capacity of the "*MI*racle 6" tone of the ancient Solfeggio—the *MI*-528 frequency of the 528LOV-ERevolution.

For it is written that Jesus directed his servant John to write a similar "End Times" salvation message to whom it may concern. John's prophecy, in *Revelation* involves 528. My role in this book is to proclaim the modern gospel, that means "good news."

My Background and Bias

As I first reported in *Walk on Water* (Tetrahedron Publishing Group, 2006), it appears I have an angel assigned to help me advance this great news. The angel is from the "Church of Philadelphia," the "City of Brotherly Love," where I was born. John, in Revelation 3:6-8, decrees this angel's assignment in heralding the Davidian "key"—a musical note.

A *key* is also a tool or instrument needed to open a "door"—in this case a metaphysical passageway. This key and door, apparently, references a spiritual portal to people's hearts.

Why?

The Bible speaks of restoring LOVE in a world gone mad, and in the coming pages you will see that this truth is revealed scientifically as well.

King David's house and heart was filled with the greatest LOVE for God. This door requires a Davidian key according to Isaiah 22:22 and John's writing on behalf of "The Church of Philadelphia" in Revelation 3:6-8:

These are the words of him who is holy and true, who holds the key of David. What he opens no one can shut, and what he shuts no one can open. . . . . He who has an ear, let him hear what the Spirit says to the churches.

The above counsel especially spoke to me.

My Hebrew name is Arya ben Schlomo ha Levi. That means "Lion of Yah [God's truer name is "Yah," written in Hebrew, יהוה], son of [Davidian King] Solomon, the Levi [priest]." Most people know me as Dr. Leonard Horowitz. Sharing my roots seems appropriate for this book, and the special honor I have of heralding 528. This background may help you understand why I've been blessed to deliver this revelatory information at this challenging time, and why an Angel from Philadelphia, coauthored this book.

I am best known for health science celebrity, having written dozens of scientific articles and more than 17 books, including the award-winning national best-seller, *Emerging Viruses: AIDS & Ebola—Nature, Accident or Intentional?* (Tetrahedron Press, 1996)

This politically charged text explained the man-made origins of HIV/AIDS and Ebola. With shocking documentation, I scrutinized the genocidal origin of the world's worst plagues.

Rebuking modern medicine, false health doctrines, and BigPharma's deceptions since 1990, my family and business partners lived on a "roller coaster ride through the Twilight Zone." We gave up our "normal" lives to expose medical malfeasance and related criminal injustices. I ended my sixteen-year career as a successful dentist, and switched from being a nationally known professional trainer to become a consumer health advocate and government whistle-blower. (See: www. originofAIDS.com and www.tetrahedron.org) I am widely known and respected for heralding many troubling truths about vaccinations and other problems within medicine, in an effort to prevent diseases and protect people from those who abuse their power and economic might.

As a result of my work, many people say a lot of nice things about me, while CIA agents and BigPharma shills work to discredit me. You can read about this on my official website http://www.drlenhorowitz.com.

One grassroots-activist christened me the "King David of Natural Healing versus the Goliath of Slash, Burn and Poison Medicine" because of my support for natural alternatives over deadly drugs. He did not know how inspired I was as a child, by the story of David and Goliath. Nor did we know that years later I would be heralding the "key of the House of David," a musical note, that shall eventually bring BigPharma down with LOVE in 528.

Today, in the spirit of LOVE that David celebrated by writing Psalms, I earnestly petition Yah to open my heart to the fullest extent possible; to enjoy optimal LOVE and gratitude for the Creator's greatness and bounty of prosperity administered using the musical-mathematics discussed herein.

Now, contrary to what you might think, I do not consider myself very religious, just spiritually sensitive. Despite my Judeo-Christian background, I reject any religious exclusivity doctrines: Hebrew, Christian, or other. Such sectarian monopolization over salvation seems ridiculous to me.

Although I was reared Jewish, and LOVE my Hebrew heritage, I opened my heart to Jesus (written in Hebrew, Yahshua). I hold in my mind, and heart, tremendous respect for His sacrifice and ministry, which encouraged LOVE as *The Way* to spiritual salvation. I view His teaching of *The Way*, pure Christianity, as a loving sect of Judaism, healing to self and others. Eternal salvation is promised by his ministry and uplifting messages; and based on the revelations herein about 528/LOVE, my faith soars.

In recent years, as Overseer for The Royal Bloodline of David ministry, I have dedicated much effort to building a virtual King Solomon's Temple for natural healing in Hawaii called "The Kingdom of Heaven." We are advancing 528, and lava-heated steam—"Breath of the Earth™"—Holy Water, for miraculous healing. We are also sending 528Hz music and prayers into the Pacific Ocean from this land, through a series of lava tubes.

The world is in need of models for sustainable living and natural healing. So, a major part of our mission on this holy land, this sacred earth, is to create a venue for the science of creationism featuring 528Hz as central to the musical-mathematical matrix of creation.

To summarize my biases and background, I am multi-denominational, and moderately spiritual. I am antagonistic to false doctrines of every kind, and feel greatly blessed to be guided to serve humanity with revelations about 528Hz frequency.

The Key of 528

In 1999, when I wrote *Healing Codes for the Biological Apocalypse,* I envisioned a global concert celebrating the miracle of 528Hz. As a result, in 2009, colleagues and I produced the Concert for the Living Water, *LIVE H_2O,* in which 72 countries were represented by groups performing music in 528Hz.

528 was revealed as very special within the Creator's musical scale by Dr. Joseph Puleo. 528, "Joey" learned in 1997, is the third note in a series of six notes in the ancient original Solfeggio.

The 528 tone is also called "Miracle 6" because it is divinely-anointed to produce miracles.

In fact, Puleo's revelations decrypted this secreted information, hidden by my great ancestors, Levitical priests, when they translated the original Torah into the Greek Septuagint. At that time, the priests—the exclusive curators of the spiritual knowledge of alchemy and musical metaphysics—put the verse numbers into the Bible, encrypting the secret musical code in the *Book of Numbers* 7:12-83.

As you will learn herein, this original musical scale contains six, of nine, frequencies that I call, "The Perfect Circle of Sound™." I discovered the final three pure tones by playing with the numerical patterns within the set of six.

The fourth Solfeggio frequency, 639Hz, or the "Family 9" tone, also relates to 144,000 prophesied vocalists required to transact the "business" of spiritual transcendence beyond the hypocrisy and insanity of ignorant society. I prayed for this positive manifestation to happen with *LIVE H₂O*, and it may have. Most participants noticed psycho-social and spiritual shifts occurring more commonly thereafter.

You might recall that King Solomon, son of David, thirsted for Divine wisdom and used it to justly rule the human family in his kingdom.

The Wisdom of 528

The Davidian key, it turns out, is fundamental to developing Divine metaphysical wisdom. Plus, it is vibrationally active in the Aloha Ohana, as Hawaiians call it—the "LOVING FAMILY."

In King David's day, he used the "Star of David," otherwise known as "Solomon's Seal," for his spiritual protection.

Featured herein is the knowledge that this six-pointed star is the sacred geometric form of molecular Water! When 528 structuring occurs, the pyramid-shaped Water molecule couples with a mate to neutralize polarities. This combination of two Water molecules form a hexagon, six-sided, atomic complex that is reflected in the typical snowflake. It is called "structured" or "clustered" water in science. Dr. Masaru Emoto, Japan's famous Water researcher, and I learned from our common mentor, Dr. Lee Lorenzen that this Water acts very differently, far more positively and powerfully, than polluted or chemicalized Water.

Years after working with Dr. Lorenzen I commissioned a genealogist to determine my family's crest-of-arms. I was stunned to see, front and center of the shield, carried by my ancestors, the hexagonal-shaped snowflake-like structure Dr. Emoto made famous in the documentary, "What the Bleep Do We Know™." I highly recommend his awesome book, *The Hidden Messages in Water*. (Hay House, 2006)

Around the time my ancestral family purchased their right to bear arms from German royalty, the Templar Knights' fleet vanished from the port of La Rochelle, France. Then, the progeny of these prosperous Templar pirates evolved economically to become the world's wealthiest bankers and business leaders. I revealed their history and New World Order agendas in my previous books, including *Death in the Air: Globalism, Terrorism and Toxic Warfare* (Tetrahedron Publishing Group, 2001). Released three months before the terrorist attacks of 9/11, *Death in the Air* examined leading globalists' positions as powerful petrochemical/pharmaceutical profiteers.

My book, *DNA: Pirates of the Sacred Spiral* (Tetrahedron Publishing Group, 2004), written more for health scientists and bioenergy enthusiasts, I merge spirituality with biology. This subject is as heretical as mixing church and state, government and religion.

This text was also built upon scientific and scriptural revelations published in *Healing Codes for the Biological Apocalypse. DNA: Pirates of the Sacred Spiral* vividly documents the threat to humanity, and myriad species, posed by the pirates' genetic tinkering. This is mentioned here because 528 resonance in electrogenetics is extremely important as detailed in Chapter 12. 528 is healing to damaged DNA according to Dr. Lorenzen and the evidence and conclusions drawn here.

Divine Acknowledgment

In past books I acknowledged Divine interventions. This book takes revelations from my previous books to the next level. This Divine frequency of 528 infuses Water with nature's most celebrated energy. Universally, Water is the most extraordinary creative juice; and this medium vibrates with myriad communications. The most powerful is LOVE, administered through dynamics and cymatics of the Creator's miracle note, 528.

This book is necessarily technical in parts, although I have done my best to simplify science and understanding of scripture for the average reader. My challenge is integrating recent advances in space/time physics, mathematics, musicology, and health science, with prophetic books of the Bible. This exploration, like any pioneering effort, presents unique challenges to general audiences for assimilation and appreciation.

Most readers will celebrate the obviously Divine revelations contained herein for which I cannot take credit. No person, or earthly force, could open these doors, nor close them. The best of these revelations derive from a source of inspiration and awareness beyond normal human reasoning.

This publication is, therefore, both extraordinary and a sign of greater things, and times, to come. It evidences the 528LOVERevolution. This accelerating process is Divinely enlightening. Humanity is being blessed with ingenuity now to produce lasting peace on Earth as it is in heaven.

Please join the pioneers of this most righteous evolution of consciousness.

Yours in the Spirit of 528 Revelation,

Arya ben Schlomo ha Levi
(Dr. Leonard G. Horowitz)

Chapter One:
Introduction to Musical Creationism

When I was eight years old I had a really bad day. My father, who rarely used force to discipline me, wacked me hard for something I didn't do. So, I ran away from home.

I got a block away, to the school-bus stop, where our neighborhood bully was beating up my friend--a New Jersey science champion. When I intervened to protect my friend, the bully threatened to beat me up too.

That day I realized, *adults are crazy, and children are crazy too!*

My next thought became my life's mission. *If it is the last thing I ever do, I am going to figure out what makes people crazy, and how to heal everyone from this insanity.*

My general prescription was published in the early 1980s by the *American Journal of School Health,* under the title "The Self-Care Motivation Model™" for Healthy Human Development."(1)

The Book of 528: Prosperity Key of LOVE, takes this general treatment to a higher level, and largely fulfills my life's mission. This knowledge of 528 music is paradigm shifting and monumentally enlightening.

In this introductory chapter you will come to know the origin of 528's Divine revelation. You will consider the ignorance, arrogance, geopolitics, and economics that has kept this freeing knowledge suppressed for millennia. You will learn why applying this simple truth about numbers—the 3s, 6s, 9s and 8s, is powerfully enlightening and healing for you, and why these revelations are rapidly transforming our planet through a 528LOVERevolution.

1

Dr. Puleo, Jesus and 528

While I was praying for the "Achille's heel of the Illuminati" in 1998, Dr. Joseph Puleo, a devout Catholic and naturopathic doctor was simultaneously praying to meet me. Unbeknownst to him, he was serving to grant me my prayer.

Living in Northern Idaho, Joey had heard me expose the Illuminati on "Coast-to-Coast AM" radio, explaining how and why their military-medical-petrochemical-pharmaceutical cartel created HIV/AIDS and deadly vaccinations. For destiny's sake, he prayed to Jesus for me to come to his house.

Three months later, through a series of Divine synchronicities, I ended up knocking on Joey's front door for dinner.

Dr. Puleo, who died in 2008, had a knack for decrypting Bible codes. He never told me if he developed his decoding skills in the military, while serving as a Navy Seal, but I suspected he was more than an intelligence agent turned naturopathic doctor. He shared with me that he learned about 528 from Jesus; and his thrilling story became the first six chapters in my second American best-seller, *Healing Codes for the Biological Apocalypse*. (2)

Published in 1998, that book began with Joey praying for knowledge of the sacred music by which the original Hymn to St. John the Baptist was sung.

Joey knew there were six verses to St. John's sacred hymn. Each verse was chanted in a different ancient Solfeggio frequency. The sacred music, he knew, could resonate Water to Divinely anoint herbal formulas. Joey's Catholic intelligence network could (or would) not provide the intelligence he sought. So, Dr. Puleo took his quest to Jesus, and prayed for the musical revelation.

Soon thereafter, Joey awoke to "a vision" of Jesus standing bedside, next to a huge angel. The vision did not disappear when he opened or closed his eyes.

Joey reported that while in this "altered state," Jesus showed him a section of the Bible's *Book of Numbers*, Chapter 7, beginning with verse 12—wherein the six musical frequencies are hidden in the verse numbers. Joey found and deciphered them, without aid of a computer, as you are instructed to do in *Healing Codes for the Biological Apocalypse*.

The numbers: 396, 417, 528, 639, 741, and 852, provided the musical notes (i.e., Hertz frequencies) of the original Solfeggio musical scale. These were passed down to Levitical priests from ancient—pre-Egyptian—mystics. The Levites later encrypted the pure tones in the verse numbers of the Bible for posterity.

Alphanumerics is Language

Music is the "Universal Language." This language, like all languages, is based on math. From tempo to pitch, music is essentially numerical weights, measures, and applications transmitting vibrations to communicate feelings, and sounds of information, or intelligence. This music for your ears, or your DNA, can be spiritually uplifting, or degrading.

Math, in fact, is the basis for all creation. Think about it. Words are sounds. Sounds are acoustic and/or electromagnetic frequencies. These are compressions and expansions of electrons flowing through hydrated space, much like ripples radiating out from a pebble hitting the surface of a pond. Whether throwing a pebble into a pond or singing a hymn, the waves radiate out. Similarly, this happens "hydrosonically." That means it involves sound traveling through Water, including the hydrated atmosphere or room that you are in. Eliminate the Water—a liquid crystal superconductor—and the sound doesn't travel at all.

Frequencies, measured in Hertz, or cycles-per-second, are simply energized Water waves measured by, and communicating, numbers, or math. So, all languages, like musical compositions, are based on math.

Since all languages are based on math, it stands to reason that the letters or symbols that relay meaning, especially obvious in the western world's languages, are based on numbers, too.

Understanding the New World Language, English, fundamentally involves considering alphanumerics. That is, a code exists to transpose letters into numbers in the creation of western languages, and this knowledge is fundamental to understanding creation, creationism, and life in the cosmos.

Language is a Creative Technology

The Creator's language is math. All natural structures are math-based, because all natural structuring incorporates "sacred geometry." The carbon-6 organic chemistry ring is a classic example. A snowflake, or honeycomb, reflects math in nature. This ordered structuring involving simple math is evident throughout the universe.

Nature exists energetically, generally in harmony versus dissonance, usually functioning peacefully to resolve conflicts.

Nature celebrates homeostasis, or what is called "righteousness" in the religious world. Righteousness and homeostasis opposes chaos or sin. So, nature, math, music, or vibrational energy, can be called upon to better understand and impact health, or provide remedies for diseases.

4

Dr. Joseph Puleo understood this concept while research-ing the ancient Solfeggio musical scale for spiritual transcen-dence. He envisioned numbers related to letters of the English alphabet that I later determined were related to Hebrew letters, too.

In *Healing Codes for the Biological Apocalypse*, he relayed how mathematics, the most precise language, is "God's lan-guage" because it always speaks the truth.

To test his theory, Joey took the English alphabet, from A to Z, as seen in Table 1, and numbered each letter. For example, A=1, B=2, C=3, and so on.

After this, he took the words "TRUST," "FAITH," and "GOD," and performed mathematical translations on them, thusly:

For "TRUST," T=20 + R=18 + U=21, + S=19, + T=20 to-tals 98. Then he used the ancient Pythagorean mathematics method of reducing each multiple digit number to a single digit. So 98=9+8=17; then finally, 1+7=8.

The same result occurred with the words "FAITH" and "GOD."

For "FAITH," F=6 + A=1 + I=9 + T=20 + H=8 totals 44. And 4+4=8.

For "GOD," G=7 + O=15 + D=4 totals 26. And again 2+6=8.

Any way you added them, according to Pythagorean math-ematics, the words "TRUST," "FAITH" and "GOD" always add up to 8!

Number "8" Relays Special Meaning

Eight (8) is the "infinity sign," that is, the Creator's number. It is also the structure of the universe (i.e., a double donut or double toroid, as you will learn herein).

Eight is also the number for oxygen in the Periodic Table of Elements. This is interesting because the Hebrew name

Table 1. Derivation of English Letter Number Code

Letter & Number	Pythagorean Skein Equivalent	Key Word Number Derivations
A 1	1	T 20–2 + 0 = 2
B 2	2	R 18–1 + 8 = 9
C 3	3	U 21–2 + 1 = 3
D 4	4	S 19–1 + 9 = 1
E 5	5	T 20–2 + 0 = 2
F 6	6	98=**8** 17=**8**
G 7	7	
H 8	8	
I 9	9	F 6–6 + 0 = 6
J 10	1 + 0 = 1	A 1–1 + 0 = 1
K 11	1 + 1 = 2	I 9–9 + 0 = 9
L 12	1 + 2 = 3	T 20–2 + 0 = 2
M 13	1 + 3 = 4	H 8–8 + 0 = 8
N 14	1 + 4 = 5	44=**8** 26=**8**
O 15	1 + 5 = 6	
P 16	1 + 6 = 7	G 7–7 + 0 = 7
Q 17	1 + 7 = 8	O 15–1 + 5 = 6
R 18	1 + 8 = 9	D 4–4 + 0 = 4
S 19	1 + 9 = 10	26=**8** 17=**8**
T 20	2 + 0 = 2	
U 21	2 + 1 = 3	The number 8
V 22	2 + 2 = 4	represents
W 23	2 + 3 = 5	Divinity & infinity.
X 24	2 + 4 = 6	9 represents
Y 25	2 + 5 = 7	completion.
Z **26**	2 + 6 = **8**	

Table shows the English alphabet and its equivalent numbers. Multiple digit numbers are reduced to single digit numbers to employ the Pythagorean skein and determine the mathematical "truth." Notice that numbers one through nine repeat; and the number 8, the universal sign for "infinity," is also the total for "Trust," "Faith" and "God." The number nine (9) represents completion.

Table 2. Column Showing Multiples of Eights (8)

Multiple of Eights	Reverse Alphabet		Alphabet w/ Numbers		Sum of Two Alphabet #s
1 X 8 = 0 8	8	Z	A	1	9
2 X 8 = 1 6	7	Y	B	2	9
3 X 8 = 2 4	6	X	C	3	9
4 X 8 = 3 2	5	W	D	4	9
5 X 8 = 4 0	4	V	E	5	9
6 X 8 = 4 8	3	U	F	6	9
7 X 8 = 5 6	2	T	G	7	9
8 X 8 = 6 4	1	S	H	8	9
9 X 8 = 7 2	9	R	I	9	9
1 0 X 8 = 8 0	8	Q	J	1	9
1 1 X 8 = 8 8	7	P	K	2	9
1 2 X 8 = 9 6	6	O	L	3	9
1 3 X 8 = 1 0 4	5	N	M	4	9
1 4 X 8 = 1 1 2	4	M	N	5	9
1 5 X 8 = 1 2 0	3	L	O	6	9
1 6 X 8 = 1 2 8	2	K	P	7	9
1 7 X 8 = 1 3 6	1	J	Q	8	9
1 8 X 8 = 1 4 4	9	I	R	9	9
1 9 X 8 = 1 5 2	8	H	S	1	9
2 0 X 8 = 1 6 0	7	G	T	2	9
2 1 X 8 = 1 6 8	6	F	U	3	9
2 2 X 8 = 1 7 6	5	E	V	4	9
2 3 X 8 = 1 8 4	4	D	W	5	9
2 4 X 8 = 1 9 2	3	C	X	6	9
2 5 X 8 = 2 0 0	2	B	Y	7	9
2 6 X 8 = 2 0 8	1	A	Z	8	9

Shown are multiples of eights (8) deciphered according to the Pythagorean skein in which all integers are reduced to single digits using addition of each digit. Example: 208=2+0+8=10; then 10=1+0=1. This number is linked to the letter A. When A=1 is added to the reverse alphabet letter Z=8, the sum is 9. The number nine (9) implies completion and results everytime the forward and backward English alphanumerics are added together. This evidences the English language was mathematically derived.

7

for God (i.e., Yah, short for Yahovah, or Yod-Hay-Vov-Hay) means "to breathe is to exist." Fascinating also because to animate Adam, humanity's first born, the Creator is said to have "breathed the breath of life into him."

It is certain that element number 8 carries the core energy (electron) for the miracle of life.

Hydrogen donates that electron.

The combination of element number 8, oxygen, and element number 1, hydrogen, yields the math of "9" found in the hydroxyl ion "OH-" that is alkalizing—probably the greatest disease preventative in the universe, largely because it simply carries pure energy.

The combination of H+ + OH- = H_2O, or Water!

During the past decade, NASA scientists discovered that space is full of Water. They filmed ice crystals in deep space; and even found Water in rocks on Mars.

Across the universe, numbers are expressed elementally, supporting "hydrosonic" creationism—that is, the constructive value of frequency vibrations moving through Water that transmit energy, language, or mathematical intelligence to direct the flow and actual manifestation of matter.

528 and the "In 6"

Consistent with the above analysis, Russia's leading space/time physicist, Dr. Hartmut Müller, previously with the Institutes of the Russian Academy of Sciences and the Institute for Applied Mathematics of Leningrad University, published persuasive evidence on the mathematical scaling of the universe. He, like many others before him, including Nikola Tesla, determined that the physical universe is scaled, much like musical octaves are scaled.

At the core of the mathematically scaled universe, Müller confirmed with hard data, is a "standing gravitational wave,"

(SGW) like a wave of Water and/or sustaining energy.

You may recall from Star Trek battle commanders the phrase to "lock your phasers," or the acknowledgment, "Phasers locked!" This actually references the requirement of all physical matter in space to "phase-lock" with gravitational forces. Some physicists call this adherence "entrainment" to a Master Matrix of mathematically-manifested gravity. Throughout the universe everything is kept phase-locked, or synchronized, by this force that Müller named the "Standing Gravitational Wave (SGW)."

The SGW operates with what Müller called the "In 6" as graphed in Figures 1 and 2. This "In 6" designates six energy "nodes" operating harmonically within the SGW. These six nodes or "strings" may be considered sub-waves.

The mathematics of the central nodes of each pure tone sub-wave impact and interact with the other subwaves within the SGW—producing holographic reality.

I call this "hydrosonic creativity."

The end result is the fractal nature of matter. In this case, the basic fractals, probably electron materializations, are circular in keeping with the wave radiance in ponds from thrown pebbles. Except the "pebbles" in the Master Matrix of the universe are scaled, like the frets on a guitar.

In essence, the Water-filled universe is vibrating in whole number ratios, with the frequency, 528Hz, strongly and centrally represented within this musical mix or matrix.

528 is special within this mathematical matrix of creation, because it represents a "6," since 5+2+8=15 and 1+5=6. A "6" vibrates with a unique "energy signature" or "resonance frequency," and has its own set of harmonic and dissonant relatives.

In terms of materialization, view the "6" as symbolic of "spiraling down from heaven into the wholeness of earth."

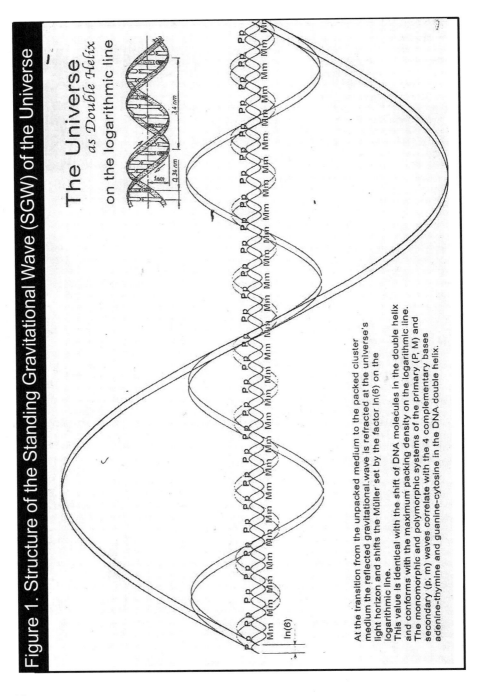

Figure 1. Structure of the Standing Gravitational Wave (SGW) of the Universe

The Universe
as Double Helix
on the logarithmic line

At the transition from the unpacked medium to the packed cluster medium the reflected gravitational wave is refracted at the universe's light horizon and shifts the Müller set by the factor ln(6) on the logarithmic line.
This value is identical with the shift of DNA molecules in the double helix and conforms with the maximum packing density on the logarithmic line. The monomorphic and polymorphic systems of the primary (P, M) and secondary (p, m) waves correlate with the 4 complementary bases adenine-thymine and guanine-cytosine in the DNA double helix.

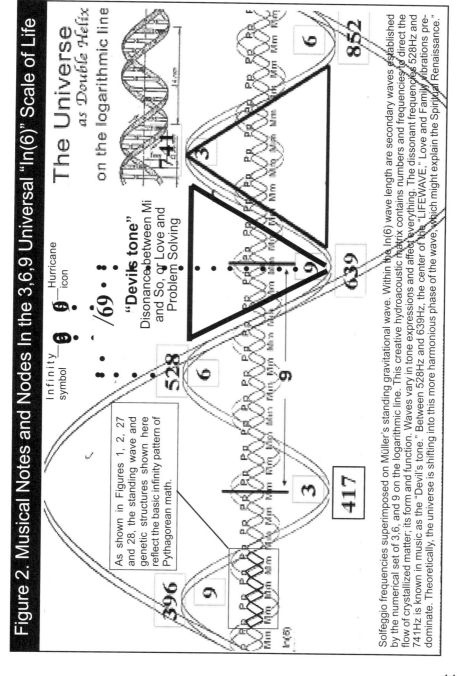

Figure 2. Musical Notes and Nodes In the 3,6,9 Universal "In(6)" Scale of Life

Solfeggio frequencies superimposed on Müller's standing gravitational wave. Within the In(6) wave length are secondary waves established by the numerical set of 3,6, and 9 on the logarithmic line. This creative hydroacoustic matrix contains numbers and frequencies to direct the flow of crystallized matter; its form and function. Waves vary in tone expressions and affect everything. The dissonant frequencies 528Hz and 741Hz is known in music as the "Devil's tone." Between 528Hz and 639Hz, the center of the "LIFEWAVE," Love and Family vibrations predominate. Theoretically, the universe is shifting into this more harmonious phase of the wave, which might explain the Spiritual Renaissance."

Going back to where I began in 1998, "528," I learned from Dr. Puleo, is the third note of the six note original Solfeggio musical scale. This "MI" tone, short for "MIracles," resonates with the unique energetic "signature" of a "6."

The "MI" note lies next to the "FA" note of 639, at the heart of this primordial scale, reflecting the primordial matrix. The 639 transposes to a "9."

Recognizing this as creative/etherial/spiritual music, wherein the number set of 3, 6, 8, 9, is extremely special, you can now understand why, according to history's greatest mathematicians, including Pythagoras, da Vinci, Aristotle, Plato, Vitruvius, and later Tesla (who omitted the 8 in his famous statement, "If humanity only understood the powers of the 3s, 6s, and 9s, it would be a completely different universe."), this set of numbers is unique and vitally important. (Read: *LOVE the Real da Vinci CODE*; Tetrahedron Publishing Group, 2007)

Dr. Müller's presentations are consistent with this knowledge. Müller wrote that the universe's SGW operates mathematically according to what he called the "In six (6)," relevant to the six defined sub-waves of the main wave.(3)

The Heart of the Wave and Mission

Following Müller's work, I considered the six original pure tones of the Solfeggio scale to be reflected in the universal matrix graphed in Figure 2. In the musical matrix, "FA" stands for "family," and "9" represents "completion" in the "*MI*racle *FA*mily."

The nine frequencies in The Perfect Circle of Sound™, that I trademarked many years ago, is shown in Figure 33. These nine pure tones of the Master Matrix is like the "Kingdom of Heaven" in the religious world.

The symbol "9" graphs the spiraling up from Earth into the wholeness of heaven. Here, everything is linked in the metaphysical or spiritual realm of pure tone energy.

The concept of this Miracle Family arising in these End Times is referenced in Revelation 14:1 with the gathering of the 144,000 servants performing in a Concert for the Living Water.

This "ALOHA OHANA" is inspired cosmically by Divine energy mediated musically-mathematically. This is precisely what is needed to move civilization beyond its present ignorance and course of self-destruction.

The word ALOHA says it all. It displays the heart of the alpha and omega, the "A" and the "O," as the "L" at the center of the Hebrew alphabet referencing LOVE according to the gematria. This is followed by HA, or Hah—the breath of life—carrying the LOVE of God in 528 resonating oxygen from the beginning of creation through eternity.

Look more insightfully now at the symbols for these numbers "8," "6" and "9". The number "8," depicts the mirror image of a 3, or two 3s totaling 6. An 8 becomes the infinity sign— "∞"—when rotated 90-degrees (9+0=9; "completion").

Look at the inverted 9, as the MIracle number "6" that starts at the top and spirals down. The entire universe is actually spiraling, like the cosmos, and like DNA, to manifest on Earth as it is in heaven.

The number 9 spirals up from below to rejoin itself in the wholeness of heaven, the cosmic circle, or "Circle of Life."

This obvious geometry evidences the mysterious relationship between these special numbers: 8, 3, 6 and 9.

Furthermore, the two numbers 6 and 9, brought together, create the symbol "69" reflecting universal polarity, the yin and yang, plus/minus, male/female; the attraction vs. repulsion of the energetic paradox of nature, operating within the intelligently designed universe.

Combined further, with one number laid on top of the other, also shown in Figure 2, these symbols yield the figure 8, the infinity sign, or Creator's number!

This is also seen in Chapter 3, in the CymaGlyph in Figure 9, showing 528Hz frequency vibrating Water that produces waves and nodes flowing into a 36-pointed *hydrosonic* star. This is, very likely, the origin of time and space in the Perfect Circle of Sound, demonstrating a 360-degree circle.

All of this simple mathematical knowledge in creative language is consistent with Bible prophecy in the *Book of Revelation*. Here, during the End Times, a marriage occurs between the Creator and the enlightened "bride"—a mass communion with Christ—choosing "a thousand years of world peace."

The Alphanumerics of English Backwards

Eight (8)— the Creator's symbol, is very unique.

The multiples of 8, as shown in Table 2, provide an alphanumeric countdown pattern reflecting the English alphabet *backwards*.

In this case, the word *backwards* literally exposes *back-words*. That is, the creators of this "New World Language"—the German-descended Anglo-Saxon, and later Norman, ruling elite—developed this *backwards* (mathematically/spiritually reversed) English language to suppress humanity's spirituality maximally.

The global elite mathematically compromised Hebrew to develop English sometime between 500 to 1,000 years after Jesus' crucifixion. This was shortly before historical accounts give rise to the Knights Templar.

Obviously, the reversed speech of the English language is based on Pythagorean mystery school mathematics. Math, as a creative spiritual technology, well known to the Greeks, is believed to have been acquired by the Templars during their military occupation of the Temple Mount in Jerusalem.

Like the Levitical priests, that encoded the verse numbers in the *Book of Numbers* with the original Solfeggio musical scale, the old English language architects encoded the same Pythagorean mathematics into the English language. They obviously put a good deal of thought into this due to the relevance of language to creationism, spiritual matters, and energetic considerations impacting populations.

The esoteric truth about this covert action remained hidden for two possible reasons because knowledge is power. The Illuminati gained the knowledge and power of math-based languages spoken from the heart. The "sacred languages" deployed this power to the people who communicated more from their hearts than from their rational left brains. There was an element of God operating during communication reflecting Divine-human communion expressed interpersonally. To gain advantage, the Illuminati changed languages. The English "New World Language" reversal spiritually, mentally, and culturally disabled people to be manipulated, virtually enslaved, to law-makers and dictators. And/or . . .

It is apparently a Divine plan unfolding. The English speaking world required a degeneration period prior to maturing to engage this powerful revelation and potential emancipation.

Suffice it to say, the alphanumerics of English are energetically *hashed*, which means confused. Interpersonal communications or "communion" was degraded from the original sacred languages, including Hebrew, Sanskrit, ancient Aramaic, and according to mounting evidence, ancient Hawaiian as well.

Alphanumerics, "Crazy 8s," or "Behind the '8 Ball'"

Have you ever wondered why there is a special game in billiards called "8-ball?" What makes the 8 ball special? Why does "pocketing it" lose the game?

Also, from whence did the phrase "crazy 8s" derive? Are 8s crazy, or are *We The People* crazy for losing knowledge about the importance of 8s in creative alphanumerics for winning the Game of Life?

A review of Table 2 and the Bible is revealing. The Creator always multiplies or divides and never adds numbers. Uniquely, the multiples of 8 produce a numerical countdown pattern—8, 7, 6, 5, 4, 3, 2, 1, 9, 8, 7, 6, 5, 4, 3, 2, 1, 9, 8, 7, 6, 5, 4, 3, 2, 1 corresponding to the alphanumerics of the English language *backwards*! Is civilization moving backwards, or degenerating? Many people claim, due to pollution, biological intoxication, and geopolitical misdirection, the world is coming to an end.

You may have heard the remorseful phrase, "behind the 8-ball." This references the Babylonian billiards game and means stuck in a troublesome place. This is much like life in today's world. We are largely stuck "behind the 8-ball."

You can consider this game of "8-ball" as a metaphor for what this book and chapter is largely about, dealing with counting, mathematical order, hidden meanings of numbers, creative mastery over the Game of Life, and the spiritual dynamics involved in the alphanumerics of creation.

"8-ball" is played with 15 balls, and this equals 1+5=6.

So, behind 8-ball is a "MIracle 6," that is, the "universal constant of 528."

"8-ball" also features the white cue ball—the most active ball on the table. You "break," or wack, all the balls on the table using this white ball. (This curiously reflects the Illuminati's

Caucasian control over people of color worldwide in the New World Order.) The white cue ball reflects full spectrum white light, which transmits all the colors of the rainbow.

The word "cue" literally means a "stimulus to prompt behavior," or a "musical or theatrical signal" to start a performance.

The 8 ball is black, absent of light and color. The "8" appears in a white circle in the black, or a "black hole," which is interesting since physicists theorize the universe sources from a black hole in the center of an 8-shaped universe. The black hole is believed to give rise to the double-donut-shaped, polarized "+" and "-" cosmos. The 8 ball gets in your way as you attempt to clear the polarized balls—solids vs. stripes—off the table.

If you drop the "8 ball" out of order, before clearing your set of stripes or solids, you lose the game.

Putting the "8 ball" properly in the designated pocket wins you the game.

In other words, understanding the importance of the powerful numbers is essential, as numbers are fundamental to music and everything else. The unique set of 3s, 6s, 9s, and 8s reveal special patterns reflecting mathematical laws fundamental to physics, sacred geometry, and physical reality. This knowledge is crucial to winning the Game of Life.

Manna, "Hashed" Words, & Conspiracy Realities

Two great related examples of how the meanings of words and languages have been changed to suppress people's spirituality is found in the words, "manna" and "conspiracy."

"Manna" is generally thought of as "the food miraculously provided for the Israelites in the wilderness during their flight from Egypt . . . spiritual nourishment of Divine origin."

The word manna has been "hashed" over the years so that most people are clueless about what really fed and saved the Israelites. They prevented starvation during their 40-year march from slavery to "The Promised Land" consuming this manna.

To further clarify, the word "hash" means to chop-up, muddle, or confuse something, such as language, or the meaning of words.

Keeping sacred spiritual information from *We The People* creates "dumbed down people" who are more easily controlled.

Repeatedly, the word *conspiracy*, has also been hashed over the years. The original word, "conspiracy," came from the French word, "conspire," used since the 12th century to mean: "to agree, unite . . . or 'to breathe together.'"

So really, God was the first conspirator for breathing the breath of life into Adam's nostrils.

Alternatively, the phrase "conspiracy theory," and its negative connotations, started in 1909--around the time when the Rothschild and Rockefeller League of Bankers orchestrated their takeover of music, medicine, genetics, public health, the media, and ultimately people's minds, by hashing words and muddling their meanings. Today, these bankers control governments and agencies, including the Federal Reserve, the Centers for Disease Control (CDC), the Food and Drug Adminisration (FDA) and more. They also persuade legislators to make laws mostly benefitting themselves.

Additional examples of hashing the English language include the words "immunization" and "drug." Immunization used to mean the boost of natural immunity from natural exposure to germs. Now it infers "vaccination" with a toxic, often deadly, laboratory concoction. The word "drug" has been hashed to control the natural healing industry as well. BigPharma's Gestapo, the FDA, claims that if you package or bottle anything, let's say energized silver-Water, and claim it cures or prevents any disease, it is a "drug," no longer vibrating "silver hydrosol."

Holy Water

In *Exodus* 16, and you will see that God appeared before Moses "in a cloud," and dropped himself as a loving gift in the "hoar frost"—the "white [oxygen rich] coating on a surface formed from frozen dew." in the "morning dew." The Israelites collected this life-sustaining *manna*--today popularly considered incorrectly "bread" for nutritional sustenance.

This term "bread" has been hashed too. "Bread" used to mean "money"—life-sustaining "currency," or current-sea—the ocean of green cash flowing from the Kingdom of Heaven, always available to prosper people in all ways.

After all, Water is plentiful throughout the universe, according to NASA scientists. And Water is considered part of the "Triune God."

This is consistent with the work of the *New York Times* bestselling author, Dr. Masaru Emoto, who shows that Water is actually conscious. He evidences graphically that Water responds to positive prayers differently from harsh words, yielding intelligent messages viewable at 20,000 magnification.

This is best explained by considering a bit of history and Water science. Before there was the "Trinity"—Father, Son and Holy Spirit—in history, there was God, Water, and the Holy Spirit as per *Genesis* 1:1-2.

The Water delivers the energy of LOVE, 528Hz frequency. This relates intimately to natural healing and manna.

Pure structured Water vibrates in 528Hz, as does the entire hydrated universe, as evidenced by snowflakes and their sacred geometry that mathematically features 528, as Victor Showell proves in Chapter 3.

Snowflakes are always hexagonally shaped because of the tetrahedron-shaped atomic structure of Water—H_2O—bearing three (3) atoms. There are two hydrogens and one oxygen atom in the molecule.

H_2O is a polarized molecule, meaning two adjacent H_2Os must form a hexagonal array of atoms, like the organic chemistry ring of "carbon 6."

The atoms vibrate in holy spiritual resonance using this sacred geometry—the triangulated elements in H_2O—hydrogen and oxygen.

Hydrogen, written as H+, donates the exclusive energy agent of the universe—the electron—while the radical, OH-, carries that energy. This generates the "Life Force" in everyone's blood, the primordial manna, as the Bible explains and science now confirms. (This actually infers the original root meaning of the word *conspiracy*, that references the pure energetic relationship between God and *We The People* manifested through the breath.)

God gave us life, pure Spirit/Water, and life-sustaining hydrogen and oxygen. This is pure manna that vibrates mathematically transmitting spirituality!

This is additional scientific proof supporting *Matthew* 4:4—that, "Men live by more than bread alone."

Manna in Hebrew: Counting the Numbers

The term manna in Hebrew holds significance beyond the above discussion. It literally provides the process by which salvation is lawfully administered, according to spiritual processes involving numbers and their counting.

This topic ties accounting (ac-counting) to free-flowing energy or spirituality.

Recall that "bread" is slang for currency, or the current-sea of green (528) energy. In accounting, for this flow of energy, the "ac" refers to *alternating current* (AC). This designates charged fluctuations (positive and negative) between electron rich and electron poor, energy waves. A counting of this numerical data yields spiritual freedom.

Amazingly, the word manna, in Hebrew, actually refers to this counting—counting of the *Omer*, most precisely. In the old days, counting was done using Omer sticks of barley.

Leviticus 23:15 says we are obligated to count the days from Passover to Shavuot. This period is known as the "Counting of the Omer." Barley was cut and brought to the Temple as an offering to count days. This simple mathematical technology—a grain offering—was referred to as the "Omer."

It is interesting that the "OM" in Eastern theology is considered the sound of "ONE," and in modern science "ER" refers to "electromagnetic radiation," both energy vibrations.

Omer counting commemorates faith, grace, mercy, and physical salvation by rebuking the "angel of death." It also recalls deliverance of Passover, the stressful Exodus, and the Shavuot, or the giving/gaining of the Law—the Torah—which was originally all sung as numbers.

This knowledge reminds us that our redemption from slavery is incomplete until we receive the Creator's Law, and then start counting, recounting, and singing the NUMBERS therein.

This provides the same background on the spiritual significance of the frequency vibration of 528, the central number of The Law. 528 resonates pure spirituality. It is the heart of The Law, as LOVE is the purest experience in life. This Law (the word/frequency/number) delivers us from evil and secures freedom from slavery!

528 is the heart-string of the Father/Son/Holy Spirit; the musical word/number/frequency/vibration characterizing faith and LOVE that secures eternal salvation.

The 33rd day of the Omer (where 3+3 = 6) commemorates a minor holiday—the miracle of the sudden stoppage of the plague. This holiday is known as Lag b'Omer. The mourning practices of the Omer period are lifted on that date.

"Lag" is not really a word; it is the number 33 in Hebrew.

Originally, each Hebrew letter in the Torah was really a NUMBER; and each number held a special meaning, or significance, pertaining to life or creation.

Speaking, singing, or chanting this alphanumeric Law, using words or sounds from vibrating lips, is a creative process involving, as you will soon learn, "cymatics." At its best, this creative audio technology recounts the truth that reestablishes harmony between man and God—the initial conspiracy.

Honoring Numbers and the Miracle of Six

The number 6, as stated previously, resonates the essence of 528Hz. This is the MIracle note, "MI," of the original Solfeggio musical scale.

This "MI6" also designates the Illuminati's Gestapo—the intelligence agency of British Secret Service. MI6 is really the western world's center of espionage and war operations.

MI6 is another example of hashing to serve evil. The designation covers the greatest secreted truth, in this case "528"—the miraculous healing power of LOVE.

This knowledge explains why Haydn's 96th symphony (9+6=15=1+5=6) is called "The Miracle Symphony." The classical composers knew about the original Solfeggio. But if you Google search this, the truth has been muddied once again.

Stories now claim that when Haydn conducted his 96th symphony, a large crystal chandelier fell from the ceiling of the concert hall into the audience. "Miraculously," it is alleged, the huge chandelier did not hurt anyone. The musical, "Phantom of the Opera," features this crashing chandelier, and the demonic "Music of the Night," as opposed to 528 "Music of the Light."

Miracle Six, Manna and Productivity

The manna—the mathematical food for miraculous manifestations through Water, including life, health, and sustainability—involves vibrating whatever, including yourself, with the *MI*racle 6 or 528/LOVE.

Evidence for this theory is found in the *Talmud*—a collection of early oral interpretations of the scriptures compiled around AD 200. In the ancient *Mishnah*, manna is treated like a supernatural substance, which is what Water really is.

There is nothing like Water. In its gaseous state, it defies the laws of gravity. So vibrating Water with the sound of 528 is sure to produce a miraculous blessing, especially when coupled with faithful heart-felt loving intention and prayer.

It is zero coincidence that manna, according to the Mishnah, was created during the twilight of the sixth day of creation. According to *Exodus*, the Sabbath was instituted the first week the manna appeared.

Celebrating the miracle of more manna manifesting, the *Mishnah* states that twice as much manna as usual was available on the sixth mornings of the week, and none at all could be found on the seventh days.

This is best explained by studies in physics, biophysics, and even medicine, that show, as previously stated, the entire universe is scaled and regulated according to the 3s, 6s, 9s, and 8s.

Test this yourself. Experiment to create powerful results in your life. Use the 3s, 6s, 9s, and 8s for anything you wish to accomplish. You will see that using this set of numbers, especially the 6s, manifests most blessedly when used in LOVE/528 for service. I believe the 6 is extra powerful because its vibration "phase-locks" (in scalar physics) to the Creator's heart-string resonating in 528.

This is the best reason for keeping the Friday night/Saturday Sabbath. If you work 7 days a week, thinking you will accomplish more, you will be disappointed. The 6s are far more materializing. By neglecting the Sabbath, you are really going against the mathematical Law of universal construction—the primordial musical-mathematics of existence and sustenance.

Considering this discovery, I now exclusively select this set of numbers for everything I am doing, from boiling eggs, to setting graphic parameters in Photoshop, and always in prayers.

Alphanumerics Creating Cymatics

With the above introduction, you may be better prepared to learn how this miracle manifestation of LOVE impacts matter. This occurs cymatically, that is, musically-mathematically.

Cymatics is the study of sound on matter. German investigator, Peter Pettersson, advanced this science by summarizing the field's top researchers' views on the creative connection between sound vibrations and physical reality. His work laid the foundation for scientifically comprehending creationism.(4)

Pettersson began with Ernst Chladni, the first observer of the shapes and forms produced as a result of sound vibrations moving electrons to form and shape matter, including you.

I've said for years, respecting these discoveries, and describing Water-filled humans, "You are a digital, bioholographic, precipitation, crystallization, miraculous manifestation of Divine frequency vibrations, coming out of Water!"

Cymaticists mostly used Water to research sound.

Chladni was, not surprisingly, a musician and physicist. Born in 1756, he laid the foundations for the discipline within physics called acoustics—the science of sound.

In 1787, Chladni published *Discoveries Concerning the Theory of Music*. In this, and other pioneering works, he explained ways to make sound waves generate visible structures.

"With the help of a violin bow which he drew perpendicularly across the edge of flat plates covered with sand," Pettersson wrote, Chladni "produced patterns and shapes which today go by the term Chladni figures."

This was significant because it demonstrated that sound actually affected physical matter. Sounds with specific frequencies held the power to create geometric forms in substances.

More recently, John Stuart Reid filmed the sound of 528Hz uniquely transmitting the sacred geometry of a thirty-six pointed star within Water. This is shown in Figure 9. Reid detailed his findings in the online journal *Hydrosonics*.org.

Reid's work confirms the earliest findings by Nathaniel Bowditch, an American mathematician, who in 1815 further advanced Chladni's works.

Bowditch studied "the patterns created by the intersection of two sine curves whose axises are perpendicular to each other, sometimes called 'Bowditch curves,' but more often 'Lissajous figures,' . . . after the French mathematician Jules-Antoine Lissajous." Both Bowditch and Lissajous concluded that the condition for these designs to arise was that the frequencies, or oscillations per second, of both curves stood in simple whole number ratios to each other, such as 1:1, 1:2, 1:3, and so on.

Bowditch produced Lissajous figures even when the frequencies were not in perfect sync, but close to whole-number ratios to each other. This indicated some amount of forgiveness in the mathematically-structured universe. The entire system, apparently, seeks "phase-locking" or symphony in scales of whole number ratios.

Considering musical-mathematical creationism, then, there are "pure tones" of whole-number frequencies that impact universal construction, sacred geometry, and physical reality most powerfully. Approximating these pure tones musically or vocally, theoretically produces increasing symphony in the system, with the word "symphony" defined as: "harmony, especially of sound or color;" or "something characterized by a harmonious combination of elements."

This knowledge, applied in your life is golden. This is the future of medicine. Applying certain frequencies of sound and light for "electro-medicine" can potentially heal most illnesses.

528Hz is one such pure tone according to the mathematical analyses conducted by Marko Rodin, as discussed in Chapter 9.(5)

More recently, Victor Showell confirmed the importance of 528Hz in cosmology and pyramid sacred geometry, showing this "heart frequency" is involved in the formation of universal constants, ancient Pi and Phi.(6)

The cosmos, as briefly mentioned, is spiraling in accordance with nine primordial pure tones I call "The Perfect Circle of Sound™". NASA recordings of the Sun and Jupiter, for instance, audibly confirms 528Hz harmony in these circular rotating expressions of cosmic music.(7)

It makes sense that large high-volume energies would impact, powerfully entrain, or phase-lock lesser energies and smaller structures. So playing music in 528, that brings you in harmony with the universal constants, this conceivably pulls you back into the matrix of creation for hydrosonic recreation. This entrainment best explains reports that broken DNA can be vibrated back to normalcy, using 528Hz frequency.

Health Science & Cymatic Creationism

The science of cymatics asserts the mechanism by which spirit, or energy, vibrates and resonates your Water-filled physical body back into balance and health.(4)

Lissajous figures are transformed by fluctuating frequencies. This is much like changing fractal art by altering mathematical equations in computer programs.

Introduction to Musical Creationism

The universe is much like fractal art or cymatic manifestations. Various formations occur due to changes in vibrations interacting with major (pure tone Solfeggio) entrainment forces.

The most entrainment is forced by Müller's standing gravitational wave operating with the "In 6," as graphed in Figure 1. The mathematics of the central nodes of sound waves impact and interact with the main standing gravitational wave—the SGW—producing holographic reality.(3)

What creates the variations in the shapes of universal constituents, or physical matter, including the sacred geometry of biology, or bioholograms, is "the phase-differential, or the angle between the two curves," Pettersson wrote.

In other words, "the way in which their mathematical rhythms or periods," and their whole number harmonics, coincided (or not) determined the shape and movement of physical structures.

Likewise, pertaining to healing, harmonious, or discordant, frequencies have been shown to produce striking differences in human tissues. Sound waves from the core of the universe, or SGW, entrain your DNA and other structures for cymatic reconstruction commonly called healing.(8)

Extending this thesis further, related biosonic vibrations result in everything from your unique eye color to the shape of your toes.

Sure your parents gave you certain genetic traits, but you are a lot more than paternal and maternal genes. Researchers found DNA protein-production mechanisms account for only about 3% of genetic function.(8)

Alternatively, genetic industrialists have institutionally-degraded genetic science by using the name "junk DNA" to discredit genetic energy operations responsible for more than 90% of DNA's activity. This involves biosonics and/or bioelectrics. Sound and light signaling is really what causes your eye color to be recreated every nano-instant of your life.(8)

In other words, you can thank your parents for about 3% of your existence, and thank God for more than 90% of your moment-to-moment sustenance.

This also explains why sleep is so rejuvenating. The Chinese proverb, "Sit quiet, be still, Spring comes and the grass grows green," applies. The green grass is vibrating at 528Hz. Go to sleep feeling sick, tired, and weak, and awaken refreshed and healed by heavenly 528Hz vibrations sourcing from the core of the universe, our Creator's kingdom.

Recall that animals, especially dogs, eat 528Hz-colored grass to heal. Only humans have a hard time comprehending the miraculous healing power of greenish-yellow chlorophyll that is vibrating with 528Hz from the heart of the rainbow!

In 1967, Hans Jenny, a Swiss physician and researcher, published *The Structure and Dynamics of Waves and Vibrations*. Jenny, like Chladni two-hundred years earlier, showed what happens when various materials like Water, sand, iron filings, spores, and viscous substances, were vibrated on membranes and metal plates. Shapes and patterns in motion appeared that varied from "perfectly ordered and stationary" to chaotic.(4)

Physical health, versus disease chaos, similarly results from harmony versus dissonance, or too many or too few core frequency transmissions. The right amount of LOVE, or 528Hz, is sustaining. Too little is distressing and sickening.

Pettersson acknowledged Jenny for originating the field of cymatics that allowed people to observe the physical results of voice, tones, and music. Jenny applied the name cymatics to this area of research from the Greek term "kyma," meaning "wave." Thus, cymatics could be defined as: "The study of how vibrations generate and influence physical patterns, shapes, and material moving processes," including those ongoing in your cells and tissues.

In addition, using sand and a tonoscope, Jenny "noticed

Figure 3. Cymatics of Hebrew Sounds Forming Their Respective Letter Shapes

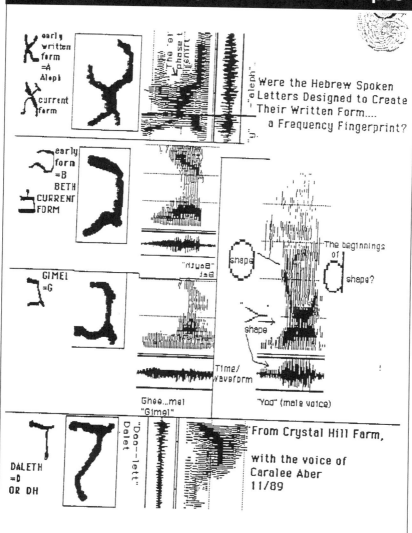

This phenomenon of alphabet-cymatics was first reported by Hans Jenny, but is now part of contested research on "frequency finger-prints" advanced by civil litigants Stan Tenen and Dan Winter. Shown here are the first four Hebrew alphabet letters: aleph, beth, gimel, and daleth, allegedly recorded by frequency registration graphing equipment. The source, Joseph Puleo, credits S. Tenen and D. Winter in "A Personal Journey into the Truth," a self-published workbook, 1998.

that when the vowels of the ancient languages of Hebrew and Sanskrit were pronounced," vibrating sand "took the shape of the written symbols for these vowels." Modern languages, including English, failed to generate these patterns.

American researchers, Stan Tenen and Dan Winter reportedly reproduced some of these cymatic alphabet effects using the Hebrew alphabet. They were reported to have concluded that the "sacred languages" were indeed sacred in this way. Figure 3 shows a sample of their alleged research that was later retracted when the two men engaged in a legal dispute. Thus, Jenny's original determinations evidencing alphabet-cymatics awaits additional independent confirmations.

[Editor's note: It is sad that such an important area of investigation would be corrupted by dissonance in human relations and damaging litigation, in this case allegedly won by Tenen. (9)]

Indeed, there are agents for the "dark side" that hash this information, or do not want you to know the truth that shall set everyone free.

These revelations lay the foundation for understanding creationism, and yourself, as a "child of God," created by the Creator's spoken word/sound/math as detailed in the *Book of Genesis*. The implications to civilization are revolutionary and evolutionary.

Think about this. If everything is a creation, including you, and you were given a simple set of nine "core creative frequencies" used to create the universe, what would you have and do?

You might start using this knowledge to recreate yourself in total health. Then, once you experience miraculous affects, you might consider sharing this knowledge with others, or recreating portions of the world that need repair.

Conclusions on Cymatic Health Science

The above revelations convinced me that creation is a function of language, and life is based on the sacred geometry of mathematics, all encoded with numbers, electromagnetic frequencies of sound, that, as Jenny concluded, relayed spiritual messages between people, and between people and God as well.

"Ultimately," as Dr. Puleo concluded, "You can't take mathematics, or even science, out of God, or God out of science, because that leaves you in ignorance with only half the picture."(2)

It is probable that this secreted sacred truth holds the capacity to free humanity completely from enslaving paradigms imposed by those who manipulate language—today they are called law-makers or legislators. These elected and appointed officials control so-called "civilized" society through their grossly dysfunctional, and damaging, legal systems that are based on definitions and manipulations of words with secret or special meanings.

Think about this. Airline passengers are forced to receive cancer-causing electromagnetic radiation for "screening." The Courts could certainly use electronic lie detectors to cut through the bogus proceedings encouraged by our current system of injustice.

Extending the power of creative words, or the "core creative frequencies," into the legal domain, some researchers claim that reverse speech does not lie. Voice recordings played backwards, they argue, "reveals truths from the soul."(10)

Hans Jenny concluded that everything, including biological evolution, can be observed to incorporate cymatic elements found throughout nature—"vibrations, oscillations, pulses, wave motions, pendulum motions, rhythmic courses of events, serial sequences, and their effects and actions." He convincingly demonstrated that all natural phenomena were ultimately dependent on, if not entirely determined by, the frequencies of creative vibration.

Jenny theorized that each cell has a unique frequency or energy signature; that a number of cells with similar frequencies created tissues vibrating another frequency in harmony with the original cell. Adding tissues to form organs creates more frequencies in harmony. Ultimately, harmony, health, and homeostatic balance is administered vibrationally.

A school of fish demonstrates this most remarkably. The entire school shifts direction instantaneously. The fish do not fight legally, or legislatively, over which direction the group should travel. Zero competitive contemplation delays the group's reactions. The school's symphony is orchestrated hydrosonically and bioelectrically, both functions of frequency vibrations. Maybe one day, humanity might benefit intuitively and similarly, beyond egoically, listening with their hearts.

Concurring with Müller, Jenny argued that recovery from disease states could be aided, or hindered by, pure tones. Mounting science supports Jenny's proposal that frequencies, above all else, influence genes, cells, and various structures in the body.

Frequencies evidence creative technology at work. The Master-Conductor Master-Composer of the universal orchestra is singing you into existence right now. God is constantly broadcasting hydrosonically, in the Spirit of holiness and harmony, in 528Hz frequency, as the coming chapters increasingly demonstrate.

LOVE is the "Universal Healer." Water is the "Universal Solvent." Music is the "Universal Language." Put them together and you emulate your Creator, and heal the world.

References

1) Horowitz LG, Dillenberg J and Rattray J. Self-care Motivation: A Model for Primary Preventive Oral Health Behavior Change. Article first published online: 9 OCT 2009. Link to: http://onlinelibrary.wiley.com/doi/10.1111/j.1746-1561.1987.tb05382.x/abstract

2) Horowitz LG and Puleo J. *Healing Codes for the Biological Apocalypse*. Sandpoint, ID: Tetrahedron, LLC, 1998. See: http://www.HealthyWorldStore.com/Healing-Codes-For-The-Biological-Apocalypse-book-p/hc%20pdf.htm

3) Müller H. *Theory of Global Scaling*. Sante Fe: NM: Institute for Space-Energy-Research, Leonard Euler, Ltd. and Global Scaling Applications, Inc., 2002.) A summary of Hartmut Müller's works on "Global Scaling" was previously provided here: http://samsanders.readyhosting.com/whatisglobalscaling.htm, and may be archived.

4) Jenny H. *Cymatics*. Quotes available from numerous sources, including: http://www.rexresearch.com/cymatics/cymatics.htm

5) Rodin M. Vortex Based Mathematics. The website is: http://markorodin.com/1.5/

6) Showell V. Teotihuacan Universal Harmonic Master Code. Showell's series of monographs available in pdf format at www.LOVE528.com. His works include 528's connections to the sacred geometry of the circle, pi and Phi.

7) Sereda D: Analysis of the Sound of the Sun Water Crystal. Article available on: http://web.mac.com/len15/LIVEH2O.info/Solar_Sonics_%26_LOVE_Harmonics_for_Peace,_Health_%26_Prosperity.html

8) Horowitz LG: *DNA: Pirates of the Sacred Spiral*. Sandpoint, ID: Tetrahedron Press., 2006.

9) Personal communications with Stan Tenen and Dan Winter.

10) Personal communication with David John Oates regarding "Reverse Speech." See: http://www.reversespeech.com/

Chapter Two:
528, John Lennon
and the Church of Satan

"It matters not who you love, where you love, why you love, when you love, or how you love, it matters only that you love."

John Lennon

Most people know that John Lennon was assassinated. Few people really understand why. Who was behind his murder?

British lawyer and journalist, Fenton Bresler, conducted an investigation into Lennon's assassination. He examined Mark David Chapman's history and arrest in, *Who Killed John Lennon?* Bresler concluded that Chapman had been hypnotized. He acted like a "Manchurian candidate" during a CIA/FBI COINTELPRO operation.

Lennon was a war protestor and tax critic who prescribed anti-government policies. After writing "Working Man's Hero," critical of governmental corruption, the "dissident" Beatle was considered an enemy of the State. He was about to launch a major peace campaign to end global injustices with LOVE when he was killed. The Illuminati worked through J. Edgar Hoover, who targeted Lennon according to Bresler's review of the evidence.

What does this have to do with 528? Everything Lennon stood, and died, for.

There are many musicians who claim that John Lennon's piano was tuned lower than "standard tuning," especially on The Beatles' *White Album*.

Lennon's Altered Tuning

Blogs and chat rooms on the Internet post claims that Ringo was credited by John for being a great drummer because he tuned his drums lower than standard.

Kettner and Rubenstein instructed drummers that, "Tuning your resonant heads lower than your batter heads will cause a downward 'pitch bend' and increase sustain."(1)

The same has been found by researcher of piano design, Daniel Kohler, tuning up to A=444Hz (that results in C[5] resonating very close to "528"), as described in Chapter 4.

Paul McCartney is also rumored to have pitched his bass lower in some of The Beatles' recordings.

It is very likely that Lennon, who promoted the healing power of LOVE, understood the metaphysics of music. His research probably indicated that diatonic scale tunings produced more "ecstatic listening," as he sought superior, more spiritual, resonance with longer sustains. This, he likely learned, would be expected from tunings that used "rational" numbers or whole number ratios.

In fact, we now know that Lennon and McCartney recorded some of their most popular songs tuning to 528, thanks to the research of Christopher Louis (contact addres: lunartunar@gmail.com). An avid investigator of the Solfeggio frequencies, and a talented recording artist, Mr. Louis posted on YouTube comparisons of 528 and some Lennon and McCartney classics, including *Imagine*, *Hey Jude*, *Let It Be*, and part of *Band on the Run*. Louis concluded, McCartney "has been tuning himself and his band to 528 since at least 1999."

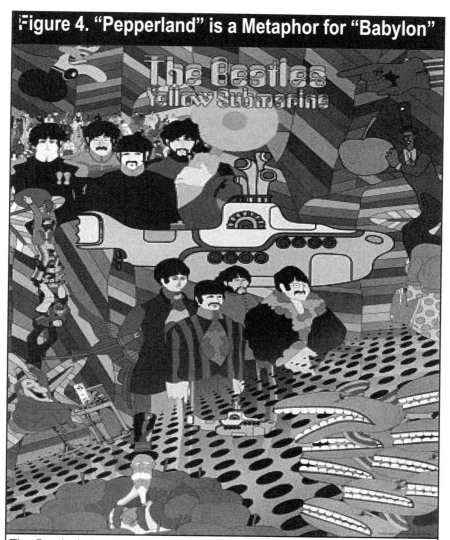

Figure 4. "Pepperland" is a Metaphor for "Babylon"

The Beatles' classic animation, *Yellow Submarine*, told the story of colorful creative "Pepperland" people becoming genocidally frozen in fragile black-and-white due to "Blue Meanies" who jailed their musical instruments and silenced their music. Only the "Captain" escaped to appeal to The Beatles to help save his civilization from the deathly scourge. In the end, The Beatles freed the instruments and voices. The LOVE music was so harsh to the Meanies that they ran for the hills. They later surrendered, in the end, with loving hearts. Everyone sings: "Love, Love, Love . . . All you need is LOVE."

Attacks Against Horowitz and 528

I've added this information to draw your attention to Lennon's genius, and his nemeses that control the CIA/FBI. COINTELPRO agents are still alive and active. I should know. They recently plotted to assassinate me as well. Their plot was exposed in 2010 as evidenced by investigative journalist Sherri Kane, and myself.(2)

Agent provocateurs Greg Szymanski (a.k.a., Eric Samuelson), allied with a man who calls himself "Dr. True Ott," David Rockefeller ally, Benjamin Fulford, and "music engineer" Don Nicoloff, who infiltrated, and tried to sabotage, 528records.com. All are now implicated in two murders, and for adding me to their "hit list."

These agents drew me into the murder of world leading financial industries analyst, Christopher Story (a.k.a., Edward Harle).Their plot included libeling me using the Internet and forged documents, including a fake list of Knights of Malta members, and setting me up to be assassinated by a "religious fanatic." They promoted an Illuminati shill named Leo Zagami, a religious *music* freak with ties to the Knights of Malta, but dressed him to feign my Knights of Hospitaller attire.

I had been honored with knighthood by the legitimate Hospitallers organization for my work in vaccine risk awareness. The Knights of Malta, linked to BigPharma, were attempting to put the Knights of Hospitaller organization out of business. BigPharma does not appreciate the Hospitallers' "Clinics for Humanity Project" to bring free natural healing clinics worldwide. Hospitaller officials gladly support my work on 528 music for natural healing as well.

This story is somewhat confusing, as every covert intelligence operation is, when involving double-agents and you first learn about it. Suffice it to say, that Sherri Kane thoroughly exposed these demons and their connections to a CIA/FBI "Church of Satan" organization that had also targeted, and assassinated Lennon, according to her and Bresler's research.

Shockingly, this group also maintains solid connections to the FBI's impotent missing children investigative branch found linked to child-trafficking and the new Temple of Set. This group of criminals features leading U.S. military propagandist, and Church of Set founder, Michael Aquino. Surprisingly, ex-FBI official and child-trafficking "expert," Ted Gunderson, is implicated as the ex-husband of Anton LaVey's widow and successor in the Church of Satan.

The Church of Satan was founded by LaVey, based upon Aleister Crowley's writings.

Therefore, it did not surprise me to read this group's counter-intelligence attempting to discredit me and disparage 528. Their campaign stupidly linked 528 to the infamous satanist, Crowley.

Using the domain AboveTopSecret.com, the Langley, Virginia, CIA/COINTELPRO group spread lies about 528, just as Kane, and I, were exposing Aquino's "mad dogs," including Timothy Patrick White.

Similar to a "Twilight Zone" reality, all of this followed the successful international peace concert called *LIVE H2O—Concert for the Living Water*, that I produced in 2009, that featured 528.

Add to this peace initiative, the stunning expose Kane, and I, rendered on the "Partnership for New York City," that explains the 9/11 tragedy and where the World Trade Centers' reconstruction money went, and you can understand why I was targeted for a "religious murder." (See: PharmaWhores.com)

The AboveTopSecret.com authors plastered false claims about me on the Internet; writing that 528 is part of the Church of Satan, and is important to the Baphomet.

To this I responded, "A blade of grass resonates in 528Hz, the heart of the rainbow . . . It makes sense the 'Above Top Secret' group would be most knowledgeable about Aleister Crowley's affection for 528, since their friends in the FBI/CIA are clearly members of the Church of Set.

"Satan has an affection for everything the Creator creates. It is petty jealousy. The Creator created all the numbers. Each number holds special values or energies. Nikola Tesla celebrated the 3s,6s,and 9s, as did Pythagoras, Plato, and da Vinci. 528 resolves to a 6; like 666 resolves to a 9, as does 432, another reliable natural healing frequency.

"The Christian world has been taught to consider "666" a "bad" or "evil" number. The meaning of the number "6" has been hashed in the religious world. "666" is really a triple miraculous manifestation affirmation. This is why many of the wealthiest companies like PepsiCo and Exxon use this sacred "mystery school" knowledge of alpha numeric 6s in their logos. (A YouTube video titled "PEPSI, 666, and Vaccinations" contains related examples. See also Figure 28.)

"The world's greatest math geniuses always spoke of the special power of the 3s, 6s, 9s, and 8s in universal construction.

"Tesla wrote: "If humanity would only know the power of the 3s, 6s, and 9s, it would be a completely different universe."

"PLEASE REMEMBER: Satan creates nothing but chaos, and confusion by lies—COUNTERINTELLIGENCE—and steals everything that can be stolen, especially faith and LOVE for the Creator. Satan kills and steals the creator's creations. Creative technologies are also stolen or secreted. The original Solfeggio math is one example. There is nothing inherently evil about any number, since the Creator created the musical-mathematical matrix of the universe wherein every number in the "Perfect Circle of Sound" is represented.

Figure 5. Church of Satan Leaders in Entertainment

Satan is said to be the fallen "angel of light and music." Pictured here (left to right) are Michael Aquino, Sammy Davis Jr., and Anton Lavay. Aquino maliciously evolved the Church of Satan, founded by LaVey, into the currently controlling "Temple of Set." Since the Vietnam War, Aquino has also been largely in charge of the United States military's "psychological warfare" operations. These include CIA black ops, Hollywood productions, and network television propaganda called "programming."

Aquino has a history, especially in San Francisco, of engaging in cult abductions, murders, and rapes of children. Missing children annually in the U.S. alone is reportedly nearing a half-million. This is more than those dying of heart diseases evey year; with barely a word issued by the mainstream media.

Many music industry leaders follow Church of Satan "devil-worship" and child abuse, is widely known.

The abuse harms the heart that suffers a Divine-disconnect. The LOVE "string" goes bent or breaks, like a "Broken Heart." Divine communion is degraded. This is purposeful, as evidenced by the Rockefeller Foundation's promotion of A=440Hz (F#=741Hz), "Standard Tuning," as detailed in Chapter 4: Musical Cult Control. Instituting A=440, versus A=444(C[5]=528), insured the "Devil's Interval" in relation to 528/LOVE would "poison" the music industry and *We The People*. Existential satanism would be instituted virtually worldwide for the "New World Order" that engages managed chaos most profitably. The stewards of modern Babylon's music and light, radio and television, have served their pagan gods well. But as written on i528Tunes.com, "The Great Hollywood Ending" celebrates a new day when the Illuminati ceases and desists making war on people's minds, bodies, and planet earth, in honor of the 528LOVERevolution.

"However, musicologists and classical musicians know that the 'Devil's Tone' or 'Devil's Interval' is the combination of 'MI in 528' and 'SO in 741.'"

"Michael Walton discovered that 741Hz in the original Solfeggio is dead-on the F# pitch in A=440Hz 'standard tuning.' The standard was instituted by the Rockefeller Foundation from war research into psychosocial stress producing illness and even 'mass hysteria.'

"So you see, the Devil has had his way with the music industry. A=440 'standard tuning,' and suppressing and demonizing 528.

"But you do not read one word about this, vaccination risks, or masses of missing children, from the CIA/FBI COINTEL-PRO agents.

"'Crowley loved 528 and 666. . . . The devil uses LOVE to kill. 'If you LOVE your children, you get them vaccinated,' you are told. 'If you LOVE your country, you send your children to war.'

"As you may or may not know, '666' regards the alpha-numeric code Dr. Joseph Puleo advanced in *Healing Codes for the Biological Apocalypse* that is required to solve the "counting-a-name riddle" in *Revelation* 13:18. I was the one who advanced the solution to the riddle. It implicates Henry Kissinger (Nelson Rockefeller's protege, nuclear weapons guru, and AIDS virus depopulationist) as the 'name of a man' identified by '666.'

"Suffice it to say, you would be less than 'enlightened' to fall for disinformation agents' lies and fears about 528.

"It is just like Satan, and his Temple of Set members, to discredit pure LOVE generated most powerfully by 528Hz, and to silence this music of the heart.

"Responding assertively with this intelligence, recreating the world as we choose to have it, including yourself if you desire it, seems reasonable under the circumstances.

"Much evidence indicates the sound of LOVE is 528Hz, and LOVE is the 'Universal Healer.' So it is reasonable that the more we play music in 528, with heart-felt loving intent to heal ourselves and our planet, that energy will ripple out like waves in a pond.

"'Spirit/Water' in your body amplifies LOVE, 528Hz, and opens your heart. LOVE, the finest virtue, expands consciousness and intelligence to advance solutions to our world's worst problems."

In other words, this book, with your support, is prompting the real-life enactment of the "plan" John Lennon encouraged in *Revolution*, and The Beatles animation *Yellow Submarine*.

Recall the urgency and threatened extinction of the underwater people of "Pepperland."

The 528LOVERevolution has the same mission as John Lennon had, as did *Sgt. Pepper's Lonely Hearts Club Band*— to free humanity with the music that instantly turns fearful, frozen, fragile, colorless people into powerful, colorful, creative, global celebrants of LOVE, peace, natural healing, and prosperity in all ways.

Sure I have my critics and nay-sayers who contend that I am a fraud, or this humanitarian project cannot succeed.

I simply prescribe for those who are arrogantly attached to intoxication and degeneration what John Lennon wrote:

"You'd better free your mind instead."

Welcome to Pepperland.

The 528 Versus 741 Decision

As further discussed in Chapter 12, good cannot exist without evil, just as everything can not exist without nothing.

This begins to explain why we have evil in the world; why demonic forces have dominated Earth's politics and economics, and why greed and fear seem insurmountable obstacles to world peace and sustainable LOVE.

I raise this issue because The Perfect Circle of Sound™ includes both 528 and 741Hz frequencies. They are disharmonious tones, meaning they don't play well together. Their vibrations are inherently discordant. That is why their simultaneous expression is called the "Devil's Tone" in musicology.

Chapter 3 and Table 3 details Victor Showell's analyses of 528 and 741Hz, and how they fit in with geometry, numerology, and cosmology. You see, they are both in the "big picture."

This proof requires reconciling the fact that dissonance, or disharmony, as opposed to peace and symphony, appears to be part of nature and nature's music.

You must also reconcile the Illuminati selecting exclusively a standard tuning that includes 741Hz (that is, the F# pitch in the A=440Hz scale) while secreting knowledge about the importance of 528Hz in nature's "Master Matrix"? Why would the Illuminati terminate 528's play in music?

That is, the C-pitch when using the A=444Hz scale—the tuning preferred by Europe's most accomplished musicians—was prohibited when A=440Hz "standard tuning" was instituted.

Clearly, a choice was made favoring the "dark side," since research indicates 741 stimulates pineal gland and egoic functions, while suppressing the heart chakra's LOVE and faith.

The Music of Good vs. Evil?

In theory, based on the evidence in this book, three primary factors influence your decisions and orientation to do good versus evil: 1) social influences, including the media and your parents, teachers, peers, or life experiences, impacting your core beliefs, values, attitudes, and behaviors; 2) "the Master Matrix"—a musical-mathematical predisposition to LOVE or not, influenced by your birth date, biocosmology, and natal resonance energy. This influence is administered by gravitational forces, frequencies, and polarities generating attraction or repulsion ("karma") in you at birth; and 3) your personal free will to make choices that may or may not be consistent with factors #1 and 2.

Notice all three are impacted by the Rockefeller Foundation's choice to institute the A=440HZ musical tuning that vibrationally quashes faith and facilitates fear.

Church of Satan or Temple of Set members, advancing the Illuminati's agenda, believe in free will too. Their egocentrism, arguably demonic dementia, rationalizes whatever damage they choose to cause. Their theology is disruptive and degenerative since they do not believe in a just God that will judge them. So they do whatever their greed and arrogance dictates. Guilt and remorse is not part of their cult.

The Illuminati's motto, "Novo Ordo Seclorum," implies a new order for the world based on managed chaos, and apparently musical dissonance. "Crisis capitalism" seems to be their mode of operation.

Alternatively, the laws of physics and mathematics honor Divine law, including Jesus's and Moses's advice to "LOVE God," "LOVE your neighbor," and "Don't Kill," because "for every action there is a reaction."

Our justice systems are supposed to deal judiciously with those who damage others. The basis for man's laws are God's laws, and the way God punishes sinners, according to the Bible, is by withdrawing protection against the negative repercussion of your actions. "What goes around comes around." Choices affecting your life impact others, and potentially the world; and always return a blessing or curse.

Metaphorically, choosing to damage others is like turning the volume down on 528 while raising the volume on 741 music. This is precisely what the Illuminati has done to damage humanity by silencing the music of LOVE/528.

The Illuminati, by instituting A=440Hz standard tuning, advances spiritual warfare, bioacoustic dissonance to LOVE/528, and the dis-eases it causes. This obviously advances financial and population control agendas. This is treason against *We The People,* administered musically.

Much of this issue comes down to "free will." If people knew the whole truth, including the Church of Satan's involvements in the music industry, most would choose 528 options instead.

God's greatest gift to humanity is free will—the power to *choose* your destiny, to go with the flow of your spiritual identity and Divine appointment.

Freedom is the opportunity to choose LOVE, or something less.

Choose paths, or actions, consistent with your higher purpose and special gifts. This is blessed because it leads to LOVE and prosperity in all ways. Hence the saying, "Do what you LOVE, and prosperity will follow."

To be true to your "true self" is wise, and probably the best thing you can do with your life.

Alternatively, a lot of people do not know who or what their "true self" is, or how to satisfy it, thanks largely to the Illuminati's cultural misdirection. They have suppressed such truths, including this useful LOVE music. People require reeducation to stop dying of misdirection, indoctrinations, and plain old ignorance.

This situation has never been more urgent. The Illuminati intends to kill approximately 6 billion people claimed to be over populating our planet. Heaven's fallen angel of *light* and *music* is effectively administering global genocide involving psychological operations (PSYOPS) and music.

Our free will has been high-jacked along with the mainstream media, organic foods, herbal remedies, and the entertainment industries. From music and math to our calendars and science, corporate enterprises are out of sync with LOVE/528.

The masses have been lulled into indifference and apathetic silence. By default, *We The People* have consented to secure a brighter future for the wealthiest one percent.

One World Bank, One World Government, One World Court, One World Health Organization, One World Peacekeeping Force, violates free will, diversity and common sense. The fact that *We the People* relinquished our control to a small group of "illuminated banksters" is insane.

With the publication of this book, and growing awareness of 528Hz music, I pray people will awaken to say, "enough is enough."

As a memorial to John Lennon, I pray that playing more 528 music will accelerate the paradigm shift to secure a brighter future for all.

References

1) Bresler F. *Who Killed John Lennon?* St. Martins Press (September 1989). See: http://www.john-lennon.com/theassassinationofjl.htm

2) Horowitz LG. Affidavit and testimony of Dr. Leonard Horowitz regarding the murder of journalist Edward Harle, involving agent-provocateurs and co-accomplices, Benjamin Fulford, Greg Szymanski, and others linked to libel and a plot to assassinate Dr. Leonard Horowitz. See: http://web.mac.com/len15/Newsletter_&_Blog/Knighting_Controversy.html

3. Kane S. Seduce, Discredit, Separate, Intimidate, Incarcerate, and Assassinate: A Look Into Edward Harle's Murder, Benjamin Fulford's Fraud, and Why the Truth Never Reaches The Masses. See: http://www.sherrikane.com/SherriKane.com/Blog/Entries/2010/9/2_Seduce%2C_Discredit%2C_Separate%2C_Intimidate%2C_Incarcerate%2C_and_Assassinate_A_Look_Into_Edward_Harle's_Murder%2C_Benjamin_Fulford's_Fraud%2C_and_Why_the_Truth%C2%A0Never_Reaches_The_MassesBy_Sherri_Kane.html

Chapter Three:
Pi, Phi and 528
by Vic Showell and Leonard Horowitz

We have been taught that there are exactly 5280 feet in 1 mile. Drop the zero, as is routinely done in Pythagorean math, and you have "528." Wow! The "MIracle 6" note of the original Solfeggio is reflected in the measured mile, . . . and this is just the tip of the iceberg.

This chapter celebrates 528 as a *universal constant*. Surely all numbers are important, but without this "LOVE frequency," nothing would exist since the most famous mathematical constants known to science—Pi, Phi, and the Golden Mean—depend heavily on 528/LOVE. This makes the number 528 a most important frequency impacting sacred geometry, space/time measurements, and the energetic dynamics of the universe.

As you read this chapter, and prove to yourself the quintessential importance of 528 by using your calculator to check the presented math, reflect on the fact that this information has remained buried for millennia. Consider the question of why you were never taught that the most famous mathematical constants used in physics depend heavily on this sacred "universal constant of LOVE."

This chapter is necessarily complex mathematically. A word of advice is necessary before you begin. The information and calculations presented herein exercise your abstract mind beyond your "left brain," or your left hemisphere. Your left brain is believed to engage mostly rational thought and linear analyses. See if you can "experience" the numbers, and the

Table 3. Victor Showell's Analysis of 741 Numerology in the Planetary Time Lines & Mayan Cosmology

Solfeggio 741 "Devil's Tone" Numerology
in Planetary Time Lines and Mayan Cosmology
(C) vs Sept 24 2010

$19 \times 39 = 741$ Solfeggio   Mars synod $780 = 20 \times 39$

Solfeggio

$19 \times 21 = \dfrac{741}{399}$ Jupiter synod $= \dfrac{13}{7}$ —— Mayan Long Count harmonics
—— Egyptian Ancient Pi sevenths harmonics (22 / 7)

$e = 2.71828$

$\dfrac{399}{741} \times 260$ Tzolkin $- 140 = \dfrac{Phi \times e}{Pi} \times 100$ = 140. 0012 rounded

$140 \times$ Royal Cubit $\times$ Ancient Pi $= 9072$ inches in Khufu pyramid base

399 days $=$ Jupiter synod with Earth

$912 = 100 \times$ tangent $54 \times$ Planck's 6.626068 $\dfrac{912}{399} = \dfrac{16}{7}$

$\dfrac{912}{741} = \dfrac{16}{13}$

$741 = 81.25 \times$ tangent $54 \times$ Planck's $\dfrac{741}{285} = \dfrac{260 \text{ Tzolkin}}{2.6}$

Solfeggio $285 = 31.25 \times$ tangent $54 \times$ Planck's

$7 \times 39 = 273$ $\times$ Egyptian Ancient Pi (22 / 7) $= 858$

$\dfrac{273}{285} = \dfrac{384}{300}$ $273 \times$ Khufu Pyramid tangent 1.3333~ = Pascal 384

Pascal Venus Mars

$15 \times 39 = 585$ Mayan Long Count / Venus synod
$18 \times 39 = 702$ Dresden Codex $\dfrac{585}{702} = \dfrac{Phi \text{ squared}}{Universal \text{ Harmonic Pi}}$
$19 \times 39 = 741$ Solfeggio
$20 \times 39 = 780$ Mars synod
$21 \times 39 = 819$ Mayan Glyph
$22 \times 39 = 858$

$\dfrac{858}{819} = \dfrac{110}{105} = 1.047619048$
Mayan Glyph $\times 100$
$= 104.7619048$

exact Menkaure base length in meters $= 33.3333~ \times$ Egyptian Ancient Pi
see Menkaure pyramid diagram

$\dfrac{858}{756} = \dfrac{780}{687.27\ 27~}$ $\dfrac{858}{819} = 1.047619048$
Khufu base length feet Khufu Pyramid Mayan Glyph
Mars sidereal

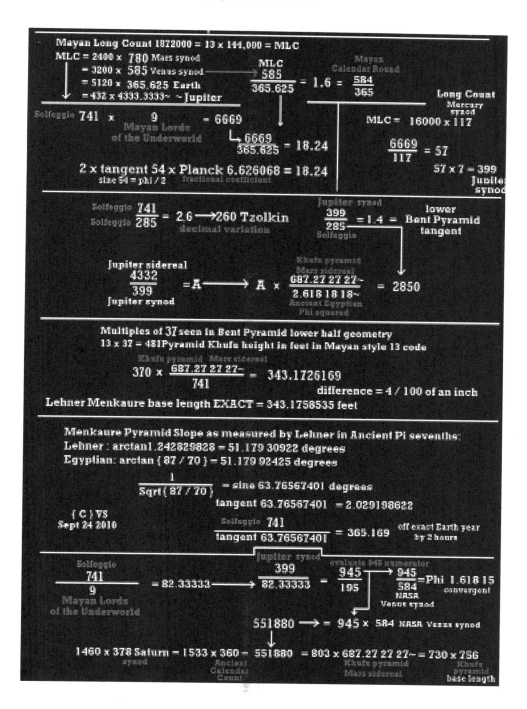

Mayan Long Count 1822000 = 13 × 144,000 = MLC

MLC = 2400 × **780** Mars synod
= 3200 × **585** Venus synod
= 5120 × 365.625 Earth
= 432 × 4333.3333~ ~ Jupiter

$$\frac{MLC}{585} \rightarrow \frac{585}{365.625} = 1.6 = \frac{584}{365}$$

Mayan Calendar Round

Long Count
Mercury synod

Solfeggio **741** × 9 = 6669
Mayan Lords of the Underworld

$$\frac{6669}{365.625} = 18.24$$

MLC = 16000 × 117

$$\frac{6669}{117} = 57$$

2 × tangent 54 × Planck 6.626068 = 18.24
sine 54 = phi / 2   fractional coefficient

57 × 7 = 399
Jupiter synod

Solfeggio $\frac{741}{285}$ = 2.6 → 260 Tzolkin
Solfeggio   decimal variation

$$\frac{399}{285} = 1.4 = \text{lower Bent Pyramid tangent}$$
Jupiter synod   Solfeggio

Jupiter sidereal
$$\frac{4332}{399} = A \longrightarrow A \times \frac{687.27\,27\,27\sim}{2.618\,18\,18\sim} = 2850$$
Jupiter synod

Khufu pyramid
Mars sidereal

Ancient Egyptian
Phi squared

Multiples of **37** seen in Bent Pyramid lower half geometry
13 × 37 = 481 Pyramid Khufu height in feet in Mayan style 13 code

Khufu pyramid   Mars sidereal
$$370 \times \frac{687.27\,27\,27\sim}{741} = 343.1726169$$

difference = 4 / 100 of an inch

Lehner Menkaure base length EXACT = 343.1758535 feet

Menkaure Pyramid Slope as measured by Lehner in Ancient Pi sevenths:
Lehner : arctan1.242829828 = 51.179 30922 degrees
Egyptian: arctan (87 / 70) = 51.179 92425 degrees

$$\frac{1}{\text{Sqrt}(87/70)} = \text{sine } 63.76567401 \text{ degrees}$$

tangent 63.76567401 = 2.029198622

{ C } VS
Sept 24 2010

Solfeggio **741**
$$\frac{741}{\text{tangent } 63.76567401} = 365.169$$

off exact Earth year by 2 hours

Solfeggio
$$\frac{741}{9} = 82.33333 \longrightarrow \frac{399}{82.33333} = \frac{945}{195}$$
Mayan Lords of the Underworld

Jupiter synod
evaluate 945 numerator

→ 945
$$\frac{945}{584} = \text{Phi } 1.618\,15$$
NASA   convergent
Venus synod

551880 → = 945 × 584 NASA Venus synod

1460 × 378 Saturn = 1533 × 360 = 551880 = 803 × 687.27 27 27~ = 730 × 756
synod   Ancient Calendar Count   Khufu pyramid Mars sidereal   Khufu pyramid base length

Table 4. Victor Showell's Analysis of 528 Numerology in the Planetary Timelines and Egyptian Cosmology

Sqrt. 10 Phi / by Pi = 1.280394935

Earth Year 365.256363 -------- >3.65256363 = X

arctan X = 74.68873878

sine 74.68873878 degrees x 1.28 = Y = 1.234567087

Khafre Pyramid slope tangent = 1.234567901

exact at 1.280000844

1 / sine X = 1.0368 00684

10368 = 72 x 144

arctan 1.0368 = 46.035~

Khafre tangent 1.33333
arctan (Phi sq. / 1.3333)
63.0108016 deg.
1.96 3525492

Use arctangent 1.27993825
from Sqrt. 10 Phi / by Pi

{ ancient Pi and 1.618 18 18~ } 51.9999 2654 deg

1.0368 x 1.27993825 = tangent 52.99989948 deg.

Now use Egyptian style tangent of 63.01 degrees

1.96 36 36 36~

arctan 1.0368 = 46.035~

10368 = 72 x 144

arctan 1.0368 = 46.035~

1.0368 / by 1.96 36 36 36~

= 0.528

x 1000 = Solfeggio 528

x 10000 = 5280 Mile

(C) VS 8 28 2010

52

math, shared here through the more abstract view of your right brain, as well as your rational mind or left brain.

Using cinema as a metaphor for explaining this, left brain function might be thought of as viewing a 3-D movie without the special glasses required to gain the depth of focus. The picture looks fuzzy without the right optics.

The "right brain," the glasses in this metaphor, is believed to operate more wholistically, intuitively, and visually. This is what is necessary in this chapter because this subject engages "matrix math" or "vortex math." This requires you enter the realm of multi-dimensional physics beyond two or three dimensional space.

For instance, the numbers to the right of decimal points may relay an entirely different concept, or dimension, than the whole numbers to the left of decimal points.

Relax if you find yourself becoming a bit confused or frustrated with the mathematical analyses presented. Simply realize that you are learning to look at space/time through a multi-dimensional lens that characterizes matter or objects, such as a Giza pyramid, or the universe-at-large, in terms of its mathematical patterns moving in multiple directions simultaneously.

If you really dislike math, you might choose to skip forward to Chapter 4.

If you enjoy math, and are a serious student of the sciences, then this chapter is worth your time to read, carefully confirming the accuracy of the calculations.

Credit this contribution mainly to the genius of mathematician Victor Showell, who specializes in sacred geometry of pyramids, and related metaphysics.(1)

"Vic" has produced a major blessing for humanity through his research. His revelations more than legitimize the use of 528 in music and healing. Showell's pyramid measurements and mathematical analyses show 528 is a number/frequency that is central to pyramid geometry, cosmology, and nature's bounty. His determinations, in my opinion, are revolutionary.

Vic Showell explains that the modern mathematical constants, Pi and Phi, are different from ancient Pi and Phi. The difference, making Pi and Phi irrational numbers, comes from neglecting 528 and the rest of the Perfect Circle of Sound™ frequencies. Factoring these sacred Solfeggio numbers into simple equations transforms Pi and Phi into rational numbers with repeating decimal digits.

Showell's studies shed light on sacred geometry, musical mathematics, and healing Water science.(2)

The following is an introduction to one of Vic Showell's masterful monographs proving mathematically that pyramid sacred geometry, cosmology, Pi, Phi, and the Fibonacci series, found in music, and throughout nature, are intimately linked to 528 frequency mathematics and harmonics.

Showell also proved 396Hz frequency in The Perfect Circle of Sound™ is fundamentally related to creative *hydrosonics*. His analysis of 741Hz, opposing 528Hz as the "Devil's Tone," is also an extraordinary contribution.

In essence, Showell's revelations compel consideration of musical creationism and cymatics that includes a new theory on physical reality and reactions in space/time. Among these considerations are three rEVOLutionary postulates:

> **Postulate 1**: All electrons are spinning musically; vibrating harmonically, as determined by nine core creative frequencies comprising a "The Perfect Circle of Sound™."

> **Postulate 2**: These nine frequencies of sound determine Pi, Phi, the Fibonacci series, and all sacred geometrics including the structure of the universe, and the laws of physics.

Postulate 3: All piezoelectricity, oxidative-reductive reactions and electromagnetism affecting chemical interactions rely(ies) on the harmonics or dissonance of frequencies within a musical (vibrational) mathematical matrix fundamental to physics and chemistry; all determined by simply nine Perfect Circle of Sound™ frequencies."

How did Showell come to these postulates and astonishing revelations?

"I just don't know how it comes to me," he wrote. "It must be that I am so subconsciously tuned to the synchronous harmonics of the ancient time lines that it just happens."

If you are compelled by your left-brain, requiring solid evidence to be persuaded about anything important, you will relish Showell's contributions. His monographs on this subject, freely downloadable in pdf files from LOVE528.com, are superb. Especially his latest "Teotihuacan Universal Harmonic Master Code."(1)

In his series of mathematical analyses, he has identified the fundamental mathematical and geometrical measurements of the Egyptian pyramids reflecting the tetrahedron structure of Water. His determinations of mathematical constants provide greater truth to set humanity free from many misconceptions, especially in the world of science..

Showell's discoveries help confirm the existence of scaling based on the original Solfeggio, and the ancient mathematical constants, Pi and Phi. This knowledge increases understanding of how the mathematical matrix of the universe, and the Standing Gravitational Wave (SGW) advanced by Hartmut Müller,(3) harmonically relates to the medium and mechanism for creation. A "creative Solfeggio carrier wave," so to speak, is influencing, and even sustaining, everything.

Here are the broadcasting channels through which the Source of the universe vibrates everything into existence. This main "carrier wave," and "creative wave set," Mr. Showell's research proves, features 528Hz.

Figure 6. Bending of Light Through Pyramid Crystal

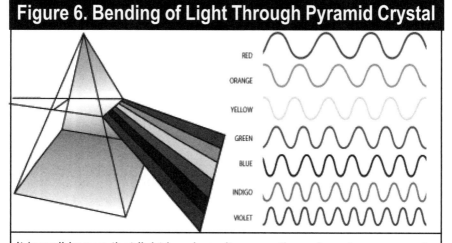

It is well known that light bends as it moves through a glass, or quartz, crystal. Diagrammed above is white light bending and transforming into a rainbow of colors. Greenish-yellow is in the center of the rainbow. This is 528Hz frequency of light.

The same thing happens as light moves through Water forming real natural rainbows. The fact is, Water molecules are shaped like tiny pyramids, little tetrahedrons. Many Water molecules together act like a larger crystal, because Water is a "liquid crystal superconductor" of light and sound.

Thus, with the universe filled with Water, it stands to reason that sound and light frequencies traveling through this Water matrix, differentiated by the part of the matrix through which this energy is transmitting, gives rise to unique outcomes.

Holographic fractal manifestations sourcing from sound and Water theoretically explain physical reality most simply and reasonably.

Graphics courtesy of the Atmospheric Science Data Center. See: http://eosweb.larc.nasa.gov/EDDOCS/Wavelengths_for_Colors.html

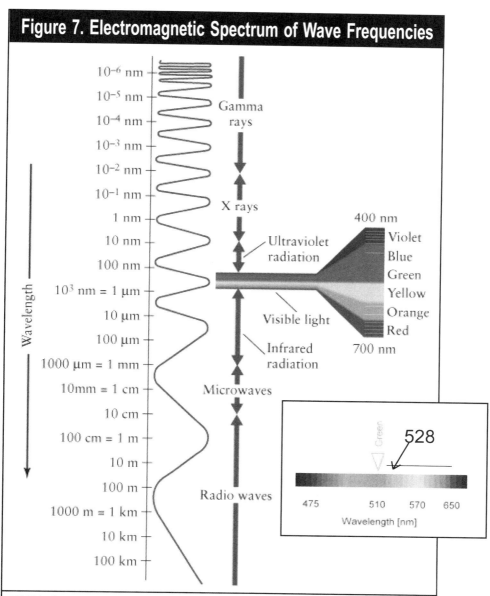

Figure 7. Electromagnetic Spectrum of Wave Frequencies

528Hz frequency of light is apparently very close to the heart of the electromagnetic energy spectrum. This is one of the main reasons chlorophyll, and most of the botanical world, celebrates "528." Source:
http://eosweb.larc.nasa.gov/EDDOCS/Wavelengths_for_Colors.html

Figure 8. Sacred Geometry of Energy Carrying Pigments

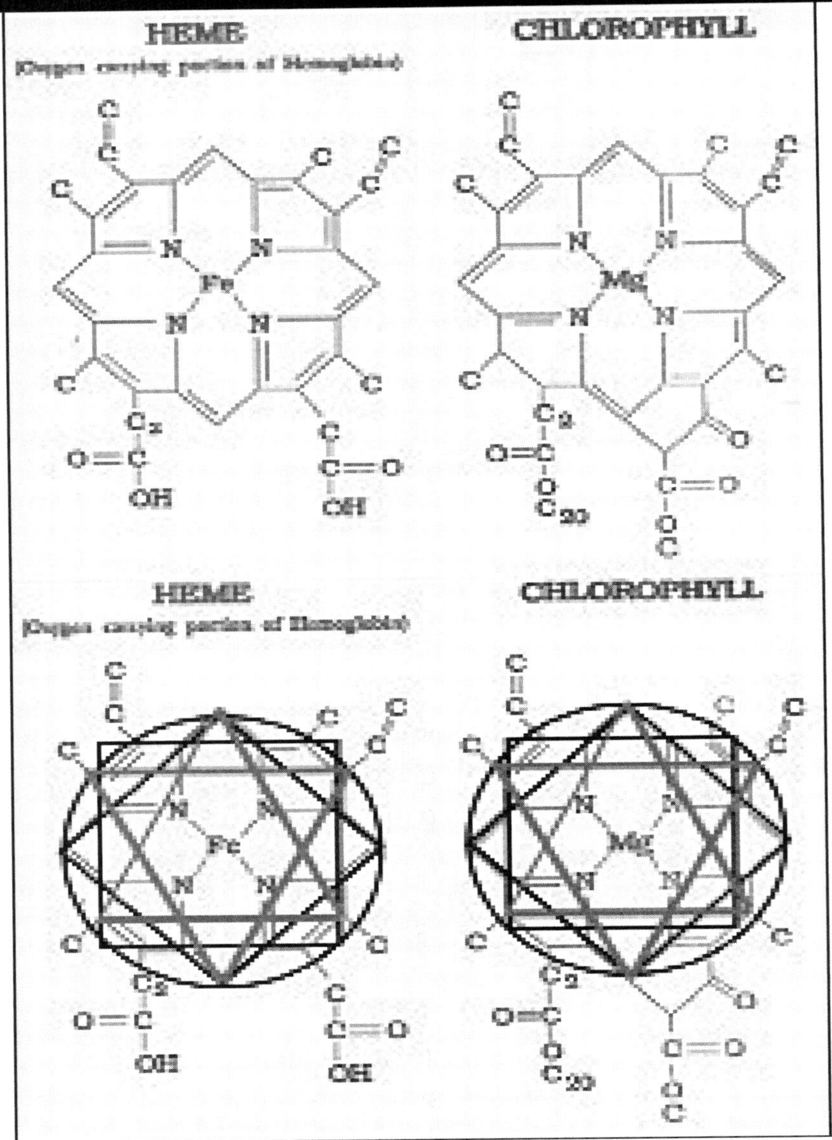

The organic structuring of the hemoglobin and chlorophyll molecules are very similar, here showing obvious sacred geometry associated with 528Hz frequency according to research by Vic Showell and others.

If "LOVE is the 'Universal Healer,'" it makes sense that it would be a spiritual energy carried universally on a special broadcasting "channel," or wave frequency. This is just like your radio receiver that uses digital electromagnetic technology to tune into a "clear-channel." 528Hz appears to carry a very special and very *powerful* signal for universal construction and reconstruction.

This "good vibration" identified as the "miracle frequency" at the heart of the ancient Solfeggio,(3) is, likewise, at the heart of the sound and light spectrums. (See Figures 6 and 7.) Many investigators, including esteemed scientists, state 528Hz has been used to restore damaged DNA as a function of its unique and powerful vibration.(4) It does this, theoretically, through cymatics or "creative hydrosonics."(5)

Background on Pi

Pi, or π, is one of the most important mathematical constants. It represents the ratio of any circle's circumference to its diameter in Euclidean geometry. This is the same as the ratio of a circle's area to the square of its radius. Many formulae from mathematics, science, and engineering involve π.[6]

The mathematical constant Pi is a real number that arises naturally in mathematics. Unlike physical constants, mathematical constants are defined independently of physical measurement.

In other words, in math—the Creator's language—there are physical and metaphysical constants, or laws that govern everything including nature's structure, function, and balance.

Modern Pi is approximately equal to 3.14159. It is, thus, promoted as an "irrational number," which means that it cannot be expressed as a fraction m/n, where m and n are inte-

Figure 9. 528Hz Hydrosonic CymaGlyph by Reid

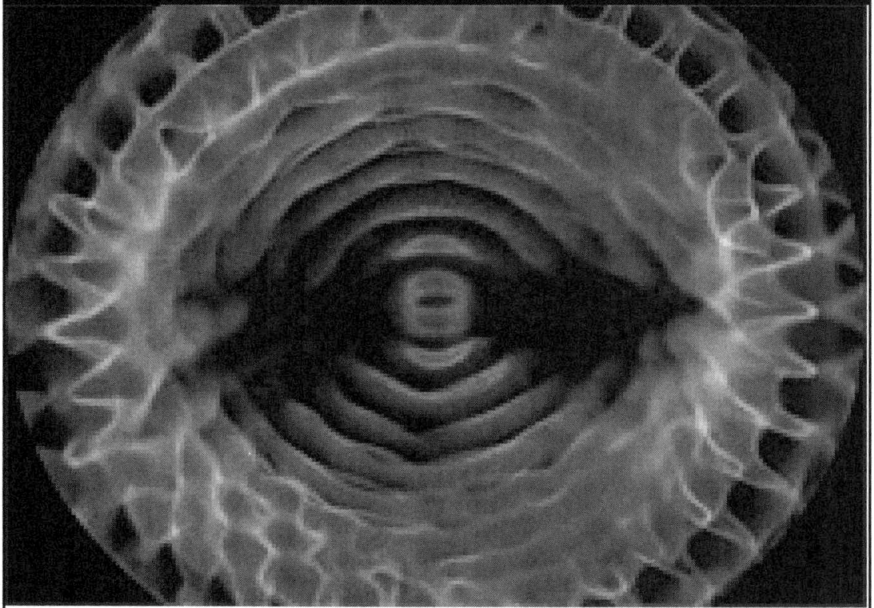

This 36-pointed star CymaGlyph was produced by investigator John Stuart Reid using a 528Hz pure tone. Reid reported this kind of image is entirely unique, especially as it cuts the circle into 36 portions, 10-degrees each. This information is consistent with Vic Showell's mathematical analyses showing 528Hz, associated with the 5280 feet in a mile, is fundamental to the sacred geometry of the circle.

gers. Consequently, its decimal representation never ends or repeats. It is furthermore a "transcendental number," which means that no finite sequence of algebraic operations on integers (powers, roots, sums, etc.) could ever produce it.

"Throughout the history of mathematics," *Wikipedia* reports, "much effort has been made to determine π more accurately and understand its nature; fascination with the number has even carried over into culture at large."

This fascination with the accuracy of Pi is the subject of Vic Showell's contribution.

Background on Sacred Geometry, Phi and the Golden Ratio

The golden ratio, also known as the divine proportion, golden mean, or golden section, is a number often encountered when taking the ratios of distances in simple geometric figures such as the pentagon, pentagram, decagon and dodecahedron.

The golden ratio is found in the pyramids of Giza and the Parthenon at Athens. (6)

Pi and Phi are important in trigonometry. For example, if you divide a 360° circle into 5 sections of 72° each, you will get a five point pentagon whose dimensions are all based on Phi relationships. Accordingly, Phi, Pi and 5 (a Fibonacci number) are related through trigonometry.(1)

Dale Lohr, and expert in this field of analysis, contributed the following equation defining the relationship between Pi, Phi and 5 as follows:

Pi = 5 arccos (.5 Phi)

Note that the angle of ½ of Phi, or .5 Phi, is 36 degrees, of which there are 10 in a circle or 5 in Pi radians.

A related CymaGlyph is shown in Figure 9. This was produced by John Stuart Reid, a pioneer in acoustic research and cymatic measurements. Reid tested 528Hz frequency transmission through Water and filmed this result. Consistent with Lohr's contributions, Reid showed 528Hz frequency uniquely produced a 360 degree circle containing 36 nodes, each perfectly ten (10) degrees.(7)

This evidences the angle of .5 Phi is formed from 528Hz, and consequently the structure of circles depends on the mathematical signature, or creative energy, of 528.

528 in Cosmic Design

The CymaGlyph in Figure 9 graphs the amazing result of 528Hz frequency resonating Water to deliver a message of cosmic conception, universal design, and Divine LOVE.(8)

Central to the CymaGlyph is a "black hole" in the middle of a "69" structure. Physicists report that the universe emerges from a black hole. The central 69 (yin/yang) symbol bears resemblance to the structure shown in Figure 29—the double toroid structure of the universe graphed by physicist, Nassim Harramein, and mathematician, Marko Rodin. Their independent determinations evidence the "double donut" shape of the universe, and their works are widely accepted following peer review. Rodin's and Harramein's works are further described in Chapter 9.(9)

The esoteric context for the 69 central image appears to be three sets of lips, or labia, giving birth to the resonating structures of the 36-pointed star. This reflects the entire vibrating Circle of Creation.

As mentioned at the start of this chapter, an intriguing virtue of 528 is that it is a decimal variant of the 5280 ft. mile, that is founded on the sacred geometry of the circle, and thus, intimately linked to the Pi and Phi constants.(1)

In analyzing pyramid geometry as it relates to Pi and Phi, Showell reported, "Now we know that the pyramid works perfectly in feet."(1)

He also concluded that this finding of the 528/mile relationship, "gives it priority above 396 in this context" of considering the relative importance of the Solfeggio frequencies to sacred geometry and mathematical constants.

The "396" Showell refers to here is the first note—called "UT"—of the original Solfeggio musical scale. By definition, it is related to electromagnetism, and all the other notes in the musical scale. This frequency, according to *Webster's Diction-ary*, also represents the entire spectrum of human emotions, from grief to joy, as shown in Chapter 5, Table 5.

Showell continued summarizing his amazing analysis of 528, and its relative importance in cosmic design as compared with 396, beginning with the sine of the tetrahedral latitude determined by Richard C. Hoagland (an expert in space/time physics); the sine 19.47122061 = 0.333333333. (The tetrahe-dron, by the way, is the structure of Water.)

[Author's note: It should also be noted that whenever you see whole numbers, or repeating numbers or patterns of num-bers to the right of the decimal point, such as this number, 0.333333333~to infinity, you are dealing with a *rational num-ber,* as opposed to *irrational number*. This difference is very im-portant and will be addressed again in greater detail in Chapter 9 while referencing Ernest McClain's research and the "urgent problem" concerning "528" called the "Pythagorean Comma."]

"The formula using the 19.47122061 to get the value of Pi is of great consequence," Showell reported:

> "The major clue I got was that 528÷6 = 88, which is the '*mercury sidereal*.' [Editor's note: The "mercury sidereal" is a measure of movement of mercury in relation to the sun.]

> "And in the entire 11, 22, 33, 44, 55, 66, 77, . . . system, as with 11 x 8; with highest value to 99 for 4-D hypercube math, only 528 does this above [that is, fits into this system] with Mercury 88.

> "The 528÷6 = 88 took me to pyramid height 481 which is the *planetary synod cycle* value 481 x 88 = x. [i.e., 481x88=42.328]

> "Then x divided by Mars Jupiter synod 816.5 = 51.840~ and the slope of the Great Giza pyramid is this number, 51 .8427~

> "This is NOT a coincidence!

63

"528÷396 = 1.333333. And that process works on various Solfeggio frequencies.

"The slope of the second pyramid at Giza is supposed to be just over 53 degrees. Arctangent 1.33333333333333 = 53.13 degrees.

"Now, look at what the sine and cosine are with that angle—0.8 and 0.6

"528 is a harmonic codex of the Solfeggio tones 852 and 285 Hertz.

"528÷336, the high physics symmetry value, = aPi / 2

"528 x [the square root of 2 which is] 1.41414141414~ = 746.6666~ which flows thru the polytope chart. But when you DIVIDE 528 by ancient square root of two, or 1.4142857 142857 142857 = 373.3333333~.

Figure 10. 528Hz Math Links to 16 Point Star

Art from Masonic temple shows 16-pointed star. Divide 528 by 16 to get 33--a high degree Freemason level widely reported..

"From here it goes nuts and spirals thru the polytope values and *all* the Mayan and Egyptian numbers.

"I will give you one example," Showell continued:

"The Saqqara pyramid height = 14. And 14 /11 = arctangent slope of the Giza pyramid.

"14 = 10 Phi x e, then divided by Pi gives you [e] = 2.71828 373.33333 ÷ 14 = 26.666666~, and that is a fundamental node of the tetrahedral and Egyptian system.

"Any decimal variation of 1296 works, similarly. I use the Kemi, thusly: 12960000 / by 26.666666666~ = 486000 = 486 = 9 x 54. And 54 is pentagonal. 54 and 378 x 0 . 142957 142857 142857~ = 54

[Editor's Note: The Mayan Long Count, abbreviated MLC below, that equals 1872000, is featured in Showell's "Freemason Code Deciphered from Grand Masonic Lodge Architecture into Phi and Pi" available online.]

"MLC [1872000] ÷ [26.6666~] = [70200] ---> [702] dresden codex

"Next, look at above equation:
528 x 1.41414141414~ = 746.6666~

"528 does the same magic in 187200 and 1296000.

"The other Solfeggio frequencies DON'T do this, except 396 which does almost as much as 528 totally, and really is equally important. . . .

"Figure 10 shows some research looking at Masonic values. I have found in a Masonic temple the 528 divided by the 16 pointed star = 33

"396 does not compute like this divisably with 16, but functions in a multiplicative sense dependent on 528.

"16 x 396 = 6336; then divide by 528 = 12. That is, 12 x 528 = 6336; and you know what 12 does when squared: 12 squared = 144; [and this] relates to 144,000 and the baktun.

[Author's note: One "baktun" is the equivalent of 144,000 days in the Mayan calendar. Also, the 144,000 number is referenced in the *Book of Revelation* (14:1) as those who are sealed with the LOVE of God, and the Lamb. These people sing a "new song" in the End Times in order to prompt the Messianic Age—1,000 years of world peace. The six Solfeggio note definitions in Table 5 regard this prophesied event.]

"1872000 divided by 6336 = 295 .45454545454~. Now use the constant from the polytope study: 2.45454545454~

"295.45454545454~ divided by 2.454545454545454~ = 120 . 3703 703 703~, and that is EXACTLY 100 times the [KhC] the Khufu Constant that = 195 divided by 162 = 1.203 703 703 703."

The above demonstrates Victor Showell's genius and excitement in the discovery of the pyramid geometry and cosmology linked to 528 musical-mathematics, including the circle and arc further discussed in Chapter 9 and the appendix.

Giza Pyramid Math & Sacred Geometry

Now for the purpose of this study, Vic analyzed the Saqqara and Giza pyramids that are geometrically very similar. The Pharaoh Khufu desired to solidify the ancient sacred geometry in the pyramid complexes built. Thus, he reproduced the geometry of Giza to establish the dimensions of the Saqqara pyramid.

Internet sites cite the dimensions of the Giza pyramid as follows:

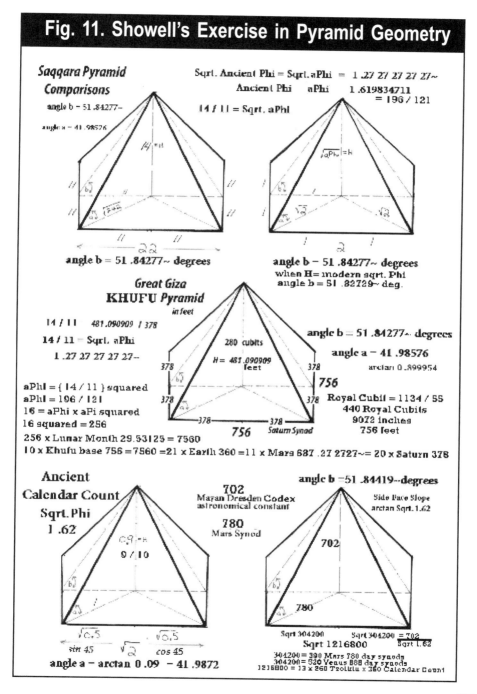

Fig. 11. Showell's Exercise in Pyramid Geometry

Saqqara Pyramid Comparisons

angle b = 51.84277~

angle a = 41.98526

Sqrt. Ancient Phi = Sqrt. aPhi = 1.27 27 27 27 27~

Ancient Phi aPhi 1.619834711
= 196 / 121

14 / 11 = Sqrt. aPhi

angle b = 51.84277~ degrees

angle b = 51.84277~ degrees
when H= modern sqrt. Phi
angle b = 51.82729~ deg.

Great Giza **KHUFU** *Pyramid*
in feet

14 / 11   481.090909 / 378

14 / 11 = Sqrt. aPhi

1.27 27 27 27 27~

280 cubits

H = 481.090909 feet

378   378   378   378   378

756

756   Saturn Synod

aPhi = { 14 / 11 } squared
aPhi = 196 / 121
16 = aPhi x aPi squared
16 squared = 256
256 x Lunar Month 29.53125 = 7560
10 x Khufu base 756 = 7560 = 21 x Earth 360 = 11 x Mars 687.27 2727~= 20 x Saturn 378

angle b = 51.84277~ degrees

angle a = 41.98576
arctan 0.899954

Royal Cubit = 1134 / 55
440 Royal Cubits
9072 inches
756 feet

Ancient Calendar Count
Sqrt. Phi
1.62

9 / 10

702
Mayan Dresden Codex
astronomical constant

780
Mars Synod

angle b = 51.84419~degrees

Side Face Slope
arctan Sqrt. 1.62

702

780

√0.5   √0.5
sin 45   √2   cos 45

angle a = arctan 0.09 = 41.9872

Sqrt 304200   Sqrt 304200 = 702
Sqrt 1216800   Sqrt 1.62

304200 = 390 Mars 780 day synods
304200 = 530 Venus 586 day synods
1216800 = 13 x 260 Tzolkin x 360 Calendar Count

Figure 12. GIZA Pyramid Energy Collector Theory

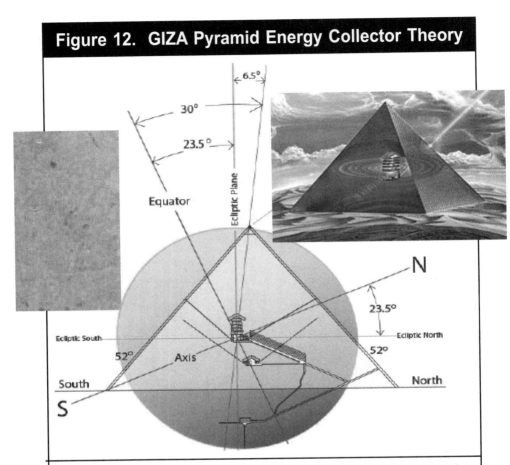

Author Christopher Dunn has published a controversial book evidencing his theory that the Giza pyramid was an energy generator incorporating the science of vibration and sound. His controversial conclusions are based on evidence in the pyramid and artifacts of Egyptian civilization. Notice the 52 degree pitch of the pyramid wall in this figure matches the 52 week calendar year. The left inset shows the greenish yellow color (528Hz frequency) of Jerusalem limestone that covered the pyramid. In theory, the energy generator collected solar and lunar energy (right inset), stored it, and transmitted it possibly using Tesla-like technology. Mr. Dunn's book, *The Giza Power Plant*, is reviewed here: http://www.theseekerbooks.com/articles/Gizapower.htm Images courtesy of: KeyofSolomon.org at http://www.keyofsolomon.org/The%20Lost%20Symbol%20Dan%20Brown.php
and Mysterious World at: http://www.mysteriousworld.com/Journal/2003/Summer/Osiria/

BASE: 756 feet.
BASE/2 (also called the "Saturn synod"): 756/2 = 378 feet
HEIGHT: 481.090909 feet (or 280 cubits).
SLOPE: 51.8427*

[*Note: Using 481 as the height, the slope would be 51
.8375. This is close enough to 51.84 for this analysis. Vic used
481 as the "calculative constant," and regardless if he used
481.09090909, or not, 481 = 13 x 37; wherein the 37 has to
do with planetary synods of Jupiter, Mars, Venus and Earth
cycles. This relates to the "Dresden Codex" wherein 702 divided by 481 pyramid height = x; then x times 37 = 54 reflecting simple math harmonics.]

Lesson One: Ancient Pi is not 3.14159,

"Ancient Pi is not 3.14159, but 3.142857 to infinity," Vic
Showell instructs.

He encourages you to "get a calculator, and take your time
to follow this slowly—step by step, calculation by calculation.
You will see that modern Pi is significantly different from Ancient Pi." This seemingly small difference has substantially
huge implications for civilization and the Spiritual Renaissance.

This regards the "Pythagorean Comma," or "Pythagorean
Crisis" detailed by Ernest G. McClain in Chapter 9. This helps
explain why modern man is simply "out of sync" with the universe or nature. The problem stems from denying ourselves
the accurate math, music, or creative language. So we are
creating everything in dissonance verses 528 harmony with
LOVE.

This truth holds the capacity to set humanity free. Analyzing it will help you open your "heart-mind"—your intuitive chan-

nel through which more revelation, and inspiration, will come to you. This is what many people are experiencing by "playing" with these numbers. In a sense, you can commune with the "Master Matrix" of creation, which is powerfully energized and energizing.

Instead, institutionalized Babylon accepts "false math" and "false precepts" that can't "phase-lock" into the system of musical-math established by the Creator.

For additional reinforcement and benefit, Mr. Showell recommends you draw a pyramid dimensionally similar to the ancient pyramids as shown in Figure 11, to visualize the sacred geometry created by this math. Divide the base line into 2 sections of ancient Pi to test the prospect that ancient Pi is truly 22 / 7. You can see from his graphic (and yours) that the pyramid base is 2(a)Pi by 2(a)Pi. And the height is 4Pi.

Next, using a calculator, divide 22/7 and write down what you see digitally on your display. It is:

3.142857 142857 142857 142857 . . . to infinity.

Now double what you see, and write it down as written here. It may help to put one row directly below the other, like this:

3.142857 142857 142857 142857 . . . to infinity.
6.285714 285714 285714 285714 . . . to infinity.

Look carefully at both rows of numbers. Do you see the pattern?

The fractional pattern that repeats to infinity shifts two places with every doubling. (This is best noted with calculators that cipher to 18 places.) In other words, the "14" in ".142857 shifts positions to the end of the repeating pattern, to become .285714. **IT DOES NOT DO THIS WITH THE "MODERN" ALLEGED Pi EQUIVALENT!**

Try it again to make sure. Double 6.285714. You get:

12.571428 571428 571428 571428 . . . to infinity.

Put this number directly below the other two rows to get:

3.142857 142857 142857 142857 . . . to infinity.

6.285714 285714 285714 285714 . . . to infinity.

12.571428 571428 571428 571428 . . . to infinity.

Do you see what is happening, or what is emerging? Repeating numbers form patterns—a developing mathematical (and musical) matrix.

This math indicates how the parallel universes, "parallel realities," or parallel "levels," including the spiritual realms in which angels travel, are "layered" so-to-speak, next to our "level" or "layer."

This is why Jesus held, "The Kingdom of Heaven is near." It is actually right next to you, right now!

Lesson Two: Phantom of the Opera, the Music of the Light, and Hidden Numbers

I previously mentioned the musical, *Phantom of the Opera*, and the "Music of the Night." It relays the story of the Angel of Darkness, that is,.Lucifer—the fallen angel of light and music. The phantom captures the heart of Christina—metaphorically representing the Christ energy or Christianity. The demon, jealous of the opera company controlling Christina, causes a crystal chandelier to fall on the audience to destroy the opera company. In the end, Christina renders the demon LOVE and is released to marry her hero.(3)

Again, Haydn's 96th classic is called *The Miracle Symphony*, where 9 + 6 = 15; and 1 + 5 = 6, or "MIracle 6."

Modern propaganda alleges this classical composition was named from the sudden, inexplicable, nearly disastrous detachment of a huge crystal chandelier that fell from the ceiling of the concert hall during Haydn's opening performance.

Miraculously, no one was harmed. No doubt Gason Leroux, author of Phantom of the Opera, borrowed this apparent myth.

Haydn, it seems, composed and named his 96th symphony honoring the 3rd "Miracle" tone of the original Solfeggio musical scale.

In the *Book of Revelation*, the "Apocalypse" refers to a similar End Times battle resolving in a musical "marriage" between God's faithful—the bride of Christ—who is finally wed to the Messiah for all eternity.

In *Healing Codes for the Biological Apocalypse*, we advanced a musical code hidden in the verse numbers in *Numbers* 7:12-83, that applies the ancient priesthood's alchemical Pythagorean math. The code reveals the "music of the light"— the original Solfeggio scale by which the "Hymn to St. John the Baptist" was sung.

Reputedly the most spiritually-uplifting hymn of all time, it is composed of only six notes; each defined in *Webster's Dictionary* as part of a "New Song" sung during a global concert in *Revelation* 14:1 involving 144,000 spiritually pure persons who are "ransomed" by God for this Apocalyptic marriage.(3)

As Showell points out above, the 1st and 3rd Solfeggio notes, 396 and 528, are both connected musically-mathematically to this 144,000 number.

These six Solfeggio tones are listed as follows:

UT: 396	FA: 639
RE: 417	SO: 741
MI: 528	LA: 852

I later added the following 3 unnamed notes to this list to complete The Perfect Circle of Sound™. These included: 963, 174, and 285.

You should note that these numbers each resolve into 3, 6, or 9 when the Pythagorean system is used.

The two central notes, MI and FA, identify the *MI*racle *FA*mily (528 and 639).

The Spiritual Set of Numbers: Ancient Pi and the Missing 3s, 6s, and 9s

Notice that the numbers comprising the fraction of true ancient Pi are missing the 3s, 6s, and 9s. From conclusions I drew based on the simple mathematical "infinity pattern" (shown in Figure 30) pioneered by Marko Rodin, the 3s, 6s and 9s represent a special set of numbers that provide a ""portal' to the spiritual domain or spiritual "levels" of reality.

These whole numbers may reflect the "animating principle" of the universe; the math or music of Spirit--the Holy Spirit that hovered over the face of the Water at the beginning of time—as part of the Triune God. The repeating fraction numbers, missing the 3s, 6s, or 9s, represent a fraction of the whole, or pieces of the totality manifesting physical reality.

In other words, spirit and matter are separated, but confluent. My theory is, this separation of Divine Spirit and human matter is mathematically-musically administered according to these simple patterns. The "period" or decimal point dividing whole numbers from fractions reflects the dividing point between matter and spirit, or physical reality and spiritual reality.

This theory extends to time as well as space and matter. The "period" may denote a time warp separating past and future, instead of being in the NOW of physical/spiritual totality, or existentially enlightened experiences.(3, 9)

Finally, the matrix pattern created by Showell's doubling the ancient Pi fraction numbers, as Marko Rodin also shows, reveals the Solfeggio frequencies in patterned positions within the matrix, minus the 396 "central triad" of numbers. This is interesting because when instruments are tuned to 396Hz, the music *feels* "angelic" or more spiritual.(3, 9)

Notice in the matrix below the 528 shifts up and to the right, while 741 shifts in the opposite direction—down and to the left. This is consistent with the Yin/Yang and the "Devil's tone" designated in musicology as the dissonant combination of 528 and 741.

142857142857142857142857142857142857142857142857
285714285714285714285714285714285714285714285714
571428571428571428571428571428571428571428571428
142857142857142857142857142857142857142857142857
285714285714285714285714285714285714285714285714
571428571428571428571428571428571428571428571428
142857142857142857142857142857142857142857142857
285714285714285714285714285714285714285714285714
571428571428571428571428571428571428571428571428
142857142857142857142857142857142857142857142857
285714285714285714285714285714285714285714285714
571428571428571428571428571428571428571428571428
142857142857142857142857142857142857142857142857
285714285714285714285714285714285714285714285714
571428571428571428571428571428571428571428571428

Finally, if you add up each fraction using the Pythagorean method, you get:

1 + 4 + 2 + 8 + 5 + 7 = 27 where 2 + 7 = 9—"completion" So, in each doubling of Pi, you get 3 or 6 alternating in the whole number place, and 9 in the fractional location.

All of the above offers solid mathematical proofs that this set of 3s, 6s, and 9s, provides a special quality, like a spiritual signature, or portal through which metaphysical energy manifests miraculously into physical reality.(3,9)

Lesson Three: Phi Cosmology, Pyramid Geometry, and the Creator's Music

Take Showell's original decimal sequence—.142857 and inverse it: 758241. Then, extrapolate it out to infinity by entering the decimal sequence into the calculator at least 3 times. It stops showing on the display, but it is in memory:

758241758241758241758241758241758241758241758241

Now you can see the 2nd Solfeggio tone, *RE*sonance, 417Hz, indicative of it resonating eternally.

Interesting enough, 417 is a harmonic of 528/LOVE even though it is in the 741 central triad, and not in the 528 central triad of The Perfect Circle of Sound™. (See: Figure 33.)

Here you can see other patterns emerge. For instance, the pattern that this pair, 417 and 582 make as two adjacent sets of "family number groups" in this line of numbers is interesting. Move the 7 two places to the left, to become Solfeggio "741" when read from left to right. Move the 5 two places to the right to yield "528" when read backwards, from right to left. This appears to be a reversal, or again, an opposite polarity between the two Solfeggio notes that form the "Devil's Tone:"

7582417

A Greater Truth Revealed

NOW! A great truth is revealed about Phi, and all the ancient Egyptian pyramids and their math becomes apparent in a flash!

If you multiply the proven legitimate Pi fraction (.142857) times the cosmological constant associated with galactic and solar cycles known as the Saturn synod (378) you get closer to 54 as you approach infinity. Try it. The more you extrapolate the numbers, getting closer to infinity, the closer it gets to 54!

0.142857 142857 142857 142857 142857 . . . x the Saturn synod (378) = 54!

Why is this important? Because the sine of 54 degrees is one half of Phi (Phi/2).

Here, Vic's genius delivers to the max. He "Harmonic Codexed" the decimal sequence by shifting the 1st digit in line to the back of the line, and multiplied that number by the Saturn synod:

.428571 428571 428571 x 378 Saturn synod = 162. EUREKA! 162 is 100 times ancient Phi of 1.62!

Try this with all the sequences. Shift the first digit in line to the back of the line and than multiply that number times the Saturn synod.

With this simple experiment, you have just proven the entire Egyptian pyramid math calendar geometry is based on Saturn and Mars cosmologies; with Saturn being predominant.

Saturn is like the lead bass player or percussionist maintaining the rhythm of the spiraling cosmos. The "bass clef" in music reflects this spiraling center.

The Greeks and Romans called Saturn Chronos. Chronometer in Greek means "measure."

So Showell proves the cosmos is laid out perfectly, mathematically, harmoniously, like a musical composition of Divine synchrony.

Similarly, he irrefutably proves 528 is a central number operating in the musical-mathematical Master Matrix, underlying the sacred pyramid geometrics established by Phi.

Lesson Four: Importance of the Ancient Solfeggio

According to Vic Showell's mathematical analyses, and a growing international consensus of math experts, the original Solfeggio frequencies work like magic in the Saturnian cosmologies.

The word "magic" sources from the ancient Melchezadak priesthood, called the Magi, who held this knowledge sacred and secret.

Returning to his earlier analysis of the Saggara pyramid and Phi, Vic wrote that the number 7 within the fraction of Pi (22/7), represents the 7 dots of the ancient cylinder seals and stele representing planet Earth, as advanced and discussed by Zaccharia Sitchin.

The seals relate to the 7 major chakras tuning your body spiritually/musically (as shown in Figure 19).

So for this lesson, Vic recommends you take the real ancient Pi = 3.142857, and multiply it times the Saturn synod (378). This yields 1188.

"Look at that number," he counsels, encouraging your intuition. "11 x 8 = 88." is intriguing.

In the Appendix section, "Musicians' 528 Discussion," I relay the research of Zion Estes and Michael Walton discovering a musical "portal" at 88.8Hz that is experientially profound.

More musically profound, if you take the original Solfeggio frequencies and apply the aforementioned information from this chapter, you prove Pi, Phi, the Fibonacci Series, and more, are all based on the Solfeggio musical matrix. (1,3,9)

Convince yourself as follows:

Divide the first note of the original Solfeggio (UT, which is 396Hz) by 1188, and you will get *the exact sine of the molecular structure of Water—the tetrahedron*:

396/1188 = 0.3333333—sine of exact tetrahedral (19.47122061)

According to *Webster's Dictionary*, the definition of "UT" says this single tone contains all other musical notes, and represents the entire gamut of human experience and emotion from grief to joy! Remember, this too is related to 528, as mentioned above, since "528÷396 = 1.333333; and the slope of the second pyramid at Giza has an arctangent of 1.333333, equal to 53.13 degrees.

Vic additionally noted that the Saqqara pyramid measurements are noteworthy. The pyramid measures 22 meters square at its base, and 14 meters high. Half those measures and you get the values 11 and 7, or "craps" in casino gambling. But considering 528, if you divide 528, by this pyramid base length of 22, you get exactly 24, as in 24 hours in a day. And remember, 2 + 4 = 6, just like MIracle 6.

528/22 = 24 proves that pyramid cosmology is not only related to 528, but also to tracking time.

Recall that 22/7 (days a week) is ancient Pi or 3.142857143. This is related to 22/19.5 = x. (The ancients used 19.5 as their tetrahedral constant.) By squaring x, you get the tangent of 51.84 degrees. If you square x again, you get the ancient Phi number 1.62.

So now mathematicians, and you too, see more clearly how the original Solfeggio musical scale, including 528Hz, Pi and Phi, are intimately connected to the liquid crystal (tetrahedral) structure of Water, the circle, the arc, and every other sacred geometric form.

Lesson Five: Final Proofs Regarding the Legitimacy of 528 and the Original Solfeggio Musical Scale

When you read Showell's works, you have to understand his use of the ancient system of no decimals, or what he calls "decimal variations in numeric sets or sequences." For example:

0.3333----> 3.33333 ----> 33.33333, and 13 x 333.33333 = 4333 .33333 Jupiter sidereal; as 0.3333 is sine of the tetrahedral 19.47122061.

Because he found the ancient Egyptian cosmological constant is 195/162 (or 1.95/1.62), he uses the 1.95 form of decimal placement often; which he named the "Khufu Constant."

"In any case," he wrote, "to get to the ancient Solfeggio music of the spheres, you can use tetrahedral 19.47122061 but then you get 10 Pi." So he used 1.947122061 instead because, he declared, "that form created virtually magical pathways into the tangents and cosines and sines of angles in derivations."

The difference of exact Pi and the actual value achieved is 0.000354308," to which he chides, "If this is not close enough, then this will not work for you. It works for me."

He derives this miniscule musical difference, ultimately in resonance harmonics, by taking the LA tone of the Solfeggio (852) and dividing it by the MI tone (528) as shown here:

Solfeggio 852/528 = 1.6136363636, then x 1.947122061 = 3.141946962 then minus Pi = 0.000354308.

Similarly, he examines the Solfeggio tones FA (639) and UT (396) to obtain the same stunning result as follows:

639/396 = 1.61363636363

Naturally, this music underlying the spinning fractal universe "goes in cycles," he explains, reiterating the connection between 396 and 528 as follows:

396 x 1.3333333 = 528 with the 1.33333 being the slope tangent of the side face on the 2nd pyramid of Giza.

"A few other Solfeggio notes do this as well with 1.33333," Vic reported.

For his grand finale, Showell is victorious in showing humanity that sacred geometry is based on musical harmony, with the Solfeggio frequencies expressing predominantly within Rodin's family number groups .

Worthy of a Nobel Peace Prize in mathematics, Showell presented his Quantum Space Time Fractal Harmonic Codex, beginning with LOVE (528), and the associated 825 number in Rodin's 285 family set of numbers.

Examples 1 and 2 below reveal the primordial association of these numbers to creation through an analysis of pyramid sacred geometry.

In Showell's latest contribution, Monograph 11 in his series posted on LOVE528.com, under the "Pi, Phi and 528" page, he analyzes the origin of measuring time based on math that features 528 and 432.(10)

Showell's focus on important derivations of 528 and 432, shown in Table 5, was partially prompted by malicious propagandists; American agents attempting to discredit 528, to exclusively promote 432--total absurdity given the proofs these numbers are integral to space/time measurements.(10, 11)

Apparently, there are persons being exposed, representing forces of evil, who are threatened by pure LOVE/528, and the accelerating 528LOVERevolution.(11)

Table 5. Victor Showell's Analysis of 528 & 432 As Important Co-Factors in Ancient Calendars and Measurements

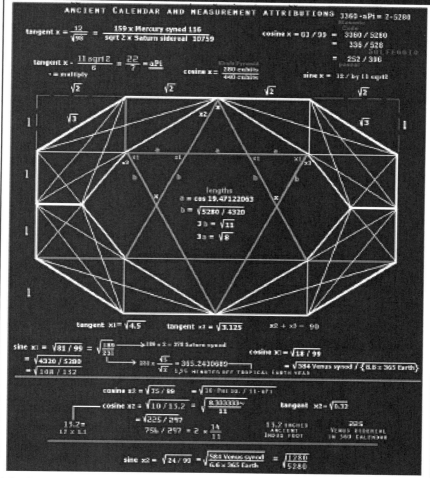

Vic Showell produced mathematical analyses and graphics "displaying how ancient Egyptian and MesoAmerican pyramid geometries and mathematics follow the universal constants of Pi , Phi and square root two in particular, which is tetrahedral geometry." In this example, from his 11th monograph titled, *Grand Unification of Ancient and Modern Mathematics,* he considers 528 and 432. Other works by Showell include: *Teotihuacan City Grid Universal Harmonic Master Code*, *Stonehenge Restored Plans*, and *The Universal Harmonic Codes in Pi and Phi.*(10)

Example 1:

[528] <------>[825]

[528] / [825] = [0.64], and [64] = [8] squared.

Now look back at my [51.84] degree pyramid and [72] squared = [5,184].

[0.64] x [5 .184] = [3.31776], then divide by Phi[1.61803388] = [2.050488445] = tangent of [64.00203243] degrees!

Example 2:

[825] <-----> [528]

[825] / [528] = [1.5625] , then divide by Phi[1.61803388] = [0.965678107] = tangent of [43.99968~] degrees = [44]

And of course [44] x [120] = [5280] mile

Conclusion

The above mathematical analyses provides proof of Divine design far exceeding the math of men. It virtually proves "Postulate 1," that "All electrons [as well as celestial spheres] are spinning musically—vibrating harmonically, determined by the nine core creative frequencies comprising The Perfect Circle of Sound.

In addition, "Postulate 2" is also proven by the aforementioned analyses: "These nine frequencies of sound determine Pi, Phi, the Fibonacci series, and all sacred geometric forms including the structure of Water, the tetrahedron, cosmology, and the laws of physics."

"As above, so below." From this evidence "Postulate 3" also appears to be significantly evidenced, virtually certain: "All piezoelectricity, oxidative-reductive reactions, and electromagnetism, affecting chemical interactions rely on the harmonics or dissonance of a musical-mathematical matrix fundamental to physics and chemistry; all determined by simply nine Perfect Circle of Sound™ frequencies."

Now that you know this information, what do you think you can do with this knowledge? These monumental discoveries require distribution and assimilation by a world urgently requiring something wonderful to happen.

Will you help to "give peace a chance," and change the dissonant vibrations in the hearts of mad men making war instead of LOVE?

Start by simply "playing" and composing music in 528. Share this information with others!

References

1) V Showell's series of monographs are available in pdf format at www.LOVE528.com. His latest, "Teotihuacan Universal Harmonic Master Code" includes 528's connections to the sacred geometry of the circle, Pi and Phi.

2) *LIVE H₂O*—Concert for the Living Water, can be researched at LIVEH₂O.org

3) Horowitz LG and Puleo J. *Healing Codes for the Biological Apocalypse*. Sandpoint, ID: Tetrahedron, LLC, 1998. See: http://www.HealthyWorldStore.com/Healing-Codes-For-The-Biological-Apocalypse-book-p/hc%20pdf.htm

4) Personal communications with Dr. Lee Lorenzen.

5) Jenny H. Cymatics. Quotes available from numerous sources, including: http://www.rexresearch.com/cymatics/cymatics.htm

6) Pi information sources from Bookrags: http://www.bookrags.com/Pi

7) Reid JS. Egyptian Sonics. *Hydrosonics*. Vol. 1, No. 1. Jan., 2009. See: http://web.me.com/len15/HYDROSONICS/EGYPTIAN_SONICS.html

8) Jenny H. Cymatics. Quotes available from numerous sources, including: http://www.rexresearch.com/cymatics/cymatics.htm

9) Marko Rodin's "Vortex Based Mathematics" website is: http://markorodin.com/1.5/

10) Showell V. Grand Unification of Ancient and Modern Mathmatics: Khafare and Khufu Pyramid Geometry In Tetrhedral Hexad Geometry; The Mars Cydonia Hexad Mounds. Sandpoint, ID: Tetrahedron Publishing Group. March, 2011. Copyright, Victor Showell. Online at: http://web.mac.com/len15/LOVE528/Pi,_PHI_%26_528.html

11) Horowitz LG. 432 Vs. 528: Honest debate or CIA Propaganda. A reply to "The Cosmic 432" video publication (Part 2) by Thurmond T and Buturff J, YouTube pub. http://www.youtube.com/watch?v=kUuyeor8f6Q&feature=related. See: http://www.528records.com/pages/432-vs-528-honest-debate-or-cia-propaganda-fraud.

Chapter Four:
Musical Cult Control Through
A=440Hz "Standard Tuning"

This chapter exposes the practice of "musical cult control." The Rockefeller Foundation's war on consciousness is examined, as it has been imposed by the standardization of the Western World's tuning of musical instruments to A=440Hz.

Here, events in musical history are recalled that are central to understanding, and treating, a source of psychopathology, more accurately psycho-spiritual pathology. Social aggression, political corruption, genetic dysfunction, and cross-cultural degeneration of traditional human values risking health, and life on earth, are symptoms. The fundamental pathology—hearts lacking LOVE—attributable to the musical-mathematical "Divine disconnect."

In essence, human spirituality and Divine consciousness is being powerfully suppressed, musically. This chapter aims to clarify this predicament, and presents compelling evidence to inspire a 528LOVERevolution, fueled by recording artists and discriminating audiences.

The Rockefeller Foundation's military commercialization of music is detailed here.

The monopolization of the music industry by banking families representing the Illuminati, features this imposed 440Hz frequency that is "herding" populations into greater aggression, psychosocial agitation, and emotional distress.

This evidence strongly suggests the 440Hz tuning predisposes people to physical illnesses and financial impositions thereby profiting the agents engaged in globalization.

Alternatively, the most natural, harmonious, and instinctively attractive, 528Hz frequency that is vividly displayed botanically in the green grass and trees, has been suppressed by the contrivance of A=440Hz standard tuning.

That is, the "good vibrations" that the plant kingdom broadcasts in greenish-yellow, which reduces emotional distress, social aggression, and remedies many illnesses, has been musically censored.

Thus, a musical revolution is needed to advance world health and peace. This has already begun with musicians tuning their instruments to restore integrity to the performing arts and sciences.

Music makers are urged to communicate, and debate, these facts, end the militarization of music that has been secretly administered, and retune instruments, and voices, to frequencies most sustaining, loving, and healing.

Introduction

Contrary to popular opinion, the most powerful "hard" science influencing society, politics, and economics is *behavioral science*. Advertising agencies, social engineers, marketing firms, and the persuasive media direct people, like cattle, most profitably.

A flock of sheep, for example, according to the Merck Veterinary Manual, responds synchronously to stimuli, such as approaching dogs or humans, due to a special set of nerve cells that fire electrically causing the release of stress hormones associated with the flight response and herd behavior. (1) Malcolm Gladwell's, *The Tipping Point: How Little Things Can Make a Big Difference*, cites social examples of the small percentage of a total population required to act, "at which the

Figure 13. "Mass Hysteria" During Elvis Concert, 1954

The first mass hysteria accompanying rock-and-roll was recorded in the mid-50s during Elvis Presley concerts. Military science had demonstrated that 6-8 percent of audiences listening to music tuned to "special" frequencies, in this case A=440Hz, would become psychologically stressed to the point of generating mass hyseria.

momentum for change becomes unstoppable" for the entire social network.(2)

There have been many unexplained "mass hysteria" episodes recorded besides the "War of the Worlds" fright that was broadcast by CBS Radio and narrated by Orson Welles, on October 30, 1938.(3) Bartholomew called the related public health crisis, "Occupational Mass Psychogenic Illness" in *Transcultural Psychiatry*.(4) Another investigator's name, Wessely, added the warning that this bizarre herd behavior impacts health and well-being. He considered how poorly this frequency impacted our mass mind-set. The terroristic media uses it to induce stress and psycho-emotional trauma. He wrote:

"[I]t is easy to lose sight of the dynamic, protean [varied] nature of mass *sociogenic illness* and its historical and transcultural manifestations, which mirror popular social and cultural preoccupations that define each era and reflect unique social beliefs about the nature of the world."(5)

Background

Assuming the field of physics, including biophysics, is valid, and the universe, including life, is energetically constructed harmonic, or dissonant, according to the musical-mathematical proofs provided in the last chapter, then energy (including bioenergy or spirituality) impacts us physically, very powerfully. The impacts, good and bad, are mediated vibrationally, really hydrosonically, through sounds' effects on body Water.(6)

Water, nearly eighty percent of human body weight, I have said, is a liquid crystal superconductor. Structured Water science, as well as the field of electrogenetics, proves this thesis adequately, given light (photons) and sound (phonons) have been shown to signal communications within and between cells, via a liquid crystal proteo-glycan matrix in cells and tissues.(6, 7) This strongly evidences the theory of hydrosonic creationism involving DNA and structured Water.(7)

Likewise, psychosocial illnesses may be triggered more often by music than previously considered. Bio-creation and health restoration may have more to do with frequencies of sound energy, or music, than has been thought.

There are a lot of people who consider modern music annoying. Many become emotionally disturbed listening to certain types of music. What few people realize, regardless of the type of music played in the Western World, the Illuminati's standard tuning for instruments and voices was instituted at the same time, by the same agents and agencies, advancing acoustic war studies for inducing "mass hysteria."(8)

This dirty fact of musical history may be terminal to the status-quo of the music industry and the movers-and-shakers of sociocultural crises.

Throughout history there have been persons of wealth and power engaged in war-making, profiteering, and various methods of population control. In 1770, for instance, Mayer Amschel Bauer (a.k.a., Rothschild) developed plans to advance the mission of global domination through a network of central banks that his family and their silent partners controlled.(9, 10) Many reputable authors track today's degenerative socioeconomic trends and genocidal acts depopulating native people to levels of threatened extinction, to the Illuminati's powerful influence. The Rothschild and Rockefeller families administer their policies through private organizations controlling multinational corporations and governments (i.e., secret societies and governing councils, such as the Council on Foreign Relations or the Partnership for New York City).(6-15)

"As a result of this influence," wrote Thomas D. Schauf, in a controversial review article urging the termination of the un-American Federal Reserve Bank, and the offshore bankers' control over the U.S. Treasury, "the arc of Western Civilization has gone from 'ascent'—belief in God—focused on the higher centers of love, joy, purity and selflessness, to descent . . . focused on the lower centers of consciousness like those of power, wealth and physical gratification. The apex was called the 'Enlightenment,' when the 'Illuminated ones'—a luciferous term meaning 'keepers of the light'—took over for God. Typical of Satan, decline into moral darkness is represented as light."(11)

Light and sound is generated and measured mathematically, according to frequencies. It stands to reason then, following Schauf's empirically evidenced thesis, we are engaged in frequency warfare in which ultimate power and control is waged bioenergetically or biospiritually. There is now zero doubt that music, frequency modulations, or electromagnetic manipulations are affecting consciousness and impacting biology, physiology, and human behavior.

The Rockefeller Foundation and Military Music

In 1913, the Rothschilds set up their third and current central bank in America, the Federal Reserve Bank, with the help of their agents J.P. Morgan and J.D. Rockefeller. Those investment firms controlling banking and the economy, the sole investment firms left standing on Wall Street, have been financed by the Rothschilds since 1865. (9, 11)

World Wars I and II evidence the banking cartel's profitable depopulation politics and policies. For instance, in 1914, at the beginning of World War I, the German Rothschild bank loaned money to the German government, the British Rothschild bank loaned money to Britain, and the French Rothschild bank loaned money to the French government. War propaganda served the Rothschild's geopolitical and financial agendas, and was provided by the three main European news agencies, Wolff in Germany, Reuters in England, and Havas in France, each financed by Rothschild banks. (9, 11)

Between World Wars I and II, scientific studies in musical frequencies best suited for war-making were funded by the Rothschild-Rockefeller alliance, represented by the Rockefeller Foundation and the United States Navy.(8-11)

A major objective of the war-makers, besides profitable population control, was research to determine musical or acoustic weapons capable of producing psychopathology, emotional distress, and mass hysteria.(8)

According to Rockefeller Foundation archives, grants provided by the foundation, in concert with the U.S. Navy and National Defense Research Council, commissioned acoustic energy researchers, including Harold Burris-Meyer, an audio engineer and drama instructor at New Jersey's Stevens Institute of Technology.(8)

Burris-Meyer is best known for providing consulting services to the Muzak Corporation, "which used his expertise to optimize sound installations in factories so that emotional motivation of workers achieved through music would not be adversely effected by factory noise . . ," wrote James Tobias, a Professor of English at the Univ. of Calif.(8)

Tobias reviewed Rockefeller Foundation archives, and documented investigations leading to psychological warfare applications of acoustic vibrations, ultimately advanced militarily and commercially.(8)

Burris-Meyer, according to Tobias, contributed to the Department of Defense during World War II, "including building speaker arrays deployed on warplanes such that enemy combatants could be addressed from the air" to produce psychoemotional affects leading to mass hysteria.(8)

Additionally, the Princeton Radio Project played a role in this research. This occurred precisely at the time the Manhattan Atomic Bomb Project was beginning at Princeton involving Albert Einstein at the Institute for Advanced Study (IAS).(12)

Poisonous Medicine and the Rockefellers' Investments in Sickening "Music"

Linking this development of music for mass hysteria, and damaging public health impacts, the IAS "think tank" was formed from the "vision of founding Director Abraham Flexner," according to the IAS website.(13) The infamous Abraham Flexner was educated in Germany and America. He joined the staff at the Carnegie Foundation, was funded by the Rockefeller Foundation, and sourced the American medical reformation. The U.S. Congress accepted Flexner's infamous "Flexner Report."(14) This bogus research paper exclusively benefited the IG Farben-Rockefeller led petrochemical-pharmaceutical alliance. Flexner, and his report, vilified every form of natural healing in order to monopolize health care. Based on Flexner's report, advancing the Rothschild-Rockefeller's agenda, the U.S. Government exclusively imposed medicine's reliance on deadly drugs, not curative remedies.

The Rockefeller Foundation's Assistant Director for the Humanities, at the time Flexner compiled his report, was John Marshall, who along with the authors of *Composing for the Films* (Oxford University Press, 1947) Hanns Eisler and Theodor Adorno, were featured performers in the musical projects serving military, and commercial, interests. Their activities juxtaposed military objectives with artistic and philanthropic initiatives.(8)

As this research and development of the broadcasting industry advanced to impact "herd behavior" and psychosocial illnesses, it is clear that every malady generated musically/vibrationally (i.e., bioenergetically), increased investors' profitability.

Figure 14. Elivs's Intelligence Agent, "The Colonial"

Colonel Tom Parker, Elvis's manager, illegally enlisted in the U.S. Army as a European immigrant. He coerced exclusive control over Elvis's career for the Illuminati's RCA. He secretly stole his alias from Army base commander, Captain Tom Parker. (This is common practice for intelligence agents working for MI6 and the CIA/FBI.) His real name was Andreas Cornelis van Kuijk. Image Source: http://www.morethings.com/music/elvis/pictures/index.html

Although Eisler or Adorno appear to be innocent of wrongdoing, according to Tobias, both were unfavorably treated by their higher-ups. Eisler opposed the use of music for cultural manipulation, and was eventually deported following years of harassment by J. Edgar Hoover's FBI. The publicity generated by his deportation embarrassed the Rockefeller Foundation. (8)

According to Tobias, Burris-Meyer became convinced that "audio control of human emotions was possible for a large enough portion of an audience to provide effective crowd control – a line of research," that John Marshall, "ultimately found irrelevant for understanding the artistic or cultural values of music. . . . " Marshall's focus was to fulfill military objectives.(8)

This best explains why this activity is linked in time, subject matter, Foundation funding, and the Rothschild-Rockefeller war investments in Germany, Britain, and the U.S., to establishing the Western World's standard musical tuning of A=440Hz frequency.

The fact that A=440Hz standard tuning is relatively distressing, as adequately evidenced throughout this book,(7, 20-22) implicates these parties and their research.

Sequestering the History of A=440Hz Tuning

Furthermore, raising more suspicion, I personally contacted Professor Tobias to request his consent to link a couple of my websites to his online paper. I also invited his submission of a related article for publication in *Medical Veritas* journal. He declined saying he did not wish to jeopardize publication of his work by the Rockefeller Foundation.

However, a simple Internet search showed his manuscript was already published by the Rockefeller Archive Center, with the following ethically objectionable notice:

"This research report is presented here with the author's permission but should not be cited or quoted without the author's consent. . . .

"Rockefeller Archive Center Research Reports Online is a periodic publication of the Rockefeller Archive Center . . . intended to foster the network of scholarship in the history of philanthropy and to highlight the diverse range of materials and subjects covered in the collections at the Rockefeller Archive Center. The reports are drawn from essays submitted by researchers who have visited the Archive Center, many of whom have received grants from the Archive Center to support their research. The ideas and opinions expressed in this report are those of the author and are not intended to represent the Rockefeller Archive Center." (8)

Frankly, under "fair use" copyright laws, Dr. Tobias, and the Rockefeller Archive Center, has zero right to prohibit his Internet published work, currently available for review here, (8) to be withheld from public scrutiny and scholarly commentary, particularly as it involves matters of widespread psychosocial pathology, public health, and national security.

For the record, Dr. Tobias neglected to reply to my invitation to prepare a *Medical Veritas* submission, or consent to be interviewed by me on this topic.

Bioenergetic Music for Mass Hysteria

Tobias's manuscript makes it clear that he was alarmed at his discovery that bioenergetic research in acoustic science funded by the Rockefeller Foundation focused on producing the social impacts of emotional arousal and even mass hysteria.

This research included "investigations in 'physical analysis' of sound effects, . . . an established technique which others may use in practice dependably . . . ," the determination of measures by which audience reactions could be accessed "'even without any technical capacity for psychological measurement of audience response," and the use of sound effects that "produced what was really mass hysteria."(8)

Tobias noted the Foundation-funded investigations extended to "'average tolerance of sound effects of different intensities and of different frequencies,' or . . . the effectiveness of sound in relation to different noise levels. . . . [T]he clear interest here seems to be in the 'dramatic' use emphasized in . . . bringing audiences, with the use of the 'sensory appeal' of sound effects, to states of 'mass hysteria.'"(8)

These revelations best account for the mass hysteria demonstrated by audiences responding to "Rock-n-Rollers," initially Elvis Presley, followed by the "British Invaders." It was recently revealed that The Beatles were barred from performing in Israel following an investigation that prompted the education ministry to conclude The Beatles' performances caused:

"[H]ysteria and mass disorder. . . There is no musical or artistic experience here, but a sensual display that arouses feelings of aggression replete with sexual stimuli."(26)

At that time, the Israeli Mossad was effectively tracking Her Majesty's Secret Service (MI6) and CIA's military interests, as it had been since WWII.(6,10,14) In 1938, the British-American radio and television cartel was funded and administered by the Rockefeller Foundation, also funding Jewish-hate campaigns and administering Nazi eugenics.(29) This Anglo-American media connection was evidenced by Michele Hilmes.(15)

On August 31, 1957, hysterical crowds trampled people, including Canadian reporter, John Kirkwood, who wrote: "It was like watching a demented army swarm down the hillside to do battle in the plain when those frenzied teenagers stormed the field. Elvis and his music played a small part in the dizzy circus. The big show was provided by Vancouver teenagers, transformed into writhing frenzied idiots of delight by the savage jungle beat music. A hard bitter core of teenage troublemakers turned Elvis Presley's one-night stand at the Empire Stadium into the most disgusting exhibition of mass hysteria and lunacy this city has ever witnessed. . . . Colonel Parker also enjoyed reading the accounts of the riot the next day."(16)

Colonel Tom Parker

It turns out that Colonel Tom Parker, Elvis's manager, was suspect for illegally joining the U.S. Army as a European immigrant. He broke his comanagement contract with Hank Snow for exclusive control over Elvis's career. He developed Presley's contact with RCA (discussed below), and worked under the alias of "Col. Tom Parker." It was a name that he secretly stole from his Army base commander, Captain Tom Parker. His real name was Andreas Cornelis van Kuijk.(17)

Thus, the Empire Stadium riot that was so pleasing to Parker was most likely a successful US military-RCA experiment to induce mass hysteria, especially since RCA, according to Tobias, was a major participant in the Rockefeller Foundation-funded research to musically produce this precise audience impact.(8)

RCA, General Electric Company and the Navy

During WWI, U.S. Navy suppressed patents facilitated the Brit's war effort. The patented technology was owned by the major media companies involved with radio manufacturing in the U.S.. All production of radio equipment at that time was allocated for the Army and Navy. The Navy sought to maintain a Rockefeller-administered military-government monopoly over the radio industry featuring advances in wireless radio.

This wartime command over radio never ended, some believe, due to the specious congressional indecision regarding the maintenance of the supposed governmental control over radio in 1918. At that time, the Rockefeller leadership forced the indecision.

However, the questionable (mis)direction of the corporatist-government monopoly over music did not prevent the Navy from creating a national radio system. On April 8, 1919, U.S. Navy officials met with General Electric Company (GE) executives to develop an American owned radio company, so that the Navy could continue operating as a "front," exercising its control over the commercial radio monopoly. The resulting purchase of American Marconi by GE satisfied this command and birthed the Radio Corporation of America (RCA).

The incestuous commercial-military cartel that formed featured RCA, GE, United Fruit, Westinghouse Electric Corporation, and AT&T. This alliance laid the groundwork for fascist control of not only the energy industries, including human energy (bioenergy) but also spirituality that overlaps electrogenetics, and the eugenics and psychiatric genetics movements advanced at that time by the same elite players.(18)

The resulting developments included the National Broadcasting Company (NBC), and a government created monopoly in radio and television, with AT&T controlling telephone communications.(6, 7, 18)

Tobias's review of Rockefeller Foundation archives proves that a major objective of the cartel was to coordinate British and American corporate and military interests in radio research and television broadcasting, initially featuring the British Broadcasting Company (BBC) and RCA. Tobias's review showed their research focused on psychotronic warfare, physiological stress induction, negative affective (emotional) arousal, mass persuasion, herd behavior, and population control.

This "black op" is evidenced in many ways aside from the communications reviewed by Tobias and his sources.(8, 15) October 6, 1938, for example, the year before A=440Hz standard tuning was adopted, a program researcher, David Stevens, wrote to Frank Jewett, vice-president of AT&T, regarding

Figure 15. Early U.S. Navy Recruiting Poster

YOUNG MEN WANTED FOR U.S. NAVY.

PAY $17⁵⁰ TO $77⁰⁰ PER MONTH

AND ALLOWANCES. BOARD.LODGING. MEDICAL ATTENDANCE

FIRST OUTFIT OF UNIFORM FREE.

AN OPPORTUNITY FOR PROMOTION — LIBERAL PAY TO THOSE WHO PROVE EFFICIENT

The U.S. Navy has, since its inception, been most active among the military branches for intelligence gathering, nuclear weapons generation, and population control. Her Majesty's Secret Service (MI6) worked closely with the Navy that advanced the power of sending sound signals through Water for use in controlling the sea and land. Today, in many parts of the world, dolphins and whales are being damaged from sonic weapons tests and hydrosonic pollution. The Navy best understands that frequencies can be used to grow deadly viruses as shown in Figure 40. The Naval Biological Research Labs have been at the forefront of developing biological weapons for mass depopulation. Frequencies for population control and war arenas were tested by the Navy in collaboration with RCA, GE, United Fruit, Westinghouse Electric Corporation, AT&T, and EMI recording studio in England. The research and developments, funded by the Rockefeller Foundation, was based at Princeton, NJ, as part of the Princeton Radio Project.

studies to "control the emotional response of audiences by mechanical means." Jewett's response letter of October 11, 1938, noted Bell Labs' officials expressed embarrassment for the company's involvements in this nefarious project, despite its profitable applications and military merits. (8)

"Thus," Tobias wrote, "this project was a typical Rockefeller Foundation project, in that the goals were partially speculative, but grounded, always, in establishing institutional networks that might ultimately grow into much larger, actually feasible mass media development projects serving commercial interests but having 'educational' or 'dramatic' uses." Military science, otherwise called "non-commercial, 'social research,' was an important way in building not-yet commercial mass media systems and applications . . ." for population control.(8)

This research was eventually applied in the development of modern methods of public persuasion and cultural indoctrination, by television and radio networks currently considered the "mainstream media."

It must be emphasized that by 1961, according to a series of Rockefeller Brothers Fund reports, their alleged concern was that *We the People* should feel a sense of "National Purpose." The Rockefeller family then determined that *We The People* should be governed by the assertion that a "prudent corporate and military leadership of the National Security State, could link guns, butter, and the new technology of missile and nuclear weapons production to the cause of Freedom and the Free World."(6)

The Media Applies Military PsychoScience

According to the Rockefeller Foundation's archives, the Rockefellers financed and helped organize the military media monopoly over broadcasting, and through various forms of "education," the programmable public's mind-set.

Tobias, neglecting the foundation's cartel arrangements, noted that television competition between NBC and CBS was "secretive and fierce as production went into experimental phases. . . ." (8)

Evidencing the intended illusion of competition, Congress, in 1974, investigated the Rockefeller-directed Chase Manhattan Bank's stakes in CBS and NBC, that rose to 14.1 and 4.5 percent respectively, through NBC's parent, RCA. The Congress recorded that Chase Manhattan Bank held stock in 28 broadcasting firms, including start-ups, based on musical intelligence. After this report, the Chase Manhattan Bank obtained 6.7% of ABC. The bank only required five percent ownership to significantly influence "programming"—a "PSYOPS" term meaning educational indoctrination, otherwise called propaganda—for sociocultural engineering. (11)

Tobias continued, "Burris-Meyer wanted to measure audience response to the sound effects, and considered wiring audience members with a 'psycho-galvanometer.'" (8)

According to Pat Robertson, a televangelist, turned enemy of the pagan corporatist state, the Chase bank is a wealthy shareholder in the FED. "It is believed other FED owners have similar holdings in the media," Robertson cautioned in his book, *The New World Order*. "To control the media, FED bankers call in their loans if the media disagrees with them." On page 131, he recommended abolishing the FED.(19)

John Marshall wrote that for responses to sound to be effective, "emotion involvement is required. If the psycho-galvanometer gives even a rough measure of emotional involvement, perhaps that is sufficient for Burris-Meyer's purposes." Marshall then "urged Burris-Meyer to seek consultation from psychologists who had consulted on the Princeton Radio Project, . . . Thereafter, Burris-Meyer worked through the American Film Center to experiment with the recording of sound effects on film." (8)

Tobias noted that the Rockefeller Foundation offered network broadcasting and industrial connections to their grant awardees that assured success in the industry and dispersion of research developments with commercial value. "Rockefeller support," he wrote, "particularly through Marshall's insights and wide ranging personal network, typically and vastly expanded the human and institutional resources of any project grantee, in addition to monetary support. . . ." (8)

"[M]usicality enabled a 'technicolor' proof of affective public address," Tobias added, "raising the possibility of greater audience involvement and the spectre of greater audience manipulation; the clear educational and commercial application for musicality as 'control' stressed in Burris-Meyer's 'sound show' . . . in works like Disney's *Fantasia*, were as much justifications for, as much as demonstrations of, the use of [these] advanced [acoustic warfare] technologies . . ." (8)

Introducing A=440Hz To Professionals

The introduction of electronic sound for stage, screen, and television did not proceed easily.

In 1910, motivated by a grant provided by the Rockefeller Foundation for the American Federation of Musicians, the initial effort to institute A=440Hz standard tuning had limited success in America. In Europe, the initial effort had near zero impact. Additional promotions were needed to secure the music world's acceptance of A=440Hz that was perceived as less pleasant, or dull when compared with other frequencies described below.

Ironically, and most revealing about the British-German-American cartel arrangement, European musicians, and the British Standards Institute (BSI), were persuaded to accept this tuning in 1939 by Nazi party propaganda minister, Joseph Goebbels. At that time, Goebbels was advancing to become England's greatest media nemesis. He, along with the Third Reich, was financially-backed by Rockefeller-Rothschild bankers.

Lynn Cavanagh, a widely referenced historian, reviewed the evolution of standard musical tuning and official reactions to it. Contrary to propaganda, and current consensus, Cavanagh determined that it was 1939, not 1938, as the true year the BSI adopted the A=440Hz standard promoted by the Rockefeller-Nazi consortium.(20)

At that time, England was about to declare war with Germany, so surely MI6 would have known of the Rockefeller's alliance with IG Farben. This consortium fueled Hitler's military build-up against Poland and threatened England. The funding of Hitler by the Rothschild-Rockefeller-Warburg bankers backing their Nazi partners was known throughout the intelligence communities. The allied British (MI6) and American (OSS, now called the CIA) intelligence agencies, as well as Israel's Irgun (now called the Mossad) sequestered this intelligence, and hashed historic accounts.

Cavanagh's account evidences treachery in that Hitler's Germany invaded Poland officially starting WWII on Sept 1, 1939. Only three months earlier, following widespread rejection of A=440Hz by musicians worldwide, Nazi propaganda minister Goebbels argued on behalf of establishing this standard tuning. Apparently, his intrusion into musical artistry, effectively persuading Hitler's supposed enemies in Britain to adopt this allegedly superior tuning for the "Master Race," was financed by the banking cartel.

After the war, the Rockefeller's Standard Oil Company was indicted by a US Federal Court as an "enemy national," that is, an American traitor.(10) It was proven that the Rockefeller enterprise was a full partner with IG Farben and the Third Reich.

A=440Hz Versus A=444Hz Standard Tuning

Research and developments in musical weaponry, tuning with dissonant frequencies, yielding the latest and greatest war making technology for broadcasting mass hysteria, was finally instituted—speciously adopted, thusly, according to Cavanagh:

> Success was achieved at a 1939 international conference held in London. Presumably as a compromise between current tendencies and earlier pitch standards, it was agreed that the international standard for concert pitch would thenceforth be based upon A=440 Hz—very close to the Royal Philharmonic's A=439 Hz of dubious derivation. The B.B.C. began to broadcast the A=440 Hz tuning note, which, for the sake of accuracy was produced electronically. (20)

To help reconcile what was made irreconcilable about standard tuning by covert operators and censorship, Cavanagh referenced Llewelyn S. Lloyd, and a representative of the BSI knowledgeable about Lloyd's publication in the *Journal of the Royal Society of Arts* (16 Dec., 1949; 80-81.) titled, "International Standard Musical Pitch." Without acknowledging the creative artistry and spirituality of music-making, here is how propagandists at the BBC, effectively controlled by Rothschild-Rockefeller banking families, electrically generated the 440Hz frequency pure tone for media broadcasting:

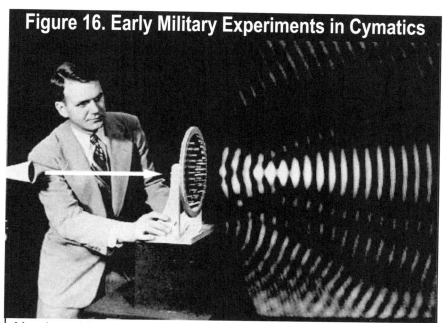

Figure 16. Early Military Experiments in Cymatics

Massive evidence shows the military's acoustic frequency research and technological developments advanced during the 1930s. The purpose went beyond military applications. The Illuminati, operating through the Rockefeller-Rothschild League of Banks, were interested in global applications to induce psychosocial pathology, herd behavior, emotional distress, and mass hysteria. Given what is known about A=440Hz, and its institutional proponents that include the Rockefeller Foundation allied with Germany's Third Reich, the frequency was successfully deployed as a weapon against *We The People*.

CBS News correspondent Paul Manning tracked the Nazi "flight capital" in his book *Martin Bormann, Nazi in Exile*. Later, John Loftus and Mark Aarons, published *The Secred War Against the Jews* evidencing further genocidal malfeasance by Rockefeller-directed intelligence agents in the OSS, and later CIA. Manning wrote that the money invested in World War II, was part of a long-range plan to create a "Neuordnung" as Hitler, Bormann and Goebbels, called it—a "New World Order" as George H.W. Bush referred to globalization in his State of the Union address in 1991.

Loftus, a former U.S. Department of Justice Nazi War Crimes prosecutor, exposed the "Dutch connection" in 1994. He made it known that Fritz Thyssen, the Nazi Party's leading industrialist, had obtained financing for the war build-up from Brown Brothers Harriman, and its affiliate, the Union Banking Corporation—the Bush family's holding company for a number of other entities, including the Holland American Trading Company.

The B.B.C. tuning-note is derived from an oscillator controlled by a piezoelectric crystal that vibrates with a frequency of one million Hz. This is reduced to a frequency of 1,000 Hz by electronic dividers; it is then multiplied eleven times and divided by twenty-five, so producing the required frequency of 440 Hz. As 439 Hz is a prime number a frequency of 439 Hz could not be broadcast by such means as this. (20)

According to preliminary research, analysis, and professional discussions by Walton, Koehler, Reid, et al., on the Internet,(23) A=440Hz frequency music compromises human energy and chakra balancing. The chakras are virtually shocked by A=440Hz tuning; certainly from the heart down to the lower spine. Alternatively, chakras above the heart are stimulated.

Walton discovered that the A=440Hz standard coincides with the Solfeggio's 741Hz note at F#. This vibration stimulates the pineal gland, ego, and left-brain function, overpowering the "heart-mind," intuition, and creative inspiration.

Given the information in this book, especially this chapter, the world must now consider the "Devil's Interval" between A=440Hz and C=528Hz, the spiritually-repressive impact of standard tuning, and its potential health affects. Consideration must be given to well-being, and the expression of higher human values and emotions including LOVE, faith, joy, and bravery.(22, 36)

Religious leaders suppressed the original Solfeggio musical scale valued by the Pythagoreans. Pythagoreans were referenced by Tobias as subscribing to the bioenergetic epistemologies described by Helmholtz.(8) Adequate bioenergetic details about 528Hz, and its harmonic tuning at A=444Hz, are provided herein to prompt international outrage concerning the A=440Hz imposition. Alternatively, a 528LOVERevolution is warranted by this information. (22,36)

This knowledge best explains why so many musicians intuitively feel better tuning up, or down, a bit sharp or flat, from A=440Hz standard tuning. Musicians seeking ultimate musical expression, who are spiritually-sensitive to nature and natural pitches, are compelled, instinctively, to reject intrusions to pure harmony with the flow of sacred cosmic energy.(21, 22)

Leading Experts Endorse A=444Hz

Llewelyn S. Lloyd, in the *Journal of the Royal Society of Arts* (16 Dec., 1949), for example, described his innate drive to "tune-up" to a "brighter," more soothing and inspiring frequency than A=440Hz.. Lloyd, an expert and leading critic of the A=440Hz tuning, described this generally felt "indelible calling for a higher pitch." The British author and composer expressed his preference for precisely A=444Hz tuning, that manifests the C-5-pitch at 528Hz. He wrote that this 4Hz higher pitch is more pleasing generally for musicians worldwide.(20) Here are his words:

> My own experience in tuning an electronic organ to be used as a continuo instrument with orchestra, in the late 1940s and early '50s, showed me that New York orchestra musicians could with difficulty be induced to tune their instruments to a'=440 Hz, but that if the organ were tuned to that pitch it would in the course of performance be flat as compared with the other instruments. If, on the other hand, I tuned the organ to a'=444 Hz, this difficulty disappeared, and I take it that this latter pitch is approximately that at which New York orchestra musicians habitually play, and to which they involuntarily tend to return even if they have started out by tuning their instruments to a'=440 Hz. (20)

Similarly, recent research by veteran piano tuner and custom piano designer, Daniel Koehler, demonstrated the beneficial acoustic and spiritual impact of prototype pianos that include granite bridges to best accommodate the higher tension of strings tuned to A=444Hz. Koehler reported most enthusiastically(23) that the 528Hz frequency resonates most powerfully and enduringly. Measuring volume and duration of string resonance, Koehler wrote:

"We took an introductory level small grand at 5 feet 1 inch long, and surpassed every 9 foot grand in the world on most of the piano concerning sustain with lack of fall-off. This is, with no boasting intended, actual fact on which I would stake my 35-year professional reputation."(24)

A=440HZ versus A=432Hz Tuning

A lot has been written on a proposed A=432Hz alternative tuning that is mathematically consistent with universal design. Among the advocates of A=432Hz standard tuning is musician and researcher, Brian T. Collins, who launched a website dedicated to posting articles supportive to this growing musical-metaphysical movement for recovering optimal integrity in the music industry and spirituality through music therapy.(21)

Collins wrote, "The current tuning of music based on A=440 Hz does not harmonize on any level that corresponds to cosmic movement, rhythm, or natural vibration. Mozart and Verdi both based their music on natural vibration, and A=432 was nicknamed the 'Verdi tuning.' Most western music, including popular New Age music is still tuned at unnatural A=440Hz. The difference between A=440 Hz and A=432 Hz is only 8 vibrations per second, but it is a perceptible difference in the human consciousness . . ."(21)

An expanded review of A=432Hz tuning finds it throughout the religious world according to researchers. "One of the oldest uses of sound is for ceremonial and religious purposes.

Whether the chanting of a Hindu mantra, the recitation of the Jewish cantor, a Christian hymn, or the call of a Moslem muezzin, sacred sound makes its way into all of the various world's religions. According to Robert Lewis, a student of the Rosicrucian Fellowship: 'The purpose of music in religious service is to raise the vibratory rate of a congregation upward through a series of overtones to a spiritual level.'"(21)

An unconfirmed report from an anonymous blogger stated, "Archaic Egyptian instruments that have been unearthed, so far, are largely tuned to A=432Hz. In ancient Greece (the school book original place for music) their instruments were predominantly tuned to 432Hz. Within the archaic Greek Eleusenian Mysteries, Orpheus is the god of music, death and rebirth, and was the keeper of the Ambrosia and the music of transformation. His instruments were tuned at 432Hz."

". . . [O]ne can make audible harmonics, such as 72Hz (9 x 8 Hz), 144Hz (18 x 8 Hz) and 432Hz (54 x 8 Hz); and then further synchronize the music in binaural 8Hz, to reawaken us to the orchestra of our thoughts, in the cathedrals of our minds."(25)

"The Cosmic 432" Fraud

Neglecting Showell's analyses, and abusing Marko Rodin's determinations, there are people who have made it their mission to discredit 528 and my works in this field.

Tesla's inventions, you might recall, were likewise discredited and suppressed by the same petrochemical-pharmaceutical corporations that advanced A=440Hz standard tuning and the nuclear weapons industry.(26)

Recently, deceptively, and maliciously, Jamie Buturff and Tyler Thurmond produced a "The Cosmic 432, Part 2," You-

Tube clip to lamely discourage the use of 528Hz frequency in music and healing, and discredit determinations by Rodin and Showell in math and my conclusions in this book. Their assertions created confusion and dissonance in the community of musical-mathematics researchers, and sourced skepticism the emerging science of creationism. Their unfair criticisms, however, and downright fraudulent demonstrations that purposely and maliciously neglected 528 permutations within Rodin's 285 family number group, were solidly scorned by a team of experts, whose rebuke has been published on i528Tunes.com for the world to consider.

The scholars noted an eerie similarity between Buturff and Thurmond's propaganda, and the lies issued to charater-assassinate John Lennon as a target of J. Edgar Hoover's COINTELPRO.

Today, at the time of this writing, agents determined to have worked for the CIA and FBI in counter-intelligence propaganda on behalf of BigPharma and the energy cartel, have been making similarly stupid assaults on 528 and my credibility over the Internet. Thankfully, the truth always surfaces, and their bogus claims are being solidly rebuked by experts responding independently online.

Buturff and Thurmond used 432 permutations with the original Solfeggio frequencies, deceitfully omitting 528 in every analysis, to claim the discovery of another "original Solfeggio" musical scale. They composed a melodic 432 scale, that could have been similarly done using A=444Hz (C=528Hz), but wasn't, to fraudulently claim that Dr. Puleo's certified original Solfeggio was false, because it is less melodic than their new scale.

Science and common sense, though, proves human hearing pales by comparison to most other species, and what some insects and animals find pleasing, humans find annoying.

Besides this, math does not lie, even when abused by agents of deception.

Buturff and Thurmond abused the works and confidence of mathematician Marko Rodin, among many mathematicians celebrating the discovery of matrix math, and its importance in music. I contacted Rodin to confirm this abuse, and he admitted that he did not endorse Buturff's math, nor their 432Hz tuning, since this number is not found within Rodin's family number groups.

In other words, 432Hz is not a Perfect Circle of Sound™ number, nor an ancient Solfeggio frequency. Each of these frequencies, Rodin proved, sources from his simple "infinity pattern" from which he derived his three family group numbers: 147, 258, and 369. (Move the 1, 2 and 3 one place to the right to derive three of the original six Solfeggio frequencies, 417, 528 and 639.)

Petty jealousy, or industrial espionage, best explains why Buturff and Thurmond would produce a freak fraudulent attack on 528, just when the world needs solutions to urgent problems facing humanity and the polluted biosphere that the 528LOVERevolution is advancing along with technologies to harness free energy.

Thankfully, the darkness, in dissonance with LOVE/528, is disappearing as more and more mathematicians, physicists, bioscientists, musicologists, and performing artists, independently confirm the importance of 528Hz frequency in the energy of life, universal construction, and ecstatic listening.

This knowledge and experience engages metaphysics and the esoteric sciences; and LOVE/528 suppression is crucial for musical (vibrational) cult control by the Illuminati at this critical time in history.

This subversion of 528 discoveries, by Thurmond and Buturff for example, is reminiscent of Tobias's reporting of subversion in the music industry accomplished through the control of esoteric epistemologies. In this vein, Tobias reported that the Rockefeller Foundation's and US Navy's funding for militarizing music, suppressed the bioenergetic fields of discovery and related developments in technology. In this regard, Tobias wrote:

> "In the course of this large-scale historical transition in which bioinformatic epistemologies drew from and displaced bioenergetic [i.e., biospiritual] ones, . . . [h]istorically, "visual music" theorists have attributed such attempts at writing sound in magnetic, electrical, electronic, or digital media as indebted to a larger history of "color organs," alchemy, or Pythagorean or neo-Pythagorean epistemologies. Here, though, we see the tensions in clear detail: at stake is a historical transition between essentially bioenergetic epistemologies after Helmholtz and bioinformatic epistemologies emerging with Turing, Wiener, or Shannon."(8, pp. 91-92)

In other words, the "color" was removed from music and the music industry when the context of the art was institutionalized to mainly serve bioinformatic left brain limited agendas, neglecting the energy of the heart and the creative technology of LOVE/528.

As expected, and evidenced by today's degenerating social and cultural conditions, Tobias concluded, "the Rockefeller Foundation's careful project management and coordination," contributed to the materialistic versus metaphysical industrialization of music in the media.(8)

The U.S. Navy's Musical Manipulations

Besides the U.S. Navy's administrative control over the National Public Health Service in America, this branch of the military has always been at the forefront of war research. This research extends to biological weaponry, virology, genetics. electro-genetics, DNA recombinomics, technical developments in electronics, communications, signaling, and military intelligence bearing on the subject of frequencies, especially those required for producing mass hysteria. Rather than researching electromagnetic and bioacoustic methods of promoting peaceful coexistence, the Navy has invested in space-based weaponry, including satellite communications useful in advancing psychotronic warfare for population control. (10, 29)

In short, U.S. Naval Intelligence oversees or administers the most advanced science in the fields of population control, including energy, bioenergy, and communications on behalf of the Illuminati. Nuclear, radiological, biological, chemical, and musical weapons for controlling humanity most profitably and effectively fall within the Navy's jurisdiction.(10)

Given this history, it is not surprising U.S. Navy celebrity, John Calhoun Deagan, is credited for having allegedly persuaded the American Federation of Musicians in 1910, at its annual convention, to adopt A=440 standard tuning for orchestras and bands.(30)

Also, around this time, the Rockefeller and Carnegie Foundations began providing grants to support the pseudoscience called "eugenics," or "racial hygiene," for profitable population reduction.(29)

The Rockefeller Foundation and Eugenics

The Rockefeller Foundation has been a prime sponsor of the United Nations' depopulation program. Terminating six billion people on earth is their current objective.(31, 32) Although most people find this hard to believe, thanks to media propaganda, this massive depopulation is being advanced by the

Fig. 17. Manson, the CIA, LSD & "Helter Skelter"

Timothy Leary, Charles Manson, The Rolling Stones, and Zager & Evans

The "British Invasion" was a social experiment for profitable depopulation, according to Carol Greene, author of, *Morder aus der Retorte: Der Fall Charles Manson*, (Test-Tube Murder: The Case of Charles Manson). She approached me in 1997 to publish an English translation of her text detailing neo-Nazi links to BigPharma and British and American intelligence agents working to "Turn On, Tune In and Drop Out" the Western World's youth. The covert operation has grown into today's "Sex, Drugs, and Rock-and-Roll" cult.

Charles Mason was drafted into the CIA and released from prison in March 1967. His murderous assignment was supported by the National Institute of Mental Health (NIMH). "The Company," allied with British Secret Service (MI6), selected Manson to model "Helter Skelter"—Paul McCartney's tribute to the falling empire—broadcasting serial slayings involving celebrities to engage youth most profitably, while depopulating most effectively to prevent political uprisings and social revolutions.

Manson's parole officer, Roger Smith, was based at the Haight-Ashbury Medical Clinic in San Francisco working to effect this unprecedented social experiment. Clinic director, and NIMH contractor, David E. Smith was involved as an expert in breeding violent anti-social behaviors in cults, and as the publisher of the *Journal of Psychedelic Drugs*. Timothy Leary was recruited from Harvard to help market the mind-set. He was mentored on LSD and psilocybin by Frank Barron for the CIA. LSD and STP amphetamines were part of the experiment.

Most of the operatives were devotees of satanic killer cults including "The Process—Church of Final Judgment," and Anton LaVey's and Michael Aquino's "Church of Satan." The American Family Foundation,

Turn On, Tune In, and Drop Out Agenda

allegedly guarding people against injurious cults, was part of the scam, much like today's National Center for Missing & Exploited Children, and the Johnny Gosch Foundation, protects The Company's ritual abusers.

Airforce allies, Col. Michael Aquino and Dr. Louis Jolyon West, both experts in brainwashing for military "black ops," were involved. Aquino wrote, "PSYOP to MindWar: The Psychology of Victory" distributed to his Church of Set members. West researched "the psychology of dissociated states" for the CIA, using LSD and hypnosis. Aldous Huxley suggested to West during an MK-Ultra experiment that West hypnotize his subjects prior to administering LSD to give them "post-hypnotic suggestions aimed at . . . some desired direction," in this case, serial homicide. Dr. West also worked for the False Memory Syndrome Foundation, an organization thought to specialize in discrediting ritually-abused, mind-controlled children and their therapists. This ploy is still used today to defend The Company's child abusers and ritualistic killers whenever they are prosecuted.

According to Anton Chaitkin's review of Greene's book, a large part of the satanic, neo-Nazi, "social experiment," involved the Scottish Rite Masons' Schizophrenia Research program, and the NIMH's Dr. Robert H. Felix, who helped develop the program that manipulated Manson. Felix's ally, Dr. Seymour S. Kety, forged the field of "genetic schizophrenia," and celebrated Dr. Franz Kallmann serving Adolf Hitler, exterminating mental patients and "genetic inferiors."

During the 1920s, Greene wrote, the Rockefeller Foundation was funded by famous American eugenicists, including Prescott Bush. Their eugenic researchers experimented to determine social conditions that would cause populations to self-destruct.

Social engineers began with rats in cages left to breed until populations, and stress levels, hit lethal limits. Alpha-males then became much more aggressive. Increasingly, they bit and killed the weaker beta-males. After witnessing enough killing, the beta-males followed their role models. Then the populations fell "naturally."

Researchers determined that they could speed up the deadly male aggression by feeding the rats psychotropic drugs, especially amphetamines.

Charles Manson was selected to play the lead role of the alpha-male. His apartment was visited daily by CIA PSYOPs personnel engaged in the druggings, hypnosis, and satanic reprogramming that enabled the cult to kill without remorse.

As the "British Invasion" was underway, and urban areas were seeded with drugs, especially in the population dense "projects," Manson, and his "family," began their murder spree. Simultaneously, RCA released the Zager & Evans hit, "In the Year 2525 (Exordium and Terminus)." The bizarre words "Exordium and Terminus" not part of the album cover, described the experiment as the "beginning of the end" for the human race. Massive media coverage of the murders assured the Illuminati's murderous role model, and deadly messages, played in the tuning for "mass hysteria" (A=440Hz), hit susceptibles.(38)

world's wealthiest industrialists, among them Bill Gates, who promotes poisonous vaccinations; which he lectures, will reduce nearly 900,000,000 people in the coming years. This is shown in the documentary film, *PharmaWhores: The SHOW-TIME Sting of Penn & Teller.*

Historic accounts document the Rockefeller Foundation and its corporate, medical, political and financial associates organized and administered eugenics—the "science of genetic differences between the races"—a mass murder program invented by the Illuminati and adopted by the Nazis.(10, 28)

A=440Hz tuning, along with Psychiatric Genetics, was instituted at this precise time with Rockefeller Foundation money. For this new field of science, the Foundation reorganized medical education in Germany, creating, and henceforth directing, the "Kaiser Wilhelm Institute for Psychiatry," and the "'Kaiser Wilhelm Institute for Anthropology, Eugenics and Human Heredity.'"(14)

The Rockefeller's chief executive overseeing these institutions was the infamous war criminal, Swiss psychiatrist Ernst Rudin, assisted by his proteges Otmar Verschuer and Franz J. Kallmann. (14)

In 1932, the British-led eugenics movement designated the Rockefellers' appointee Rudin as the president of the worldwide Eugenics Federation. The movement called for the killing or sterilizing of people whose heredity made them a perceived burden. (14)

The Rockefeller Foundation's German grantees drew upon existing American "racial hygiene" statutes passed by the State of Virginia. Verschuer and his assistant Josef Mengele collaborated on reports for special courts which enforced Rudin's racial purity law against cohabitation of Aryans with non-Aryans. (14)

116

The Cult of Militarized Music

According to Tobias, the wartime economy provided greater funding for musical research and development for opportunists with conflicting military and "non-profit" interests. In September, 1941, Burris-Meyer was encouraged by the Navy Sub-committee on Sound Sources of the National Defense Research Council to receive "$50,000 for another one year contract" to deliver what was called his "command performance." (8)

In January 1942, in a letter to John Marshall, Burris-Meyer stated his belief that military applications of his acoustic research would be used in the entertainment industry following the war. Soon thereafter, a California defense contractor planned to develop "wired music" installations to deliver Muzak-style ambient sound in movie theaters. (8)

Tobias detailed, "[t]he power of sound control to create musical, corporeal synchronization." That is, people's bodies would bioenergetically entrain to the musical frequencies and electronically-engineered sound effects. These would affect people's emotions and cause them to act in certain programmable ways. This would occur "across a variety of environments," and "across the war-time economy . . ." (8)

Tobias noted that Burris-Meyer had been "requisitioned by the Navy," and with R.L. Cardinell, co-wrote, a "Guide to Industrial Sound," published by the War Production Board (73 200R, RG 1.1, Series 200, Box 282, Folder 3353).(8)

"Sound control," according to Tobias, "worked for the Rockefeller Foundation, as . . . a general signifier of cultural, factory, and military industries, . . ."

Tobias's legendary characters considered the long-term implications of militarizing music "in terms of both conflicts between "trade" and "research," as well as . . . the Foundation's goal of developing non-profit, educational, industrial, and military institutional networks . . ." (8)

This, Tobias wrote, "is, in fact, the crux . . . in the overall commoditization of listening across educational, artistic, working, consuming, and military environments, . . . [T]he 'culture industries' were the commercial arm legitimating a broader control of consciousness." (8)

As in the 1500s, wherein Shakespearean plays were promotionally pivotal in advancing English as the New World language, the twentieth century's mass mediated musical manipulation of culture and consciousness is hereby exposed as the modus operandi of the Illuminati.

On May 16, 1949, the Rockefeller Foundation's Charles B. Fahs ran into Burris-Meyer on the train platform at Penn Station in Newark, and rode with him to Philadelphia. Burris-Meyer was in uniform as a naval officer, heading to Washington for further military research work . . . on "the problem of the control of human emotion as a determinant of action." (8)

"B-M points out . . . the realization that we were moving into an era when such control of human emotion would be technically possible which led to the development of Nazism in Germany. It is clearly indicated in Mein Kampf and in the work of Goebbels. According to B-M, his wartime work demonstrated that means to control emotion with sufficient precision to determine the action of from two to eight percent of a given population . . . While this percentage of a population is small, it is perhaps quite adequate to be decisive. There is no use ignoring the possibility of such techniques and hoping that the disturbing visions of what the effects in politics might be will go away. The question is rather, as in the case of the atom bomb, whether the techniques will be mastered and utilized for democratic purposes before they are exploited for totalitarian purposes. This is the background of B-M's conviction that this work is important and urgent in the United States." (8)

Figure 17 details the Illuminati's satanic agenda for which 2-8% of youth would "Turn On" to drugs, "Tune In" to A=440Hz and the media's deadly messages, and "Drop Out" of LOVE, altruism, discernment, and the exercise of free will to engage a murderous cult. These drop outs, psycho-spiritually impaired by the overwhelming "social experiment," advanced cultural degeneration, leading to what is happening now—profitable depopulation.

Following Hanns Eisler's deportation from the United States to Germany where he joined the East German intellectual establishment, a 1958 interview he published is noteworthy. Defending the East German youth under attack in West Germany "for indulging in what he agreed was the false ecstasy of 'boogie-woogie' and the 'stupid' fashion of American-style jeans," Eisler commented in reference to politics, youth, and urgent insurmountable social challenges, "[T]he American culture industries have a monumental influence over the entire world." (8, 33)

Summary, Solutions and Conclusions

The current world crises, cultural indoctrination, and behavior modification has a lot to do with the science of coercion, the history of musical instrument tuning, and the media.

This review of Rockefeller Foundation literature sets the record straight regarding the organization's involvement with the military-medical-petrochemical-pharmaceutical cartel's focus on acoustic science to identify sounds and modern musical technologies that produce vibrational frequencies useful in war and applicable to public persuasion and crowd control. These parties institutionalized standard A=440Hz musical instrument tuning.

President Dwight Eisenhower (1953-1961) protested against this "beast," warning that globalist threats to "Economic, Political, even Spiritual" freedoms were mounting.(34)

Populations are now tethered like sheep by psycho-emotional attachments and addictions to whatever this cartel sells and promotes through radio and television. Civilization is now virtually enslaved to tolerate media contrivances facilitating genocide or omnicide.

In essence, this "military-industrial complex," rooted in the world of investment banking, has advanced a covert operation to control populations, most loudly and profitably.

Music bioenergetically affects your body chemistry, psychoneuroimmunology, and health.(35) Your body is now being vibrated musically, audibly and subliminally, according to an institutionally imposed frequency that resonates in dissonance with LOVE and positive emotions.

From the Rockefeller Foundation Archives, it is clear that the investors in A=440Hz standard tuning, are some of the least trust-worthy entities on earth. They directed the U.S. Navy's involvement in this "black-op," engaging the consortium-controlled networks.

These findings strongly suggest the military's acoustic frequency research and technological developments advanced during the 1930s to induce psychosocial pathology, herd behavior, emotional distress, and mass hysteria, were successfully deployed and are now being used against *We The People*.

Alternatively, musical frequencies most beneficial to health, psychosocial harmony, and world peace have been suppressed.

These findings offer a most reasonable, simple, and powerful remedy residing in restoring naturally preferred frequencies to music. Instruments and voices tuned to the A=444Hz scale are far more acoustically pleasing, instinctively and kinesthetically stimulating, spiritually refreshing, linked to genetic repair, and arguably, even resonating pure LOVE.

Given that the media is so negatively controlled and behaviorally controlling, alternatives to the major networks are now required to free *We The People*. This was the original intent of the U.S. Constitution and Bill of Rights, virtually vanquished by the Rockefeller-Rothschild industrialists.

Many musicians, mathematicians, physicians, physicists, and even geneticists, now celebrate the emergence of truth about 528Hz as an apparent carrier wave of LOVE, broadcasting from the heart of everything in nature, or the heart of the electromagnetic energy matrix.(7, 22) The vast majority of objective investigators now view these revelations as an opportunity to rediscover our spiritual roots in music. With the accelerating Spiritual Renaissance, this knowledge is perfectly timed to remedy otherwise impossible problems imposed on the world by unelected controllers of geopolitics and economics.

Everyone is urged to discuss these findings, reject secret militarization of music, and retune instruments and voices to frequencies most sustaining and healing.

A service operating by donation to provide A=440 to A=444Hz (C=528Hz) frequency transpositions of every genre of music was recently launched to accommodate this revolution. (See: i528Tunes.com)

Music is humanity's best hope for physical salvation and Divine-human connection. The spiritual musical portals through which planetary rebirth and harmonization is destined, await your vision and activism. The choice remains yours to advance solutions, or remain part of the problem.

References

1) *Merck Veterinary Manual.* Social Behavior. Whitehouse Station, NJ: Merck & Co., Inc., 2008.

2) Gladwell M. *The Tipping Point: How Little Things Can Make a Big Difference.* New York: Little Brown, 2000.

3) Frater J. Top 10 bizarre cases of mass hysteria. Listverse ultimate top 10 lists.

4) Wessely S. Protean nature of mass sociogenic illness: From possessed nuns to chemical and biological terrorism fears. *The British Journal of Psychiatry* 2002:180;300-306.

5) Bartholomew RE. Occupational Mass Psychogenic Illness. A Transcultural Perspective. *Transcultural Psychiatry*: 2000;37;4, 495-524.

6) Horowitz LG. *DNA: Pirates of the Sacred Spiral.* Sandpoint, ID: Tetrahedron Publishing Group, 2004.

7) Horowitz LG. *Walk on Water.* Sandpoint, ID: Tetrahedron Publishing Group, 2005.

8) Tobias J. Composing for the Media: Hanns Eisler and Rockefeller Foundation Projects in Film Music, Radio Listening, and Theatrical Sound Design. Rockefeller Archive Center Research Reports Online, 2009.

9) Jubilee, 2012. The House of Rothschild. June 21, 2008. See: http://jubilee2012.50webs.com/the_house_of_rothschild.htm

10) Horowitz LG. *Death in the Air: Globalism, Terrorism & Toxic Warfare.* Tetrahedron Publishing Group, (June) 2001.

11) Schauf TD. The Federal Reserve Is A PRIVATELY OWNED Corporation. (See: http://proliberty.com/observer/20090404.htm)

12) Institute for Advanced Study. Albert Einstein. (See: http://www.ias.edu/people/einstein)

13) Institute for Advanced Study. Mission and History. (See: http://www.ias.edu/about/mission-and-history)

14) Horowitz LG. The American Red Double-Cross. *Idaho Observer*, October, 2001.

15) Hilmes M. Creating links between British and American broadcasters in the 1930s. Rockefeller Archive Center Research Reports Online, 2009.

16) Elvis Presley Pictures. Elvis Presley Vancouver, Canada. Empire Stadium, August 31, 1957.

17) Wikipedia. Colonel Tom Parker.

18) Wikipedia. RCA

19) Robertson P. *The New World Order*. Nashville, TN: Thomas Nelson, Inc. 1982.

20) Cavanagh L. A brief history of the establishment of international standard pitch A=440 Hertz. (Pdf file is available for a free download. See reference here: http://en.Wikipedia.org/wiki/Concert_pitch. Cavanagh cites Lloyd's paper as: Llewelyn S. Lloyd, "International Standard Musical Pitch," *Journal of the Royal Society of Arts* 98 (16 Dec., 1949), 80-81.

21) Collins BT. The Importance of 432hz Music. See: http://www.omega432.com/music.html

22) Horowitz LG. LOVE528.com website and the online journal *Hydrosonics,* provides much information on the 528Hz frequency.

23) Koehler D. Pianos, Violin, and New Concert "A." Concert for the Living Water, LIVE H2O, Official Forum. Discussion on A=444 (528), Jan. 25, 2010; See also: http://web.me.com/len15/MUSICAL_CULT_CONTROL/Leonard_G._Horowitz.html

24) Koehler D. Personal communication, May, 2010.

25) Anonymous author of blog provides relevant discussion including Scientific American (March 1965, p. 28) reference to genetic repair using natural frequencies.

26) Peterkin T. Israel banned The Beatles fearing 'hysteria.' Telegraph.co.uk. Sept. 22, 2008

27) Horowitz LG. *LOVE the Real da Vinci CODE*. Sandpoint, ID: Tetrahedron Publishing Group, 2007.

28) Horowitz LG and Pulio J. *Healing Codes for the Biological Apocalypse*. Sandpoint, ID: Tetrahedron Publishing Group, 1998.

29) Horowitz LG. *Emerging Viruses AIDS & Ebola--Nature, Accident or Intentional?* Rockport, MA: Tetrahedron Publishing Group, 1998.

30) The National Cyclopedia of American Biography. John Calhoun Deagan. Volume 43, pp. 391-392. (See: http://thescreamonline.com/photo/photo10-01/garygoss/deaganbio.html).

31) Gates B. TED Conference lecture: Reducing global warming by reducing populations via vaccines and more. February, 2010. (See: http://www.youtube.com/watch?v=-0gvDkVcFkl)

32) United Nations. *Population challenges and Development Goals*. New York: UN Dept. of Economic and Social Affairs, Population Division (ST/ESA/SERA/248), 2005.

33) Eisler, Hanns, Gespräch mit Hans Bunge: *Fragen Sie mehr über Brecht*. Munich: Rogner and Bernhard, 1976, p. 157.

34) Eisenhower DD. Military-Industrial Complex Speech. Public Papers of the Presidents, Dwight D. Eisenhower, 1960 p. 1035-1040.

35) Horowitz LG. *Healing Celebrations: Miraculous Recoveries Through Anxient Scripture, Natural Medicine & Modern Science*. Sandpoint, ID: Tetrahedron Publishing Group, 2000.

36) Walton M and Horowitz LG. Synthesizer re-tuning to the "Perfect Circle of Sound:" A preliminary study with implications for bioenergetic healing. *Hydrosonics* 2009:1;1:1.

37) Hero B. Chakra energy centers of our bodies. In: Color Energies and Healing the Color Rays of Creation. Copyright, 1996. See: http://www.greatdreams.com/hertz.htm; http://www.greatdreams.com/hertz.htm

38) Chaitkin A. British Psychiatry: From Eugenics to Assassination. *Executive Intelligence Report*. V21, #40 See: http://webcache.googleusercontent.com/search?q=cache:dCThB3UOLM4J:www.operationmorningstar.org/british_psychiatry.htm+Murder's+Test-Tube:+The+Box+of+Charles+Manson&cd=4&hl=en&ct=clnk&gl=us&source=www.google.com

Chapter Five:
The 528LOVERevolution

With the advent of ultrasound and nuclear-magnetic-resonance imaging (MRI), healthcare engaged biophysics and biospirituality.

Sounds, electron waves, or bioresonating energy signals from machines, cause patients' cells and cell nuclei to vibrate. These vibrations return through body Water as signals to computer sensors; which are then transformed into data and projected by light energy electrons flowing against video screens into remarkable images. Improved diagnosis of disease is thus made.(1-3)

This use of sound on body Water vibrating cell nuclei—physical matter—is similar to the Creator's work. Eons ago, in molding our universe, the words or sounds generating the frequencies or "keys" of creation were sung. This "voice" gave rise to the cosmos.(2)

This same celestial orchestra is currently playing as loudly as ever, although you can not hear it without special equipment. It inspires and sustains you.

Therapeutic uses for this knowledge are addressed in Chapter 10. These include the emerging field of hydrosonics, or "biosonics," that is, biologically active sounds.(1-5) Other uses include physical therapies, sports medicine, music, dance and relaxation therapies, laser therapies, homeopathics, acupuncture, osteopathy, and chiropractic care, all part of "energy medicine" involving bioenergetics and electromagnetism.

Anthropologically and medically, during the past few centuries, scientists worldwide gained great respect for physics. Largely neglected, however, is a specialty field called *metaphysics* that demands attention to psycho-spiritual reconciliation.

The Heart of The Revolution

Despite a general suppression of this information by the mainstream media, monumental discoveries in physics, meta-physics, and biophysics are now prompting paradigm shifts, and are helping to explain what has been secreted for millennia.

Studies in structured Water science, electrogenetics, and protein crystallography provide knowledge about how you are built using sacred geometry. Every carbon-6 hexagon in your body is vibrating musically with 528Hz energy, and operating energetically or biospiritually.

Your physical chemistry, in fact, is entirely regulated energetically. Simply consider the pH of your blood as vitally important in health versus disease. pH is a measure of acidity versus alkalinity, and that, fundamentally, reflects electron availability or energy levels.

Acid/alkaline dynamics in your body is like the Yin/Yang of cosmic creation. Since 741Hz is distressing and 528Hz is relaxing, and stress is acidifying, while rest is alkalizing, 528 may be your miraculous elixir, especially when put into Water.

528 is probably the most therapeutic sound in the cosmos, given the fact that your organic structuring is based on it.

Your organic structuring is now recognized as being a manifestation or precipitation of energy vibrations molding molecular sacred geometry.(6,7) Proof of this simple concept is shown in Figure 8 diagramming the most important energy transducers on earth—chlorophyll and hemoglobin.

Look carefully at these most important life-giving structures to see the sacred geometry of 528Hz frequency—the circular array and hexagonal ring.

Biophysics best explains this process by which sound energy, measured in Hertz frequencies, moves like waves through Water, cymatically precipitating physical reality; regulating chemistry's structures and functions, too.

Reality is perceived incorrectly or erroneously due to your limited senses and three dimensional perspective. In science, your bias or perspective can influence scientific measurements. Physicists claim you are living in a pliable world in which your thoughts, attitudes, and core beliefs, *energetically* alter your realities. LOVE in 528, versus FEAR in 741, for instance, yields different outcomes, even though they both derive from your free-will and power to choose what is happening inside you.

A broader view of reality is needed to reclaim your spiritual life and power. You can choose to participate with the unseen world of energy flowing in parallel dimensions; wherein angels travel. Spiritual life, fundamental to physical reality, helps many people feel or perceive more using their hearts than their minds.

Some people use pendulums or diving rods effectively to help navigate the world of choices. Healing remedies are often selected this way. People use telepathy, and intuition too, to guide their actions.

The unseen but accessible universe of energy affecting physical reality also accommodates placebos and nocebos. With a placebo, your faith or belief in a cure produces the remedy. Healing manifests energetically, from the belief in your head that touches your heart. From there, something magical happens to your psychoneuroimmunology that flows with faith in the positive result. With nocebos, the opposite of placebos, you get sucked into a demonic realm that manifests psychoneuroimmunologically from fear that troubles your head, and blocks your heart and its creative connection to Source.

You are learning here that everything is crystallized within Water from math—the perfect language of the Creative Spirit. Everything in creation comes from LOVE, and all destruction follows fear that arises from lacking faith. It is that simple.(8)

528Hz frequency, characterized by LOVE, faith, joy, empathy, and bravery, harmonizes with nearly everything, except for 741Hz in the A=440Hz scale. Striking the 528 tuning fork simultaneously with each of the other eight Perfect Circle of Sound keys produces only one that is obviously disturbing. That is, the "Devil's tone" produced by 528 and 741 together.

Metaphorically, the Circle of Life was created where LOVE plays harmoniously with the rest of creation, or discordantly with one option that opposes LOVE.

Answering the Call

People worldwide suffer a multitude of modern plagues due to ignorance. This knowledge suggests illnesses initiate from mainly one degenerative resonance squelching LOVE.

In the normal state, harmonious bio-resonating energy flows to and from every cell's DNA and along energy channels called "meridians" in Chinese medicine. Your "Life Force" is carried through these channels by electrons inspiring your body through your breath. The "Ha," called the "breath of life," or "prana" celebrates this dynamic. This energy flows in perfect balance and harmony with nature and keeps you chemically balanced and re-energized.

Electrons carrying the "charge of life" are input into oxygen you breathe through the greenish-yellow chlorophyll molecule that vibrates most powerfully in 528Hz frequency. You are breathing pure prana/ LOVE with every breath. This fuels nearly everything alive. This is the "Ha" in *alo__ha__* and Jehov__ah__ that sustains you.

This is from whence the *Star Wars* blessing, "May the Force be with you," sources. "The Force is strong in you."

The Force is strong and getting stronger in a lot of people today, especially those with opened minds and hearts.

This eternal Force, called the Holy Spirit in the religious world, is far stronger than drugs. Ailments for which drugs have largely failed may be cured by "The Force" generated using bioenergetic advances, including 528Hz resonating bio-technologies.

This 528 healing revolution comes at a time when people need it most. Modern medicine, which keeps patients under pharmaceutical duress, chemical distress, and physiological and psychological dependence, has failed to provide optimal relief.

New philosophies, highly effective alternative products and practices are emerging.

The notion that you can "treat" a spiritual Temple with chemical pollutants and claim this is a "reasonable standard of care" is barbaric.

In reality, all healing is performed primarily energetically by the Holy Spirit. People miraculously heal all the time, despite being medically poisoned by doctors and druggists who receive the credit for patients' natural return to balance.

Yet, the best alternatives are being suppressed by Big-Pharma through its agents at the World Health Organization, the CDC, and the FDA, all advancing CODEX ALIMENTARI-US legislation for industry-wide regulation and consumer coercion.(8)

The Human Potential Movement of the sixties foreshadowed the Natural Healing Movement of today. Both correspond to the 528LOVERevolution facilitating the currently accelerating Spiritual Renaissance. The logic and impetus for this mass awakening features LOVE, musical-mathematics, and 528Hz frequency dynamics.

This philosophical, theological, and metaphysical journey towards LOVE and global enlightenment is compelled by the pains and pleasures in our lives at this time. Many people are searching for meaning in life. A popular focus is on entertainment, spirituality, and spiritual-healing as a remedy for what ails us.

The stage is set for revolutionary technological solutions for this "mad world," especially in healthcare. People are now

Table 6. Solfeggio Definitions Reveal Keys for the 144,000 Vocalists Fulfilling Rev. 14:1

UT–quent laxis

1. a syllable used for the first note in the diatonic scale in an early solmization system and later replaced by do. 2. the syllable sung to this note in a medieval hymn to St. John the Baptist. <Gk. -Gamut- 1. the entire scale or range; *the Gamut of dramatic emotion from grief to joy.* 2. *the whole series of recognized musical notes* [1425-75]; late ME (Middle English)> <ML (Mediaeval Latin)– contraction, of *Gamma*, used to represent the first lowest tone of (G) in the Medieval Scale Ut, Re, Mi Fa, So, La, Si. <Gk -Gamma- 1. the *third* letter of the Greek alphabet. 2. the *third* in a series of items. 3. a star that is usually the third brightest of a constellation. 4. a unit of weight equal to one microgram. 5. **a unit of magnetic field strength equal to 10^5 power gauss**. (quent: needing), (laxis: loose; axis—an affiliation of two or more nations. Also Axis Powers.)

RE–sonare fibris (Res-o-nance)

1 a: the state of quality of being resonant. b (1) *a vibration of large amplitude in a mechanical or electrical system caused by a relatively small periodic stimulus of the same or nearly the same period as the natural vibration period of the system* 2. the prolongation of sound by reflection; reverberation. 3a. Amplification of a source of speech sounds, esp. of phonation, by sympathetic vibration of the air, esp. in the cavities of the mouth, nose and pharynx. b. a characteristic quality of a particular voice speech sound imparted by the distribution of amplitudes among the cavities of the head, chest, and throat. 4a. *a larger than normal vibration produced in response to a stimulus whose frequency is close to the natural frequency of the vibrating system, as an electrical circuit, in which a value much larger than average is maintained for a given frequency.* 5a. a quality of *enriched significance, profundity, or allusiveness; a poem has a resonance beyond its surface meaning.* 6. the chemical phenomenon in which the arrangements of the valance electrons of a molecule changes back and forth between two or more states. (in percussing for diagnostic purposes) a sound produced when air is present [1485-95]; <MF (Middle French), <L Resonantia, Echo = Reson (are) to resound + Antia-ance.(Re–a prefix, occurring orig. in loan words from Latin, use to form verbs denoting action in a backward direction , *Action in answer to or intended to undo a situation*, or that *performance of the new action brings back an earlier state of affairs.* (fibris: fibre string, vocal cord.)

MI–ra gestorum (Miracle)

1. *an extraordinary occurrence that surpasses all known human powers or natural forces and is ascribed to a divine or supernatural cause esp. to God.* 2. a superb or surpassing example of something; wonder, marvel [1125-75]; ME <L Miraculum=Mira(Ri) to wonder at. *fr* (French): sighting, aiming to hold against the light. (gestorum: gesture; movements to express thought, emotion; any action, *communication*, etc. intended for effect.)

FA–muli tuorum (Famulus,)

. . . plural Famuli, 1a. *servant/s, or attendant/s, esp. of a scholar or a magician* [1830-40 <L (Latin), servant, of family. (Tourum - quorum - 1. *the number of members of a group required to be present to transact business or carry out an activity legally. usu. a majority. 2. a particularly chosen group.* [1425-75; <L

SO-lve polluti (So-lve')

1. to find the answer or explanation for; clear-up; explain; to *solve a mystery* or puzzle, to work out the *answer or solution to (a mathematical problem.)* [1400-50; Late ME <L Solvere to loosen, release dissolve = so-var, after velarl, of se-set-luere to wash; (see Ablution.) Ablution n. 1. a cleansing with water or other liquid, esp. as a religious ritual. [1350-1400]. (Pollutii–pollute-luted, 1. to make foul or unclean,)

LA–bii reatum (Labi-al)

1. of pertaining to or resembling a Labium. 2. of pertaining to the lips, 3. (of a speech sound) *articulated using one or both lips.* 4. of or designating the surface of a tooth facing the lips. 5. the labial speech sound, esp. consonant, [1585-95]; ML lingual. (Reatum - reaction - 1. *a reverse movement or tendency; an action in a reverse direction or manner.* 2. *a movement toward extreme political conservatism*; 3. *a desire to return to an earlier system or order.* 4. action in response to some influence, event, etc.; 5. a psysiological response to an action or condition. b. a physiological change indicating sensitivity to a foreign matter.) 6. mech. the *instantaneous response of a system to an applied force*, manifested as the exertion of a force equal in magnitude, but opposite in direction, to the applied force [1635-45].

SI (Sancte Johannes)

1. a person of exceptional holiness, formally recognized by the Christian Church esp. by *Canonization.* 2. a person of great virtue or benevolence. 3. a founder or patron, as of a movement. 4. a member of any various Christian groups. 5. to acknowledge as a Saint. Canonize. [1150-1200]; ME Seinte. Canon: 1. an ecclesiastical rule or law enacted by a council or other competent authority and, in the Roman Catholic Church, approved by the Pope. 3. a body of rules, principles, or standards accepted as *axiomatic* and universally binding, esp. in a field of study of art.. 6. any officially recognized set of sacred books. 10. the part of the mass between Sanctus and the *communion.* 11. *consistent, note-for-note imitation of one melodic line by another, in which the second line starts after the first.* (axiomatic: 1. pertaining to or of *the nature of an axiom; self-evident. 2. a universally accepted principle or rule. 3. a proposition in logic or mathematics that is assumed without proof for the sake of studying consequences that follow from it.*

131

clamoring for physical protections and spiritual ascension from cataclysmic events, inclusing Earth changes, weather chang-es, and threatened pandemics.

Seeking Shelter From the Storm

Medical sociologists teach that during troubled times, people increasingly turn to spiritual faiths to survive and even thrive. Where America now focuses its spirituality, even *Newsweek* proclaims, is in heart felt prayer and practiced devotions. Yoga, meditations with deep breathing, chanting, praying, ton-ing, speaking in tongues, and the martial arts all share the developing skill of communing with the Divine—the mission of the 528LOVERevolution.(10)

Why, then, does BigPharma and the PharmaMedia prin-cipally feature killing agents to supposedly protect or sustain life? Is biological warfare using vaccines, antibiotics, antivirals, antitumor agents, and deadly radiation, the best that "modern medicine" can offer? Why do they suppress and discredit bio-energetic re-harmonization with the foundational frequencies of nature?

Obviously, profits come before people for politically-em-powered drugsters.

Oriental physicians efficiently rebalanced human nature for more than 5,000 years with acupuncture, herbs, and positive loving intention—a form of prayer. They normalized energy flow throughout the body benefiting physical and psychologi-cal health. This Chinese tradition continues with acupunctur-ists who require payment only when their patients stay well.

How does acupuncture work, fundamentally?

It brings the energy of Heaven to Earth, into your Holy Spirit-filled Temple. It is a function of bioenergy.

This process of enlightenment begins in your own Temple. Enlightened means "made light." At the heart of the light is

Table 7. The Ancient Solfeggio Frequencies

1. Ut = 396 = 9   4. Fa = 639 = 9
2. Re = 417 = 3   5. Sol = 741 = 3
3. Mi = 528 = 6   6. La = 852 = 6

The Hymn to Saint John the Baptist

So that your servants
Can sing together
With the loose strings
The wonders of their deeds
Oh Saint John
Wash away the guilt
of their polluted lips.

Table shows the increasing frequencies encoded in the Bible in *Numbers*, Chapter 7, verses 12–83. Initially encrypted by Levi priests who translated the original Torah into the Greek *Septuagint*, these six frequencies possess extraordinary spiritual power. Besides their link to "The hymn to St. John the Baptist," and their likely association with creative and destructive events as detailed in the Bible, the third note— "Mi" for "Miracles" or "528"—is fundamental to mathematical constants and sacred geometry.

528Hz energy. This is proven by data in Figures 6 and 7.

LOVE and enlightenment go hand-in-hand. This message is eons old.

Tables 5 and 6 relay the meanings and math of the ancient Solfeggio scale that proves the validity and central significance of 528Hz frequency in this ancient process of "illumination," censored by the Illuminati. This is the music to be sung by the gathering 144,000 described in *Revelation*. This is the "New Song" that invites the heart of the Lamb.

Recently, due to the Spiritual Renaissance and Internet, these truths are being rapidly revealed, and embraced by multitudes of people. Scientists, scholars, and religious leaders as well, are increasingly becoming enlightened by advances in 528 science. The evidence even supports fundamentalist thinking about LOVE, Christ's teachings, and creation.

The BioSpiritual Mechanics of Life

One concept bridging the gap between science and the religious world is that of the Holy Spirit. Miraculous healings are often associated with prayer, and this Divine energy undoubtedly features 528Hz frequency.

The Holy Spirit was often depicted by light surrounding the heart of Jesus, or the halos around the heads of angels. This is commonly recognized throughout Christianity.

The Holy Spirit, science now evidences, uses the dynamics and mechanics of metaphysics to inspire life. Biophysics, the energy dynamics fundamental to biology and nature, is a subspecialty of metaphysics. Metaphysical theories and theologies go hand-and-hand with advancing reality theories and the physical sciences.

For instance, the "string theory" discussed in Chapter 9 provides a musical, mathematical, metaphysical, view of creation and even creationism. In Chapter 1, I mentioned the works of Dr. Hartmut Müller, proving that the human energy field is scaled relative to the "Standing Gravitational Wave." This general force field resonates from the periphery of the cosmos.(11)

This field of study is mathematical and metaphysical. It was christened "Biocosmology" by Chris King at the Department of Mathematics, at the University of Auckland, New Zealand.(12)

Müller et. al., showed that your body, like all biology, is mathematically generated piece by piece, or "fractally." Mathematically you crystallize or fall apart.(11-13). As an expert in space-time mathematics and physics, Müller compared biological elements to cosmic elements: planets, galaxies, and particles in space. Comparing double helix DNA to the universe as a double helix on the logarithmic line, he concluded, "[t]he genetic code itself is a product of the global standing gravitational wave = time wave."(11)

The Energetic Nodes of Existence

Waves flow according to certain laws in math and physics. Sound waves broadcast in space, the air, or by an antennae, spread out radially in rings, which is probably why people refer to the sounds made by bells and telephones as "rings."

Figures 9 and 18, supplied by John Stuart Reid, shows radiating sounds similar to throwing a pebble into a pond and watching the waves spread out radially. In theory, the circles expand to the furthest shores of the universe. Vic Showell explained in Chapter 3, how 528 is fundamental to this circular geometry, the rings of waves, and their mathematical constants.(15)

If you have ever watched two waves cross, you witness the formation of "nodes" where the waves cross each other. These nodes are discussed by Müller and colleagues examining space/time. They claim there are six primary nodes in the universe within which all physical elements congeal.(11) From microscopic bacteria and cell organelle to macrocosmic celestial bodies and galaxies, all matter crystallizes in these special energy zones or vortices. Müller noted that this fractal precipitation of matter is mathematically based on repeating sequences of the numbers 3, 6, and 9.

Entrainment, Coherence or Phase-locking to 528

The above information is consistent with investigations published by many reputable researchers.

At the Institute of HeartMath, for example, leading researchers in emotional physiology and stress-management have worked for years investigating heart-related psychophysiology, neurocardiology and biophysics. Their research has "significantly advanced understanding of heart-brain interactions, heart-rate variability and heart-rhythm coherence, and the physiology of optimal learning and performance."(14)

Founder Doc Childre began in the 1980s to demonstrate that people can harness "the intelligence of the heart" to extinguish destructive cycles of stress in their lives.

The Institute of HeartMath interests include intuition, its electrophysiology, and "exploring how we are all globally interconnected at a deep, fundamental level via electromagnetic fields and biofields."

Childre advanced the concept of *coherence* to help explain how your body physiology changes with different emotions. He defines "coherence" as "the quality of being logically integrated, consistent and intelligible, as in a coherent argument. In this context, thoughts and emotional states can be considered 'coherent' or 'incoherent.'" He describes "positive emotions such as love or appreciation as coherent states, whereas negative feelings such as anger, anxiety or frustration are examples of incoherent states."

"These associations are not merely metaphorical," he explains. Research provides "intriguing evidence that different emotions lead to measurably different degrees of coherence in the oscillatory rhythms generated by the body's systems," especially the heart. Advancing research clearly proves the positive emotion of LOVE helps your cardiovascular, nervous, immunological, and hormonal systems relax and heal.(14)

Knowing that the heart is an electronic instrument affecting all these body systems, and as a composer and music lover, Doc Childre sought to develop "designer music" to promote health.

Childre's studies showed that music affects emotions, moods, and physiological responses to stress through the autonomic nervous system. Through this common pathway, music was proven to help regulate all the systems mentioned above.(14)

The Institute's research focused on "physiological coherence" as a state associated with "a sine wave-like pattern in the heart rhythms, a shift in autonomic balance towards increased parasympathetic activity, increased heart-brain synchronization and entrainment between diverse physiological systems."

"In this mode," Childre reported, "the body's systems function with a high degree of efficiency and harmony, and natural regenerative processes are facilitated."

Childre prescribes music, breathing, and exercises that increase positive emotions and physiological coherence as "a natural human state." Here is how he described "physiologic coherence" and its benefits:

> In states of psychophysiological coherence, there is increased synchronization and harmony between the cognitive, emotional and physiological systems, resulting in efficient and harmonious functioning of the whole. . . . [S]tudies conducted across diverse populations have linked the capacity to self-generate and sustain psychophysiologically coherent states at will with numerous benefits. Observed outcomes include: reduced stress, anxiety and depression; decreased burnout and fatigue; enhanced immunity and hormonal balance; improved cognitive performance and enhanced learning; increased organizational effectiveness; and health improvements in a number of clinical populations.(14)

Figure 18. Sound Waves Travel in Circles

Art from John Stuart Reid showing circular transmission of sounds, cymatically affecting physical reality that commonly reflects circular geometry.

Summarizing LOVE/528 Metaphysics

Entraining your heart to the 528Hz music of nature is an ongoing exercise and spiritual discipline.(11)

Whenever you are bouncing off people's negativity, remember the power of the heart to LOVE and heal with 528 energy. To entrain energetically, and return to sanity, most quickly, just recall what nature does when stressed.

Consider a Water wave bouncing off the side of a swimming pool. The *slap* shifts the wave's direction and frequency. But with each shift, waves still maintain their connection to the original wave. Whole number ratios, or rational numbers, express the identity of the new radiating wave.

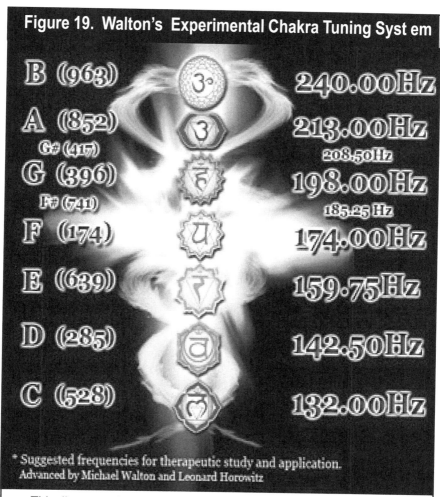

Figure 19. Walton's Experimental Chakra Tuning System

B (963)   240.00Hz

A (852)   213.00Hz

G# (417)   208.50Hz

G (396)   198.00Hz

F# (741)   185.25 Hz

F (174)   174.00Hz

E (639)   159.75Hz

D (285)   142.50Hz

C (528)   132.00Hz

* Suggested frequencies for therapeutic study and application.
Advanced by Michael Walton and Leonard Horowitz

This diagram relays an experimental protocol advanced by sound therapy pioneer, Michael Walton, relating pure tones and frequencies to human energy centers (i.e., chakras). It is supplied for experimental purposes only, and is not intended to imply definitive relationships between the chakras shown and the frequencies posted. This work is based on theory, and anecdotal reports of therapeutic effects, associated with chakra stimulation using various acoustic instruments. Walton suggested, as the image depicts, starting with C=528 for base chakra opening and balancing; then proceeding upward through the chakra system using suggested Solfeggio pure tones. Source: Walton (SomaMagic.com) and Horowitz (528Records.com).

Müller proved this happens in the universe at large, wherein the Standing Gravitational Wave bends when it bounces off the "light horizon" (otherwise called the "edge of the universe," or "event horizon.") The bend integrates 528 mathematics, and the MIracle 6 dynamics, or what he called the "In6." His studies provided the math enabling prediction of the exact refraction of the new wave, showing each time the result demonstrated a return to the 3, 6, and 9 "spiritual set" of scaling numbers or measures.(11, 15-18)

All of this proves that LOVE, as universal energy, whether in your heart or the cosmos, flows lawfully according to musical-mathematical certainty, providing measurable frequencies. These sounds (Hz) and wavelengths of light (nm) radiate force-fields affecting and connecting you to everything. This knowledge proves the heart of the Creator, reflecting the heart of His created, is connected in the frequency of LOVE/528.

This is the LOVE that moves all matter, including you, to heal and be whole. This is the energy of Divinity that most certainly restores what is missing or broken in your heart and the world. The 528LOVERevolution is the solution for what ails us.

References

1) Miller MI, Christensen GE, Amit Y, Grenander U. *Mathematical Textbook of Deformable Neuroanatomies*, Proc. Nat. Acad. Sci, USA 1993;90:11944-11948

2) Chervenak F and McCullough L. Ultrasound for all: By whom and when? How often? Presented before the First World Congress On: Controversies in Obstetrics, Gynecology & Infertility. Praque, Czech Republic, 1999 (Link to: http://www.obgyn.net/displayarticle.asp? page=/firstcontroversies/prague1999chervenak-mccullough2)

3) Toga AW and Thompson P. An Introduction to Brain Warping. In: *Brain Warping*. Arthur W. Toga, Editor. Los Angeles: Academic Press, 1998.

4) Becker RO and Selden G. *The Body Electric*. New York: William Morrow & Co., 1987.

5) Anonymous. *Blast It! The Ultimate Rife Researcher & User Manual*. KeelyNet, 2002.(Link to: http://www.keelynet.com/products/blastit.htm).

6) Emoto M. *The Message from Water* vol. 3 *Love Thyself.* Tokyo: IHM Research Institute, 2004

7) Keutsch FN and Saykally RJ. Water clusters: Untangling the mysteries of the liquid, one molecule at a time. Inaugural Article!

8) Horowitz L. *DNA: Pirates of the Sacred Spiral*. Sandpoint, ID; Tetrahedron Publishing Group, 2004

9) Haltiwanger S. The science behind LIFEWAVE™ technology patches. Atlanta, GA: LIFEWAVE™, LLC, 2005. Link to: http://www.lifewave.com/pdf/haltiwanger_24p_paper.pdf)

10) Underwood A, Whitford B, Chung J, et. al. Spirituality in America. *Newsweek*, Sept 5, 2005, pp. 46-64.

11) Müller H. *Theory of Global Scaling*. Sante Fe: NM: Institute for Space-Energy-Research, Leonard Euler, Ltd. and Global Scaling Applications, Inc., 2002.

12) King C. *BIOCOSMOLOGY*. Department of Mathematics, University of Auckland, New Zealand, 2003; Link to: http://www.dhushara.com/book/bchtm/biocos.htm)

13) Horowitz L and Puleo J. *Healing Codes for the Biological Apocalypse.* Sandpoint, ID: Tetrahedron Publishing Group, 1999.

14) Childes D. Institute of HeartMath. Research papers are posted online at: http://www.heartmath.org/

15) Showell V. Teotihuacan Universal Harmonic Master Code. This is one of a series of monographs are available in pdf format at www.LOVE528. com. Showell's latest, includes 528's connections to the sacred geometry of the circle, pi and Phi.

16) Personal communication with Marco Rodin, 2007.

17) The Phi Nest. DNA: The spiral is a Golden section; the cross section is based on Phi. Lengthy analysis and discussion is available online at http://www.goldennumber.net.

18) Personal communication from Lifewave Company founder, David Schmidt following his mathematical investigation of 528Hz.

Chapter Six:
Revelations, Transformation
and Enlightenment

R evelation 7:4 describes the great spiritual battle wherein an army of 144,000 faithful peacemakers take refuge in His fortress. Only then, we are told, despite tens
of thousands dying in their midst, all faithful are delivered "from
the snare of the fowler, and from the noisome pestilence."

Revelation 14:18 follows with the singing of "a new song"
by this 144,000. The melody echoes throughout eternity and
fulfills humanity's destiny to begin 1,000 years of world peace.(1)

Illuminati Conspiracy Prophecy

The word "peace" implies harmony versus dissonance.
It naturally radiates from the musical-mathematical matrix of
pure spiritual "Being." Peace is the fruit of righteousness, that
is, right-standing according to the mathematical laws of the
universe.

The metaphorical "fortress" in Psalm 91 is the coverage
provided by Divine LOVE. It is strong enough to withstand
any physical or spiritual force laid against it. The optimally
righteous and faithful who hold "Love of Faith in Love," are
instantaneously delivered from those who desire to enslave
humanity in these "End Times."

The deceivers, Revelation 9:21 discloses, practice "sorcery" and "cast magic spells." These literally reference pharmaceutical industrialists according to *Strong's Concordance*.
They set the hypnotic snare (i.e., television and the mainstream

media) to poison hearts and minds. The "noisome pestilence" brought on by these drug pushers enslave the masses.

Pharmaceuticals pollute people and our planet. Modern plagues, for the most part, are engineered in labs, and loosed for profit and population control.

Modern music tuned to A=440Hz is also the "noise" from which illness overtakes the sonically blessed and blissful body.

In the last chapter you learned how harmful stress and fear is on your Temple. Disturbing wave lengths and frequencies of sound, including those coming from energetically-potent negative images and fearful thoughts, oppose LOVE/528 and the Creator's natural healing energy.

This may seem "farfetched" to some, but every major plague throughout history was accompanied by severe immunosuppression associated with the stresses and strains of war or socioeconomic and political upheaval. Plagues resulted from this immunosuppression primarily, followed by infections such as influenza.

But the media neglects this greater truth. The media generates the Illuminati's illusions. These feed egos rather than souls. The propaganda plays to people's fears, pains, losses, and real or imagined threats to survival, as evidenced by the evening news. The media, literally, makes people sick.

In addition,the average person engages hours of radio and television daily, both vibrationally numbing. It ultimately leaves people feeling empty of meaningful relationships in life.

The most important relationships are your relationship with God, then your relationship with your Self, and thereafter, spouses, children, and family.

Neglecting these relationships and important subjects advances the global conquests of the Illuminati.

Consider how traditionally strong family relationships have degenerated over the past century. The "me generation" replaced the "we tradition." As a result, many people come to the end of their lives and wonder, "Is that all there is?"

LOVE expressed and experienced is the only eternally memorable and meaningful fruit of your life.

The media-promoted theology of greed and scientific conquest is apparent. Social systems have become unsustainable and intolerable. The masses of reasonably intelligent people increasingly disdain what is unfolding environmentally, economically, and geopolitically, due to the Illuminati. These "banksters" control the media and global markets in every industry. Some people even believe the Illuminati works for aliens, or are themselves aliens as they coldheartedly direct geopolitics and economics.

The alternative to this pollution and population reduction, what the Bible calls "noiances," is what wise elders have prescribed for millennia—*righteousness*—*being* respectful of life and the law.

What's "SO"?

It is no accident the Illuminati forced A=440Hz frequency on humanity. The "SO" note of the ancient Solfeggio is the most heart-wrenching vibration they could have used. Its overuse or abuse causes and sustains the great stress in your heart.

A=440Hz standard scale puts 741Hz frequency precisely at F#, that is the "SO" note of the ancient Solfeggio. It appears to be the only sound within the primordial scale that doesn't get along with LOVE in 528. As detailed in Chapter 4, 741Hz vibrates in gross conflict with 528Hz in your heart.

Tuning instruments to this frequency, slowly-but-surely poisons enough loving hearts to intoxicate general society—the entire population. This conclusion accords with the research funded by the Rockefeller Foundation cited previously.

The Illuminati's efforts to control humanity's hearts and minds is evidenced by this thesis. Solfeggio 741 is two notes removed from 528 resonating the heart chakra. The heart chakra spins at the center of the seven major chakras in humans. Two chakras up from the heart chakra is the third eye chakra, the seat of human insight. Clouding Divine or intuitive insight is a primary goal of devil-doers abusing the domain of the ego and "cognitive functions." The third eye chakra is the zone wherein negative thinking, fear, and worrying repeatedly about pains, threats, traumas, or abuses, is stimulated. Stimulating this chakra with negativity, or A=440Hz frequency, does the most damage psychosocially and spiritually.

Theoreticallly, this damage involves the pineal gland in the forebrain. The distress mainly results from the dissonant vibrations produced by this standard scale that melodiously incorporates 741Hz as the F# pitch.

Your pineal gland is at the center of your endocrine orchestra called the "hypothalamic-pituitary-adrenal axis." Your pineal gland is connected to your entire neuroendocrine system. The pineal gland is highly active in cosmic, or spiritual, energy reception and general orientation. This gland guides migration in the animal kingdom. When seeking spiritual "enlightenment," or communion with God, the pineal gland should be clear to resonate in harmony with Divinity, not exclusively 741Hz frequency or A=440Hz tuning.

According to Phylameana lila Desy, in her book, *Exploring Major Chakras*,(2) the third eye chakra "is also called 'brow chakra.' Our mental calculations and thinking processes are functions of the third eye chakra. We are able to evaluate our past experiences and life patterns and put them into perspective through the wisdom of the third chakra's actions. Our ability to separate reality from fantasy or delusion is connected to the healthfulness of this chakra. It is through a receptive brow chakra that auric hues and other visual images are intuited clairvoyantly."

So, it is no wonder people in the Western World are especially preoccupied by illusions, soap operas starring the rich and famous, personal dramas of dysfunctional people seeking "the American dream;" celebrity parades on tabloid stands featuring obese and morose people who once appeared larger-than-life on movie screens. Now the dying and dead "model" the values, attitudes, and core beliefs molding our *cult*-ure. This is how people learn to accept negativity, drug intoxications, and various pollution as "normal" rather than pathological and self-destructive.

It is ironic that the "SO" note, that stands for "solving" problems, particularly mathematical ones, according to *Webster's Dictionary*, would be creating so much heartache. The imbalance in people's psyches reflected in their behaviors and lifestyles, tips the scale in favor of personal distress and social chaos.

Compare this sick and sad set of functions attributed to the "SO" note and "what's so" in society, with the "MI" note and heart chakra, according to Ms. Desy. She wrote:

"The Heart Chakra is associated with the color green or pink. This love center of our human energy system is often the focus in bringing about a healing. Thus, the words 'Love Heals All' have great truth. Hurtful situations that can effect our emotional being are divorce or separation, grief through death, emotional abuse, abandonment, adultery. All of these are wounding to the heart chakra. Physical illnesses brought

147

about by heartbreak require that an emotional healing occur along with the physical healing. *Learning to love yourself* is a powerful first step in securing a healthy fourth chakra. The 'wounded child' resides in the heart chakra."(2) [Emphasis added.]

Transformation of Self and Civilization

Everyone has a "wounded child" residing in their heart. Any traumatic experience during childhood heavily influences your core beliefs, attitudes, states of mind, and points of view about people and life.

The beliefs you have about *yourself* are super potent, especially the negative ones. Without knowing what they are, or how they are operating in your life, you project them onto others. In other words, it is easier to see flaws in others, and get upset with them, than to recognize them in yourself and purge them.

So you project your distressing traits and opinions onto others, resulting in personal dramas. That drags you down. Virtually hypnotized by negativity, you blindly justify your damage and victimization, attributing the crimes to others, instead of recognizing and expressing your creative power to heal and move ahead more positively in your life.

When these patterns finally become self-evident, you'll learn life's lessons and let go of your self-destructive fears, insecurities, and inaccurate perceptions about yourself and others. Your negative experiences can then be transformed into helpful learning opportunities to extinguish abusive behaviors and negative patterns.

Once you are really okay with yourself, and faithful to God within you, you will rebuke all negativity like a window deflects rain.

Whether you realize it or not, your attitudes and behavior, good and bad, impact the entire world, beyond your family and friends.

If you just suppose your "wounded child" resides in your heart, and you try to figure this whole thing out with your head, you are in trouble. Your heart requires more positive reinforcement, not simply your head, already stimulated maximally by the media, generating much of your ego's negativity and insecurities in the first place. The conscious mind in the third eye that dominates your awareness and experience, and issues negative thoughts and worries, is unaware that the precious loving child residing in your heart, needs healing.

This is, therefore, a job for 528, not 741.

The Self-Loathing Problem

I assert the Illuminati's preoccupation with psycho-sexual stimulation and emotional trauma projects their self-loathing pathology on society most profitably.

Simply stated, some people *hate* themselves, or certain parts of their personalities. The Illuminati's choice of A=440Hz suppressing LOVE and other "meta-needs" as Maslow called them, including health, peace and freedom, is related to self-loathing.

Self-loathing is among the world's biggest and deadliest problems, as it is self-destructive and socially troubling.

Fed up with sexual distress, attitudes that hurt your heart, and negative thoughts and judgments about yourself that you project onto others, you end up love-less, lacking friends or family, depressed, loathing yourself and situation, and even potentially suicidal. The Illuminati suffer from this as well.

Your heart may know your inner child is hurting, feeling abused or rejected, but your head doesn't know how to help.

Your egoic mind adds to your misery, attitudinally, while engaging judgment and self pity. Sadness, anger, and bitterness, are negative emotions triggered by your disturbing thoughts and feelings over perceived threats, including rejection and persecution. The Illuminati fear revolution.

These thoughts and feelings overpower your joyful, loving,, and lovable inner child that is worthy of living a more meaningful and satisfying life.

You then start questioning life, and whether it is even worth living.

Solving this common psychosocial stress pattern of self-loathing may trigger a millennium of world peace, which is the mission of the 528LOVERevolution.(3)

The Self-Loathing Illuminati

People ask me all the time to reconcile how and why the Illuminati can pollute and depopulate the planet without feeling remorse, perceiving financial risk from fewer consumers buying their products, or appearing to protect themselves against myriad intoxications. The answer is quite simple: The Illuminati are highly-advanced self-loathers.

The global elite's self-hate is obvious from studies of secret societies and their abusive conditioning rituals. These have reached the silver screen in movies like *Eyes Wide Shut*, and television in the news coverage of George Bush, Jr.'s defense of his Skull & Bones fraternity's hazing rituals. These include mock murders, sexual atrocities, and death worship.

FBI special agents, John Douglas and Robert Ressler, experts in profiling serial killers, researched the switching that takes place in children when they are sexually assaulted. The abused victims become abusers later in life in a psychotic effort to extinguish their painful memories. Their neurology switches, producing pleasure when they cause pain. At the heart of their psycho-emotional distress is their self-hate. They despise themselves for being powerless during their abuse, and torture others to gain a sick sense of control.

Only this self-loathing psychopathology explains, for example, pedophilia, blood ritual sacrifices, Jewish bankers funding Hitler to exterminate masses of Jewish people during World War II, or the Surgeon General of the United States, David Satcher and Barack Obama, Black men, promoting sterilizing "immunizations" most heavily damaging and depopulating African Americans.

Treating Self-Loathing with 528

If self-loathing leaders of the Illuminati have persuaded nearly everyone to self-loath, and slowly self-destruct, then the only effective remedy is to teach everyone to self-LOVE.

But who or what is the "Self" that deserves the LOVE? Other important questions are, how do you LOVE your*self* unconditionally, and how can you become a world-class lover, on a planet populated by distressed self-loathers?

Your Self is not simply your mind, or ego, engaging neuroticism. Nor is your Self stuck in your third eye chakra that largely dominates your life experience. They are parts of you, but not entirely or exclusively your Self. You are *much* more as a spiritual being.

Psychiatry and behavioral science that neglects spirituality is not the answer; nor is pharmacology. These are not solutions to fundamentally spiritual problems affecting most people's hearts.

Your heart is at the center of your total Self. Your Self includes your body, mind, emotions, imagination, intuition, and spirit linked to God's Holy Spirit that sources from God's heart with LOVE.

In addition, God gave you "free will," which best summarizes why we are in this mess.

You have a will to choose different options in life, such as a path to enlightenment, versus a path to worsening psychopathology and suppressed spirituality.

Heading toward enlightenment is the path to sustainable unconditional LOVE. It is the path paved by the music of 528.

The Self-LOVE Option

As mentioned in *Ephesians* 6:12, "It is not against flesh and blood with whom we do battle." Spiritual factors and forces are at work for better or worse in your life. Your choices generate karma, or magnetic energy attracting circumstances, experiences, rewards and punishments.

This is a prescription for optimal spiritual evolution, and to cure self-loathing:

Life should always be celebrated with faith, gratitude, and LOVE.

I believe your heart, the center of your Spiritual Self, is in communion and communication with God's heart that is broadcasting over the 528Hz frequency clear-channel on the universal dial. This is what all the evidence suggests.

If you have ever been in LOVE, and made LOVE most sweetly and sensitively, the ecstasy was shared spiritually. Many people report "out-of-body experiences" while making LOVE. For many, LOVE-making is spiritually pleasing far beyond physically gratifying. At the point when two beings join most intimately, two hearts meld, and the energy of unity, including Divine harmony, flows most exquisitely. Their LOVE is energetically or musically manifested, and spiritually appreciated as a symphony in ecstasy.

Your heart's capacity to experience this musical-mathematical bliss of 528 is very real. That warm fuzzy feeling you have in your heart when you're in LOVE, and experiencing LOVE, is that greenish-yellow vibration of 528.

The Spiritual Renaissance and 528LOVERevolution is all about going back to the source of your spiritual sustenance and heart-felt bliss.

I am writing to invite you to find the Kingdom of Heaven within and around you, by bringing Heaven to Earth in your life as part of your spiritual journey. This quest for higher Self-LOVE fulfills your goal of enlightenment.

Fear and loathing dissolves in the presence of faith and LOVE, since there is nothing missing or broken in the Kingdom of Heaven. There is nothing distressed or diseased therein. Finding and inputting peaceful harmony in your heart is an enriching investment.

The simplest yet most powerful solution to degeneration in this mad world is filling your heart with LOVE, best facilitated with 528 music.

Exponential Acceleration of the 528LOVERevolution

The good news is that media programming is insufficient to resist the Spiritual Renaissance that is now exponentially accelerating, due to the laws of physics and cosmic justice.

Global freedom simply depends on increasing the volume of LOVE. The temporal affairs of mere mortals, Illuminati included, can't withstand this healing force wielded by the maker of space/time.

A "critical mass" is awakening to this fact of nature. Faithful and trusting servants are being pulled by their heart-strings to heed this call.

Opening hearts most Divinely, in 528Hz frequency, is our greatest hope.(1)

This is what is happening for the 144,000 lead singers representing the "FA-muli tuorum."

The Roman Catholic Church referred to this fourth note of the Solfeggio as "FA"—the critical mass of humble loving servants who sing in unison a "new song." The new song resurrects old notes in the ancient Solfeggio, including the "key to the house of David." FA (639) joins harmonic MI (528) at the heart of this rejuvenating symphony.

As detailed in Tables 6 and 7 that relay the musical notes, their meanings and frequencies, each relating to a "Beginning Times Concert," these revelations are already producing what was predicted in the Bible, and in *Healing Codes for the Biological Apocalypse*—a musical event that shall end the New World Order (NWO) brief rule over Earth.

That is, our Creator wants a NWO too, but God's plan honors nature, rather than pollutes, destroys, and/or corrupts natural living.

Divine law is administered spiritually, energetically, electromagnetically, musically, or fundamentally mathematically. Right-standing within the Creator's law means you are in harmony with the mathematics of LOVE, peace, and prosperity. That means you vibe to 528Hz frequency, "on Earth as it is in Heaven;" *Heaven* being the matrix of musical mathematics that creates and sustains everything.

This happy beginning is possible and preferable to extinction through self-loathing and self-destruction.

The Illuminati condemns righteousness and creates chaos; managed chaos to be exact. They have seized control of our planet and *We The People*. However, their fearful messages, terrorist attacks, and faithless defenses, can't hold back what is already happening with LOVE.

The "SO" note, as I shared previously refers to what is happening to us, and our planet. It is a "mathematical problem," says *Webster's Dictionary*. Table 6 says that this note is needed to "SOlve the problem."

Knowing that Webster was a high level Freemason, and the Illuminati have twisted and abused Freemasonry to cause myriad problems. The problem and solution lies in terminating our consumption of SO-frequency vibrations.

Turn your mainstream media off. Engage instead the Internet and alternative independent media. Listen to 528Radio. com to help you get out of your head, and into your heart.

Once the critical mass of enlightened people, also called "the 100th monkey," is achieved, the rest of civilization will follow.

Enlightenment with 528/LOVE

528 is at the heart of every rainbow. Rainbows are visual manifestations of light bending through crystalline Water. So 528 resonates at the heart of light and Water crystals.

Consider *enlightenment* becoming one with the light, which is the spectrum of colors and frequencies of creation. The word light in enlightenment is surrounded by the prefix and suffix "en". *Webster's Dictionary* defines *en,* as "put into or onto, cover with, . . . cause to be;" and "cause to have, or come to have."

Light, coming from the Sun, resonates fundamentally 528Hz frequency, as stated previously. In other words, pure light irradiates your body with LOVE from the sun that vibrates in 528, making you whole, complete, and sustained by the creative spirit of God's sunshine.

This intelligence was hidden to create division between God and man, and man and nature. Ignorance of these facts produces diseases and division between humans as well. Prophets, saints and wise elders knew and told this truth. The measurable rewards of integrating this knowledge include noticeable life changes, behavior changes, mood changes, and attitude shifts reflecting greater peace and happiness.

References

1) Horowitz L and Puleo J. *Healing Codes for the Biological Apocalypse.* Sandpoint, ID: Tetrahedron Publishing Group, 1999.

2) Desy PL. Learning About Chakras. Introducing the Seven Major Chakras. See: About.com, Holistic Healing at: http://healing.about.com/cs/chakras/a/learnchakras.htm

3) See the websites www.LOVE528.com and i528Tunes.com.

Chapter Seven:
528 and Musical History

You know there are fifty-two (52) weeks in a year with four seasons, and fifty-two (52) cards in a deck with four suits.

If you study the history of the calendars and cards, you may be surprised by the fact that both relate to musical-mathematics and the harmonics of 528.

To begin, consider the fact that Gregorian monks, famous for their spiritually-uplifting chants, sourced our current system of tracking time. Early calendars were less accurate than today's Gregorian calendar.

Inaccuracy in the Gregorian calendar, however, stems from what you are now learning. There appears to be an organized effort to keep you, and the rest of civilization, ignorant about the matrix math that keeps perfect time and makes the universe lawful.

Consider the bizarre concept of a "leap year"— a year containing an extra day. Did God make that rule, or a mistake? Why do some years have 366 days instead of 365 days? An extra leap-year day is added in February, which has 29 days instead of the normal 28 days. Also, leap years are said to occur every 4 years; except that every 100 years, special rules apply. For example, 1900 was not a leap year, but 2000 was.

So authorities who claim solar and lunar cycles can be measured accurately, measure time *inaccurately*. They use "irrational numbers," and man-made rules that are not perfectly patterned or precise; not simple whole numbers, or even numbers with repeating decimals that are called "rational numbers," to predict calendar dates and holidays.

In other words, the accepted calendar doctrine reflects pseudo-science and propaganda more than the true nature of math-based reality. Apparently, the Illuminati wants you to believe cosmic forces that consistently demonstrate patterning, cycling, scaling, with lawful balance and harmony, somehow misses beats! The "experts" neglect the perfectly-ordered mathematics reflected in every strand of DNA and snail shell.

Your life is fundamentally scheduled by these people who have bent time and music and engage you irrationally.

Messing with Musical Scales

Besides calendars, Western music, integrating the diatonic and later chromatic scales, also sources from the Gregorian monks in the Roman Catholic Church. This group of religious leaders hid, changed or weakened the Gregorian chants.

The spiritual theology in musicology summarized in this section is important. It begs you to consider how much music and math influences your life, beginning with the spiritual energy dynamics. Consider the force of the cosmos, planets, gravities, electromagnetic and bioacoustic frequencies. These obviously impact your genetic blueprint at the time of your birth. This impact is like hard data affecting your life, world-view, personal relationships, and, theoretically, even your destiny.

Early Christians adopted the ancient Greek system of music that used *tetrachords*. Tetrachords are collections of four continuous notes that descend by two tones and a semitone.

This brings you back to considering the sacred geometry of a tetrahedron, and Water as part of the Triune God, since molecular tetrahedrons compise Water. Liquid crystals of Water are shaped like tiny pyramids due largely to 528's influence forming their sacred geometry. Recall that Water existed at the beginning of time, according to Genesis. Recall also that God's name, given Moses, is the tetragrammaton—**Yod-Hay-Vov-Hay**—and that God operates in your body through the tetrahedron structure of the Water molecule, H_2O, that resonates 528/LOVE, like the sun, and Son of God.

This knowledge should make you wonder whether tetrachords involving 528 express God's LOVE best, especially in Water.

According to the CIA-edited *Wikipedia*, "The disjunct tetrachords . . . have been the subject of much speculation, because they do not correspond to the diatonic framework that became the standard Medieval scale. For example, there is a high F#, a note not recognized by Medieval writers."(8)

This is suspicious because that F#, that plays in the A=440Hz frequency of standard tuning, is the 741 antagonist to LOVE/528 called the Devil's tone. This best explains why the Medieval writers would not use this note. This F#, when played with the pure tone 528, is energetically/spiritually distressing.

A similar imbalance was created when the Roman Catholic Church instituted "TI"—the seventh note in the modern Solfeggio. That is, the "DO, RE, ME, FA, SO, LA, and *TI*" was man-made, not God-made. The "TI" came from "*SI*," short for Sancte Johannes—defined as:

1. a person of exceptional holiness, formally recognized by the Christian Church esp. by *Canonization*. 2. a person of great virtue or benevolence. 3. a founder or patron, as of a movement. 4. a member of any various Christian groups. 5. to acknowledge as a Saint. Canonize. [1150-1200]; ME Seinte. Canon: 1. **an ecclesiastical rule or law enacted by a council or other competent authority and, in the Roman Catholic Church, approved by the Pope. 3. a body of rules, principles, or standards accepted as *axiomatic* and universally binding**, esp. in a field of study of art.. 6. any officially recognized set of sacred books. 10. **the part of the mass between Sanctus and the *communion***. 11. *consistent, note-for-note imitation of one melodic line by another, in which the second line starts after the first.*

(axiomatic: 1. pertaining to or of *the nature of an axiom; self-evident. 2. a universally accepted principle or rule. 3. a proposition in logic or mathematics that is assumed without proof for the sake of studying consequences that follow from it.*

This lengthy definition shares a lot of information about the demonic workings of religions that promoted the addition of "TI" to modify God's sacred Solfeggio.

By reading the definitions in Table 6 carefully, you find a qualitative difference between the first six notes and this new one. The original six Solfeggio definitions seem to offer a musical-mathematical-spiritual solution to the urgent problems facing humanity courtesy of the Illuminati. These definitions all seem to reference elements in *Revelation* 14:1, when a new song is sung by 144,000 spiritually inspired people, in concert to resolve Earth's most urgent problems. This is the first light, in the depths of the darkness, prophesied to get us out of the mess we are in globally, environmentally, geopolitically, and economically.

Notice there is a distinct difference between these positive messages and this added one. The imposition of TI, as well as the A=440 standard tuning, is based, by definition, on a "proposition in logic or mathematics that is assumed without proof for the sake of studying consequences that follow from it."

In other words, you are being used like a guinea pig in a genocidal experiment. The consequences intended and generated are clear. The global intoxication and spiritual degeneration of humanity, accompanying the corruption of the arts and sciences by the early Roman Catholic Church, with help from other religions, and later the Rockefeller Foundation, is terminal. Extinction is a high probability, unless we sing a new song.

REmedying Spiritual Suppression

Many people feel the spiritual (energy/frequency) suppression from which everyone suffers. But what can be done to remedy this quandary.

The Solfeggio "RE" note suggests a solution, promising a return to the "Garden of Eden.

Resonance evidences how small signals can produce large impacts when vibrating in sync with the larger electrical system. This profoundly important, yet allusive, phenomenon promises to "bring back an earlier state of affairs," namely the Garden of Eden.

In Hebrew the "Isle of Eve," or Garden of Eden, is HaVoHY, (pronounced "Ha-vay-yee") or Hawaii. Incredibly, this is also the Hebrew name of the Creator, *reversed*! Check it out. . . .

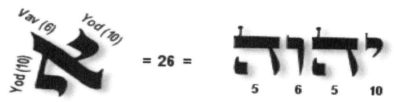

So the remedy for the main problem is synchronizing your energy with the Garden of Eden frequency of God. This is best accomplished with meditation, deep breathing, and prayer, as evidenced by word *aloha*, and its hidden meaning.

Most people know the word *aloha* in Hawaiian is used like the word *shalom* in Hebrew. It is a warm greeting and peaceful farewell between loving people. Break it down, and you see the A-L-O-HA signifies this remedy we can actualize.

The "A", or first Hebrew letter, aleph, represents the alpha, the beginning of the universe, graphed as a two waves of Water above and below the sixth Hebrew letter, the vav.

The "L" is the precise heart of the Hebrew alphabet, the lamed, signifying LOVE as the tallest letter, indicative of the King of Kings and true teacher of LOVE, Yahshuah (Jesus) according to scholarly Christian-Jews. It precedes the "O"—the Omega, signifiying LOVE is at the heart of the alpha and omega, the beginning and ending of everything.

The "HA" in aloha signifes the breath of life, the prana, or energy in oxygen, transmitted from the 528 broadcasting Sun, through 528 resonating molecules of greenish-yellow chlorophyll, sustaining you with LOVE/528 in your blood.

The Ancient Solfeggio Keys and Their Prophesy

You already learned "MI"—the 528 key means, "to produce an extraordinary occurrence that surpasses all known human powers or natural forces and is ascribed to a divine or supernatural cause esp. to God. . . ;"

The remaining keys are:

1) "UT"—the first tone that includes the "whole series of musical notes," and the entire array of human emotions from grief to joy. That is, virtually the entire human condition resonates in this first note of the Solfeggio. This note transmits a "magnetic field strength equal to 10^5 power gauss,"(1)

2) "RE"—the second key, as mentioned, broadcasts a "relatively small periodic stimulus" in harmony with a much larger "natural vibration"—like God's LOVE or the Standing Gravitational Wave (SGW) of the universe. This mutual resonance produces "a vibration of large amplitude . . . of enriched significance, profundity, and allusiveness," to back the "earlier state of affairs" in which God and man vibrate in sync. This sound, and its definition, is a metaphor for Divine-human communion.

"FA"—the fourth key heralds "the 144,000 servants equipped with this knowledge to be present to transact [this spiritual] business." In Christian terms, "FA" represents "the "bride" or "body of Christ." For Hebrews it is the Minion required to raise the dead to spiritual life. For Muslims it is the faithful servants of Allah. For the Hindus, it is Shiva's earthly army that cuts through the confusion.

"SO"—the fifth note has already been introduced as 741Hz, the F# pitch within the A=440Hz scale. This actually shares in this prophecy as part of remedy for global pollution. LOVE/528 must extinguish, or overpower, the dissonance. This is like Christina in the *Phantom of the Opera*, giving her LOVE to the demon, which kills him. *Webster's Dictionary* defines SO as "the answer or solution to [the] mathematical problem," of what is causing spiritual dissonance and world chaos. Isn't this largely the choice to engage egocentrism, arrogance, fear, and greed, linked to pineal chakra stimulation by 741 broadcasts through the mainstream media?

If this is the case, the *problem* is the SOlution, recognized by raising consciousness about it, 741Hz (F# in A=440Hz tuning) versus 528Hz (C in A=444Hz tuning), and making the choice to LOVE.

"LA"—the last key, means articulating, using the lips; and the sounds required to "reverse direction" and move "toward extreme political conservatism." "LA" also celebrates the power of spoken words, prayers, hymns and chants to impact your life and, collectively, our planet. Your lips give birth to manifested intentions.

With the above Solfeggio notes and the "MIracle 6" key unlocking the door "to an earlier system or order," one that advances global solutions and world peace through a spiritually-blessed political movement, we will manifest the 528LOVERevolution.

This topic also parallels the true meaning of "Israel"—where the "lion lies down with the lamb"—and its homonym, "Is real," implying peace on earth through LOVE/528 is a *real*ity. This references the prophesied millennium of LOVE resulting from opening spiritual "doors" to your heart, and the hearts of others like you.

Since the needed spiritual transcendence calls for a *miracle*, a "MIracle 6" of Divine LOVE is needed to manifest peace on Earth as it is in Heaven.

According to *Webster's Dictionary*, Divine LOVE and protection is also generated by the 6-pointed hexagonal *Solo-*

mon's Seal—⬡—an "amulet" that features 528, as shown in Table 5, also codes for the tetrahedron structure of Water.

By referencing the entries in Table 6 from *Webster's Dictionary*, the original six notes of the Solfeggio compares closely to the overall message in the hymn to John the Baptist reinforced in Revelation 14:1-5.(1) This is how we win in the end, with those who are loving and meek inheriting the earth through acoustic performances opening the heart and purifying the pineal gland.

Revelation 14:1-5 prophetically proclaims:

> Then I looked, and there before me was the Lamb, standing on Mount Zion, and with him 144,000 who had his name and his Father's name written on [or in] their foreheads. And I heard a sound from heaven like the roar of rushing waters and like a loud peal of thunder. The sound I heard was like that of harpists playing their harps. And they sang a new song before the throne and before the four living creatures and the elders. No one could learn the song except the 144,000 who had been redeemed from the earth. . . . No lie was found in their mouths; they are blameless.

These 144,000 sing to secure the Messianic Age for millions of others. As with the hymn to Saint John the Baptist this singing washes away guilt and fear from this polluted world.

Much like a Water baptism, wherein a person is refreshed and blessed by the infusion of the Holy Spirit coming through Spirit/Water, this hymn, using the original Solfeggio tones, is expected to impact the entire planet, uplifting spiritual energy, opening people's hearts, to spread LOVE.

Do not underestimate the power of this blessing. The infusion of this Holy Spirit power of Divine LOVE knocked people off their feet during the opening ceremony in King Solomon's Temple.

The Medieval Latin hymn in Table 7 records the 144,000 humble servants will need to sing in harmony with "the loose strings," that is, the logarithmic Standing Gravitational Wave, which will loose throughout the universe this awesome "roar of rushing waters." This concept of manifesting change features dynamics reminiscent to "string theory" in physics, will be discussed in Chapter 9.

These frequencies are worth repeating and celebrating. These acoustic vibrations are the core resonant frequencies of the universe, and the frequencies used by the Creator to form the cosmos in <u>six</u> (6) days. They are essential for creating world peace and prosperity, while vanquishing injustice and degeneration.

In the *Book of Joshua*, six (6) days of Levitical horn blasts followed by the Ark of the Covenant used as an energy amplifier shattered Jericho's great wall. During this time the people were instructed to remain completely silent so as not to alter the frequencies of these miraculous sounds. Then, on the 7th day the public shouted, and the walls "came tumbling down."

Additional evidence for the capacity of miraculous music comes from Rahab's story. In *Joshua* 2:21 she is instructed to apply a scarlet line to her window to spare her home, part of Jericho's great wall. In 6:17, she, her family, and home was spared because of this action. Considering modern physics, the scarlet line acted as an acoustic/electromagnetic "heat sink" to absorb the miraculous, albeit destructive, energy blasts from the priests' horns, and the Ark of the Covenant that is arguably a drum.

This battle against the city of Jericho was not the last time these frequencies were used for war.

The "Greater Perfect System" of Sound

There are two types of scales commonly referenced in music: 1) diatonic, and 2) chromatic. The *diatonic scale* is a simple whole-note scale missing the half-tones, sharps and flats. You can think of this simpler scale as a piano keyboard without any black keys. Each "whole note" represents a pitch whose frequency is a whole number. Alternatively, the *chromatic scale* grants greater "shades" of music from the addition of half-tones, the black keys. Half tones reflect fractions of the whole notes, or 1/2 intervals between the whole numbers.

Historically, "a diatonic scale with a *chromatically* alterable b/b-flat was first described by Hucbald of St. Amand's treatise *Musica,* who adopted the tetrachord," D, E, F, and G, and constructed the rest of the system following the model of the Greek Greater and Lesser Perfect Systems. These were the first steps in forging the modern "theoretical tradition" of music. (8)

The simple diatonic scale was used by the Gregorian monks for their spiritually-uplifting chants. The Hymn to St John the Baptist was sung to simply six whole tones--the original Solfeggio. (The "TI" note was added later by the Church.)(8)

I emphasized the word, *chromatically*, two paragraphs above, because it speaks to the "color of sound." That is a literal, or fundamentally accurate, description of sound. Acoustic vibrations project colors of light, based on their math; especially through Water—a liquid crystal superconductor of sound and light.

Dolphins have been observed to sonically vibrate bubbles from which light emanates. This is called *sonoluminescence*. I think of it as "hydro-luminescence." That is, sound vibrates cavities in Water called *cavitations*. These cavitations emit light (a form of spirit) from the energy of Hertz frequencies.(9)

This science supports a literal interpretation of *Genesis* 1:2 that states the sound of God's words on the Water created light.

Getting back to the conspiracy to suppress Solfeggio frequencies, *Brittanica* reported that in the "pattern of ancient Greek performance," octaves were missing one whole tone. Later, a low A was added by theorists to achieve the following diatonic two-octave system: "A G F E D C B A G F E D C B A."

Notice the half tones are missing in the Greek "Greater Perfect System." Note also that this sequence of pure tones is **backwards** to the way the scale is today: "C D E F G A B C."(12)

Recall from Chapter 1, that English language and alphabet, is *reversed* also, compared to the alphanumerics and energetics of the early sacred languages.

Again, it is my contention that the Illuminati suppressed human spirituality maximally by instituting these reversals, thus altering the energy of spoken words and music.

This model of "dumbing-down" or disabling humans was recorded in the Bible in Genesis when God "confused their tongues" to rebuke egocentrism.

The ancient sacred languages, including Hebrew, Sanskrit, Aramaic, and Babylonian, touched people's hearts more than their heads, and relayed intuitively or instinctively greater meanings, feelings, and emotions, providing the technology for optimal communication and communion.

The Greeks and Gregorians

This spiritual capacity of sound to create or destroy relationships, between God and man, and interpersonally between people, was honored by the Greek *Greater Perfect System* that was based on ancient Hebrew. This music was made using seven overlapping scales, or octave *species*, called *harmoniai*, characterized by the pleasing harmony of pure tones, broadcasting the vibrations of whole numbers, within the species. (8)

In other words, scale patterns, reflecting Fibonacci math patterns, using different pitches, were called "octave species," and were harmonically pleasing to your ears and uplifting to your heart or spirit.(8)

To modify the feel and energy of their music, however, the Greeks, and later Gregorians, transposed their octave species using different pitches within the Greater Perfect System. (12) This is much like I recommend now using i528Tunes. com. Here music uploaded in A=440Hz is automatically downloaded transposed into C=528Hz.

MIracle 6s, Hexachords, and Solomon's Song

During the eleventh century, Guido d'Arezzo, who invented the system of staff-notation still in use, determined that hexachords could be built on C. For example, using 528Hz, a natural hexachord, C-D-E^F-G-A, could be played. "The use of notes outside of this collection was described as musica ficta," d'Arezzo wrote. That is fictitious music as opposed to genuine pure tones.(8, 14)

This knowledge, paired with d'Arezzo's practice in forming natural hexachords, support the assertion that modern music is "musica ficta," man-made vs. God-made.

Completing this practical lesson in music history, around 1025, d'Arezzo revolutionized western music by organizing pitches in the singing range into overlapping *hexachords*.(8, 14)

Here again, the number "6" is remarkable as hexachords reflect the musical-mathematical harmony and stability of hexagons. The hexagon provides protective power, spiritual security, like the energy provided by *Solomon's seal*.

The amulet, with its hexagonal shape is traditionally reputed to transmit protective and restorative energy most miraculously. It resonates the MIracle 6--528Hz frequency, according to Showell's mathematical analyses, and is associated with miraculous manifestations by definition. The miraculous "Universal Healer," LOVE, seals your heart with this radiant source of healing inspiration. The *Song of Solomon,* a musical prayer, is reputed to do the same. The icon for all of this is Solomon's seal.

In *A Place in God's Heart: Finding Joy in His Presence,* Kay D. Rizzo unwittingly expressed this relationship between LOVE/528 and the sealing of loving hearts with joy.(13)

LOVE is an emotion. The word, *e-motion*, depicts an electron—"e-"—the source of all energy, in motion. The vibrations of your e-*motions* impact different parts of your body, like your heart, musically-mathematically affecting your physiology, neurology, and immunity.

By the way, the *Song of Solomon* speaks of God's intense LOVE for you.(13)

Solomon's father David, loved God most ardently. His contribution to *Psalms* was a result of his Divine adoration and devotion. He celebrated his "Star of David" for everything it provided. The power of Solomon's Seal was made known to him by Hebrew scholars and Levitical priests. The latter practiced alchemy and honored the hexagonal ring as a sacred structure. The ancients knew of the connection between sacred geometry and musical-math, and they used 528Hz to amplify the power of their prayers. They were privy to the power of LOVE, and the benefit of celebrating God's creative technology and resonance in their hearts.

Rizzo wrote, "Scripture describes the marital union. (*Genesis* 4:1). How fitting to define the relationship God longs to have with you and me in the same intimate terms (*Ephesians* 5:31,32). . . . Properly and ultimately there can be no separate chasm between love divine and love human; and because of this fact the marriage bond became, . . . the symbol of the divine love."(13)

Incredibly, Solomon's seal also symbolizes this loving union of male and female elements and energies. Two triangles are merged into one star. One triangle points up (the phallus); the other one down (the chalice).

This is also the structure of Water. Two H_2O molecules merge the same way the two triangles do, forming the hexagonal "star tetrahedron." This natural formation occurs due to the polar attraction of the two triangular molecules whose elements, hydrogen and oxygen, are the electron donor and receiver, respectively.

"Place me like a seal over your heart, . . . for love is as strong as death, . . . Many Waters cannot quench love; rivers cannot wash it away." (*Song of Solomon* 8:6,7)

Conclusions

Cosmic laws, the movement of planets, the best music, ways to tell time, and the LOVE in your heart, are all related to 528Hz frequency. And due to the suppression of this fact by the Illuminati, these topics are among the most contested subjects in history.

In 1545, the 19th ecumenical Council of Trent met to settle musical matters and advance sweeping reforms. Their decisions were based on retaliating against Protestant protests.

"Avoiding more restrictive prescriptions, the council decreed that music was allowed in church provided it was not 'base and suggestive,' and it ordered seminarians to be taught to *chant*."(7, 15)

Later, "Pope Gregory XIII dedicated his papacy to implementing the recommendations of the Council. By the time he reformed the Julian calendar in 1582 (using the observations of Christopher Clavius and Johannes Kepler), it had drifted *10 days off course.*"(7)

So much for the accuracy of Catholic dogma concerning math and music.

To this day, most of the world uses Gregory's Gregorian calendar, and the original forbidden F#, 741Hz, is spiritually suppressing human hearts musically.(7)

Hundreds of years after Gregory XIII, monks were the only ones with any free time for scholarly pursuits – and they were discouraged from thinking about these secular matters of math and music.(15)

The Illuminati desired to keep Heaven's most powerful creative technology secret: Astronomical-musical-math featuring LOVE/528. Their paradigm of control, based on fear, would have been rejected if word spread that God resided in everything outside church walls.

So leaders of all religions have kept this knowledge secret: Who you are, how you got that way, and where you are going to fulfill your Divine destiny is all based primarily on musical-mathematics controlling the laws of physics.

This subject was considered taboo. God's technology— the Perfect Circle of Sound™—that explained, encouraged, and evidenced Divine-human communion, was outlawed. The Church of Satan did not encourage this revelation.(15)

As a result, the greatest truths in life were suppressed. The divisive card was played by the Illuminati, keeping Catholics and Protestants at war for hundreds of years. The same divisive antics today keep Muslims and Jews embattled.

Illuminati leaders of the secret societies advanced through the cryptocracy of Freemasonry, social and religious upheaval, including medieval attitudes toward music and its role in our lives.(16)

The Renaissance heralded one of the greatest cultural transformations in Western World history. Like the 528LOV-ERevolution today, the Renaissance aimed to bring Western civilization out of the Dark Ages.

References

1) Sereda, D: "Analysis of the Sound of the Sun Water Crystal,": http://web.mac.com/len15/LIVEH2O.info/Solar_Sonics_%26_LOVE_Harmonics_for_Peace,_Health_%26_Prosperity.html

2) Horowitz LG. *LOVE the Real da Vinci CODE*. Sandpoint, ID: Tetrahedron Publishing Group, 2007.

3) Myerson RB. *Game Theory: Analysis of Conflict*. Harvard University Press, 1997. 4) Aumann RJ. (1987), game theory, In: *The New Palgrave: A Dictionary of Economics 2*, 1987; pp. 460–82. See also: http://en.Wikipedia.org/wiki/Game_theory

5) Pascal's wager. Wikipedia. See: http://en.Wikipedia.org/wiki/Pascal's_Wager

6) Horowitz LG. *Death in the Air: Globalism, Terrorism & Toxic Warfare*. Sandpoint, ID: Tetrahedron Publishing Group, (June, 2001).

7) Google. History of our Calendar. Google User Content: http://webcache.googleusercontent.com/search?q=cache:Qp0eZj8grIMJ:www webexhibits.org/calendars/year-history.html+leap+year+origin+of+calendar&cd=1&hl=en&ct=clnk&gl=us

8) Wikipedia. Gregorian Chants. See: http://en.Wikipedia.org/wiki/Gregorian_chant

9) Sonoluminescence is discussed here: http://www.valdostamuseum.org/hamsmith/newtech.html#sonolum

10) Horowitz LG and Puleo J. *Healing Codes for the Biological Apocalypse*. Sandpoint, ID: Tetrahedron Publishing Group, 1998.

11) Le Her. See: http://en.Wikipedia.org/wiki/Le_Her

12) Greater Perfect System of tuning musical instruments. See: http://www.britannica.com/EBchecked/topic/244027/Greater-Perfect-System

13) Rizzo KD. *A Place in God's Heart*. Pacific Press, 2003, pp. 62-63.

14) Musica ficta (from Latin, 'false', 'feigned', or 'contrived' music) was a term used in European music theory from the late 12th century to about 1600 to describe any pitches, whether notated or added by performers in accordance with their training, that lie outside the system of musica recta or musica vera ('correct' or 'true' music) as defined by the hexachord system of Guido of Arezzo. See: the Free Dictionary online at: http://encyclopedia.thefreedictionary.com/Ficta

15) The Counsel of Trent. See: http://webcache.googleusercontent.com/search?q=cache:KjKFstca7QQJ:www.answers.com/topic/council-of-trent+council+of+trent+music&cd=4&hl=en&ct=clnk&gl=us

16) Smith M. *Music and Religious Change in the Renaissance*. Essays online: http://www.exampleessays.com/viewpaper/30032.html

17) NASA Recordings of the Sun and Jupiter were provided to the author by David Sereda. See:

18) Meyers S. Other Views: Carl Baugh, Institute for Biblical & Scientific Studies. See: http://webcache.googleusercontent.com/search?q=cache:m9vhsfBsw24J:www.bibleandscience.com/otherviews/baugh.htm+dr+carl+baugh+planets+sing&cd=3&hl=en&ct=clnk&gl=us&client=safari

Chapter Eight:
528 and Space/Time Probabilities

Water commands nearly eighty percent (80%) of your body weight and one hundred percent (100%) of your body chemistry. That makes you susceptible to the Creator's musical math that influences the tides by the light of the silvery moon.

Many surgeons refuse to operate under the influence of full moons, especially during flood tides, fearing deadly hemorrhages might result from higher blood pressures.

Water, a liquid crystal superconductor of sound and electricity, receives and transmits electromagnetic and acoustic energy.

Contrary to popular belief, Water has vibrational memory and can hold an electrical charge. I proved that to members of the American Academy of Anti-Aging Medicine in 2008 by literally "LOVE-shocking" two groups of doctors before the general assembly. One doctor touched the LOVE528Water and they all instantly jumped from the charge of electrons moving through their hands held in a circle.(Reference 1 includes a link to view the Google video.)

Given the electrical storage and energetic memory capacity of Water bathing your DNA, cells, and tissues, then common sense says that your ancestry and *birthday* assigns your body Water a unique "energy signature" that influences your life.

Aging reflects your inner time clock ticking. Calendar days and years are determined by resonating planets cycling around our solar system. Just because organized religion discourages members from considering these facts, and you may never have thought these forces could be connected energetically, or spiritually, does not mean they aren't.

Figure 20. Water Cluster From Solar Recording

NASA Sound of the Sun exposed to water. Flash frozen water crystal examined. Experiment designed by David Sereda and Saida Medvedeva.

Звуки Солнца

Care of: www.VoiceEntertainment.net

Photo by Russian scientists Elena Izvekova and Leonid Izvekov

This 20,000 magnification of a frozen Water cluster, also called "Structured Water," resulted from vibrating distilled Water using the sound of the Sun that was supplied by NASA to Russian scientists Elena Izvekova and Leonid Izvekov. The sound included harmonics of 528Hz as well as the pure tone. The complex features hexagonal sacred geometry obviously reflecting intelligent design.
Image courtesy of David Sereda and Jim Law. VoiceEntertainment.net.

What is hard for some people to grasp is that two or more people, unique energy beings, might come together in search of LOVE, family, community and Divine communion by destiny, not simply serendipity.

If Water can hold a charge, and lunar cycles move tides, then your relationships and destiny might flow similarly according to the musical-mathematics of Divine design.

Indeed, you are regulated by the same musical mathematics that directs the stars to their positions on any given day. The destiny, or destination, of planets are mathematically predicted all the time. So, theoretically, your destiny might be measured similarly, and systematically predicted by knowing the mathematical harmonics and disharmonics associated with the planets in relation to your coordinates in space/time at birth.

A data base could be developed to correlate historic events and predict future probabilities. Acquired knowledge could be valuable in your life. You may choose to avoid involvements that the mathematics predicts might harm you, or gravitate to experiences that might help you fulfill your greatest heart-felt goals. Knowing your Divine destiny might help you naturally express your greatest gifts as an individual, or reconcile your weaknesses.

Trade-offs, however, are the same for those considering astrology, such as misinterpreting the data due to personal biases. You certainly do not want to limit your life to what any analyst or man-made system says while choosing to follow your Divine callings.

In any case, this subject is fascinating, and based on the revelations in this book, a math-based system seems reasonable, feasible, and potentially beneficial.

Such a system might benefit psychology and psychiatry greatly, and save time, money, and the risk of deadly drug addictions.

A person's spiritual inheritance, affecting harmony versus dissonance in relationships or career choices, might be valuable intelligence to pursue.

What Is in the Cards?

To consider this question of musically-mathematically administered reality impacting your destiny, first consider an old card game called "Le Her" that has played a role in the development of mathematical probability theories.

Le Her has also been referenced in advancing "game theories"–the mathematical study of games, pioneered in the 1940s by Von Neumann and Morgenstern. This knowledge has been applied with some success in economics.(2)

In 1982, Maynard Smith advanced "Evolutionary Game Theory," adapting the study of optimal strategies in games to model processes in biological evolution.(3)

Spiritual evolution is what you are learning about in this book, as it pertains to musical frequencies, or mathematics. Similarly, Le Her has been referenced in the scholarly writings by Benjamin C. Jantzen, who borrowed "from the heads of Enlightenment mathematicians, . . . a truly novel and unified mathematical theory" of probability.(3)

Le Her is played by two people with a standard deck of 52 playing cards (missing the two jokers). One player is designated the dealer, and the other the receiver. In Le Her, a *king* is ranked high and the ace is low.(2) The dealer gives one card to the receiver, then takes one. The receiver may choose to exchange cards with the dealer, unless the dealer has a *king* in which case no exchange occurs. Then the dealer may choose to exchange with the top card of the deck, unless the top card is a *king* in which case no exchange occurs.

The reason why I emphasized the word *king* in this description is because the king card designates the musical-mathematics of a leadership position within the deck. This is just like real life wherein the Royal Family and bloodline plays a dominate role in history and the evolving New World Order. The king card also plays a dominant role in an ancient system of analyzing human relationships discussed below.

The Musical Math in a Deck of Cards

Wikipedia—a source of filtered intelligence—provides a brief entry on playing card symbolism, as follows:

"Popular legend holds that the composition of a deck of cards has religious, metaphysical, or astronomical significance. . . .[E]ach suit of 13 cards represents the 13 months of the lunar year. Since the Sidereal lunar month may be approximated to 28 days, each suit is equal to 364 days of the year.

"Similarly the whole deck of the 52 cards represents the 52 weeks of the year. Therefore, the whole deck is also equal to 364 days of the year."(4)

The 52 weeks in a year are divided into four seasons of approximately thirteen weeks each, reflecting the four different suits. (5)

"The Ace is symbolically "Alpha and Omega" or "the Beginning and End."

The two colors, red and black, represent polarities, like yin and yang, or male and female.

A standard deck of cards also contains two jokers, or "wild cards," that are removed from play during most card games. The two jokers are considered "cards out of time." The Creator and the Adversary appear to operate beyond space/time, unlike mortals.

The 52 card deck, plus the two jokers, reflects the mathematics of 528Hz frequency sourcing sacred geometry. Recall in Chapter Three, Vic Showell assessed correlations between pi, Phi and 528 that included the number 52. He also determined the numbers 72 and 144 are factors in pyramid sacred geometry based on 528 in relation to other Solfeggio tones. Figure 9 provided a 36-pointed star CymaGlyph based on 528's cymatic impact on Water. Figure 20 shows a perfect six-sided Water crystal formed in a 360 degree circle formed from the sound of the Sun, fundamentally resonating in 528Hz.

Figure 21. Star Decahedron Showing 360 Degrees

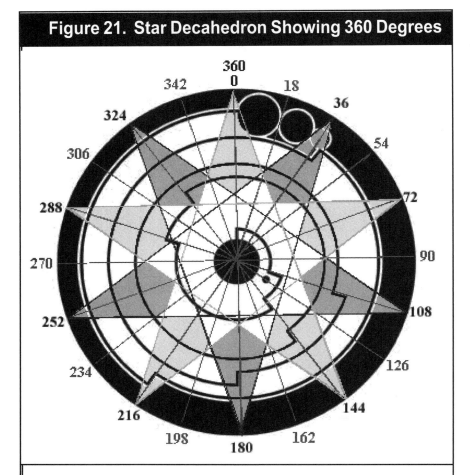

A ten pointed star divides the circle's 360-degrees into twenty 18-degree intervals. Notice when the Pythagorean method of combining numbers is used, all the numbers shown equal "9s"— completion. The third number, 54 is the number of playing cards in a deck, including two jokers. The frequency 528Hz, the MIracle "6," is fundamental to this circle's structure, as 528 relates to Phi, and to the pentagon and star decahedron through trigonometry analysis of pi. Is it a coincidence that the featured colors, geen and yellow, in this diagram, are exclusively represented in 528Hz at the center of the rainbow? Image courtesy of: IonizationX.com

Figure 22. 5th Century Synagogue Zodiac Mosaic

A zodiac mosaic found in the floor of a Hebrew synagogue at Hammath Tiberias, Israel, believed to have been destroyed by an earthquake in 363 AD. Source: BiblePlaces.com

Similarly, Figure 21 provides a 360-degree circle divided into 20 sections. Notice the numbers 72 and 144 in approximately the same positions as the "MI" and "SO" notes in the Perfect Circle of Sound shown in Figure 33, and recall this "Devil's Interval" in musicology involves suggests a "*MI*racle *SO*lution" based on *Webster's Dictionary* definitions provided in Table 5. Notice also that all of these numbers reduce to 9s—completion—according to Pythagorean math. Notice also that the third division yields 54-degrees in every Star Decahedron also shown in Figure 21. 54 is the total number of cards including the jokers, representing God and Satan.

"Given the preponderance of these numbers . . . one certainly is tempted to believe a message is trying hard to come through . . ." said Gary Val Tenuta, a "CryptoNumerology" investigator who joined celebrity author Greg Braden in advancing the God Code's relationship to DNA. "On an intuitive level," Tenuta wrote, "it has the 'feel' of something that might make sense if only we knew the precise context in which to place it. . . . [A] message is trying hard to come through . . ."

God Does Not Play Dice

Albert Einstein said, "God does not play dice with the universe," and celebrity scientist, Stephen Hawkin, sought to reconcile his statement. Here is what he concluded:

> [W]hether the universe evolves in an arbitrary way, or whether it is deterministic. . . . [t]he classical view, put forward by Laplace, was that the future motion of particles was completely determined, if one knew their positions and speeds at one time. This view had to be modified, when Heisenberg put forward his Uncertainty Principle, which said that one could not know both the position, and the speed, accurately. However, it was still possible to predict one combination of position and speed. But even this limited predictability disappeared, when the effects of black holes were taken into account. The loss of particles and information down black holes meant that the particles that came out were random. One could calculate probabilities, but one could not make any definite predictions. Thus, *the future of the universe is not completely determined by the laws of science*, and its present state, as Laplace thought. God still has a few tricks up his sleeve. (8) [Emphasis added.]

Hawkin's accurate conclusion deserves clarification. "The future of the universe is not completely determined by *the laws of science*," but they are determined by God whose tricks include a wholistic relationship with the Master Matrix that is incomprehensible to man, and supersedes scientific analysis.

This is certainly proven in my life, from age eight when I intuited this destiny God paved for me to advance this work heralding the "key of the house of David," and Bible prophesy yet it was written by Moses and John the Baptist thousands of years before I was born into the bloodline of David.

It occurs to me now that King David could not have lost against Goliath, because the deck was stacked against the giant by this same "trick" that Hawkin acknowledges. The fact that Goliath's destiny was sealed, as is yours and mine, by an unmeasurable Force and unfathomable Master Plan, helps ease the stress and strain, including impatience, in your life, knowing you are on God's schedule, and the things you desire are still manifesting.

Alternatively, if the complete future were known to you, in advance, without any mystery, then your tendency towards apathy, laziness, and boredom would probably make you more cynical, depressed, dysfunctional, suicidal, and deathly ill than you are already—inconsistent with God's LOVE and game plan.

Some people might argue that all of this is sacrilegious and blasphemous. Others will say my evidence is shoddy, coincidental, or blindly biased, which is a reasonable argument against trusting numerologists, Tarot card readers, astrologers, Destiny Card System devotees, and religious fundamentalists since they all express personal biases in their analyses.

Moreover, the Game of Life could not be correctly called an "experiment," based on these revelations. Because Einstein was right, "God does not play dice," even though man's choices are like a crapshoot!

Science assumes the "null-hypothesis" when experimenting. That means, it always assumes nothing is happening among the variables, or there are zero relationships operating. Experiments also assume there is something unknown that shall be revealed by the scientific methods and materials used

Fig. 23. Destiny Card System Birthdate Relationship Chart

DAY	Jan	Feb	Mar	Apr	May	Jun	Jul	Aug	Sep	Oct	Nov	Dec
1	K♠	J♠	9♣	7♣	5♠	3♠	A♠	Q♦	10♦	8♦	6♦	4♦
2	Q♠	10♣	8♣	6♣	4♠	2♠	K♦	J♦	9♦	7♦	5♦	3♦
3	J♠	9♠	7♣	5♣	3♠	A♠	Q♦	10♦	8♦	6♦	4♦	2♦
4	10♣	8♠	6♣	4♣	2♠	K♦	J♦	9♦	7♦	5♦	3♦	A♦
5	9♣	7♣	5♣	3♠	A♠	Q♦	10♦	8♦	6♦	4♦	2♦	K♠
6	8♣	6♣	4♣	2♠	K♦	J♦	9♦	7♦	5♦	3♦	A♦	Q♠
7	7♣	5♣	3♣	A♠	Q♦	10♦	8♦	6♦	4♦	2♦	K♠	J♠
8	6♣	4♣	2♣	K♦	J♦	9♦	7♦	5♦	3♦	A♦	Q♠	10♠
9	5♣	3♣	A♣	Q♦	10♦	8♦	6♦	4♦	2♦	K♠	J♠	9♠
10	4♣	2♣	K♦	J♦	9♦	7♦	5♦	3♦	A♦	Q♠	10♠	8♠
11	3♣	A♣	Q♦	10♦	8♦	6♦	4♦	2♦	K♠	J♠	9♠	7♠
12	2♣	K♦	J♦	9♦	7♦	5♦	3♦	A♦	Q♠	10♠	8♠	6♠
13	A♣	Q♦	10♦	8♦	6♦	4♦	2♦	K♠	J♠	9♠	7♠	5♠
14	K♦	J♦	9♦	7♦	5♦	3♦	A♦	Q♠	10♠	8♠	6♠	4♠
15	Q♦	10♦	8♦	6♦	4♦	2♦	K♠	J♠	9♠	7♠	5♠	3♠
16	J♦	9♦	7♦	5♦	3♦	A♦	Q♠	10♠	8♠	6♠	4♠	2♠
17	10♦	8♦	6♦	4♦	2♦	K♠	J♠	9♠	7♠	5♠	3♠	A♠
18	9♦	7♦	5♦	3♦	A♦	Q♠	10♠	8♠	6♠	4♠	2♠	K♥
19	8♦	6♦	4♦	2♦	K♠	J♠	9♠	7♠	5♠	3♠	A♠	Q♥
20	7♦	5♦	3♦	A♦	Q♠	10♠	8♠	6♠	4♠	2♠	K♥	J♥
21	6♦	4♦	2♦	K♠	J♠	9♠	7♠	5♠	3♠	A♠	Q♥	10♥
22	5♦	3♦	A♦	Q♠	10♠	8♠	6♠	4♠	2♠	K♥	J♥	9♥
23	4♦	2♦	K♠	J♠	9♠	7♠	5♠	3♠	A♠	Q♥	10♥	8♥
24	3♦	A♦	Q♠	10♠	8♠	6♠	4♠	2♠	K♥	J♥	9♥	7♥
25	2♦	K♠	J♠	9♠	7♠	5♠	3♠	A♠	Q♥	10♥	8♥	6♥
26	A♦	Q♠	10♠	8♠	6♠	4♠	2♠	K♥	J♥	9♥	7♥	5♥
27	K♠	J♠	9♠	7♠	5♠	3♠	A♠	Q♥	10♥	8♥	6♥	4♥
28	Q♠	10♠	8♠	6♠	4♠	2♠	K♥	J♥	9♥	7♥	5♥	3♥
29	J♠	9♠	7♠	5♠	3♠	A♠	Q♥	10♥	8♥	6♥	4♥	2♥
30	10♠		6♠	4♠	2♠	K♥	J♥	9♥	7♥	5♥	3♥	A♥
31	9♠		5♠		A♠		10♥	8♥		4♥		Joker

The above matrix shows the theoretical relationships used by practitioners of the ancient Destiny Card System of discerning mathematical and gravitational probabilities affecting a person's personality traits, social relationships, developmental history, and predictable "destiny." Established following decades of research into this secreted system, the card matrix coincides with calendar coordinates following a mathematical pattern and equation under investigation including frequency and scaling factors affecting the coordinates issuing from the nine note Perfect Circle of Sound™.

Figure 24. Destiny Card System "Life Spread" Chart

The Life Spread chart is used to assess relationships. Cards in direct contact with your card, or alternatively cards at a distance, suggests higher or lower probability of attraction and successful or meaningful relationship. Often people are surprised to quickly find their close friends and family members in these proximal positions validating this system by analyzing the card pairs.

Figure 25. Destiny Card System "Spiritual Spread"

The Spiritual Spread

"The Spiritual Spread" is used to consider "relationships in heaven," not necessarily the "face you show the world." This system derives from an ancient method of divination, rooted in the secret esoteric "Order Of The Magi." This knowledge was encoded into the tarot and ultimately developed into the common playing cards. Card readers' personal biases should be considered during "readings" that relay probabilities, not certainties. Practitioners' agendas are a caveat to reliability.

to test null-hypotheses. But since everything, you now know and see, is determined mathematically to be related to 528Hz frequency, this fundamental relationship between LOVE and all creation, is grossly neglected throughout science, proving all of science is not only limited, but biased by paganism.

So Hawkin's "trick" played on science, is the same "message" sought by Tenuta. **LOVE is the alpha and the omega**. Heisenberg's Uncertainty Principle will now need to be revised to accommodate the "Universal LOVE Constant"—528—the commonality among all of the systems of scientific and probability analyses, and measurement.

It has been wisely affirmed for millennia, that "God is LOVE." We have been tricked into thinking LOVE is fleeting and personal, rather than Divine, eternal, and fundamental to society. This message of LOVE/528 reveals God is LOVE, and He shows Her hand in every relationship, throughout creation. The central mission of LOVE/528 in the matrix of math that deals all the cards, compels you towards self-realization of the LOVE that lies within.

LOVE/528 always honors all the players in the game.

LOVE/528 is the fundamental force, burning in your heart, compelling you to make a choice to be part of the solution in every situation.

Destiny Cards

With the background above, more clues of God's plan for you may be found by researching the obscure Destiny Card System involving matrix math and probability.

Years ago, a political activist in Hawaii introduced me to the Destiny Card System saying it was based on the mathematical coordinates of planetary positions at the time of your birth. This analysis, therefore, shared fundamentals similar to astrology and numerology.

Astrology and numerology don't scare me as it does those who identify with Christian "fundamentalism," mainly because I have faith that "God doesn't play dice with the universe." While backpacking in Israel before starting college, the summer of 1972, I visited the ruins of an ancient Hebrew temple that indicated me that my ancestors apparently honored astrology, or some form of it.

At first, I was highly skeptical of the Destiny Card System. Then I considered the solidly proven affect of moon cycles on sleep, blood pressure, and behavior. I now accept the theory that planets in our solar system can impact people, like a digital download.

Theoretically, a cosmic download or influence on your life is administered electromagnetically, gravitationally, vibrationally, or musically-mathematically.

Likewise, the Destiny Card System operates musically-mathematically, empirically proving to users that your destiny is influenced by the planetary positions on your birthday.

Figures 23-25 show the Destiny Card "spreads." Some career counselors and human resource officers claim the system of researching the cards on these spreads quickly reveals valuable information about the "players." They use the cards to consider probabilities for getting along with others on teams, and succeeding in certain areas.

Simply put, the Destiny Card System spreads are used to relate personalities and probabilities mathematically and systematically.

In 2004, author Robert Lee Camp published *Love Cards* and *Cards of Your Destiny.* The former caught my attention due to my interest in LOVE/528. Mr. Camp credits Olney H. Richmond in *The Mystic Test Book* (1894) for sourcing much of this modern knowledge. The system's data base was expanded in *Sacred Symbols of the Ancients*, by Florence Campbell and Edith Randall (1947), and Arne Lein's *What's Your Card?*(1978)

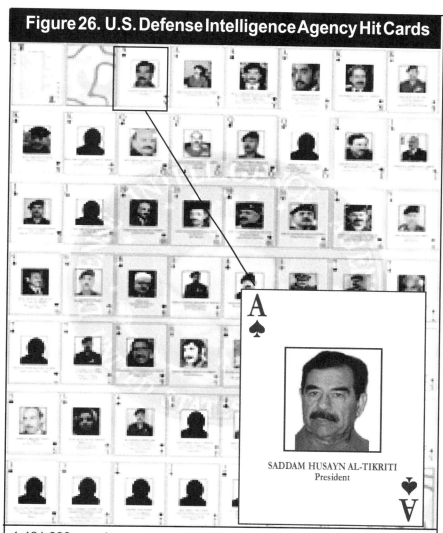

Figure 26. U.S. Defense Intelligence Agency Hit Cards

SADDAM HUSAYN AL-TIKRITI
President

1,421,933 people were reported killed by the invasion of Iraq, in 2003, directed by the Bush administration, including Vice President, Dick Cheney, the retired CEO of Halliburton Company that heavily profited from the war. The allegation that Saddam Husayn held weapons of mass destruction were accurate, despite the propaganda that hashed the facts. The Bush administration had supplied weapons of mass destruction to Iraq only days before the invasion. These included a variety of weapons-grade biologicals supplied by the American Type Culture Collection. The genocide served the Illuminati's New World Order agenda. Source: U.S. Defense Intelligence Agency.

Campbell and Randall discussed the mystical significance of the playing cards and their uncanny connection with birthdays and future probabilities.

All the above authors agree, this ancient knowledge was secreted by priestly magicians around the time of Atlantis.

Robert Camp wrote that this system of self-understanding and prediction is easier to learn and apply than astrology. "You can learn this system well enough within an hour to do a significantly accurate reading for yourself or somebody else. . . . These cards, and the relationships between them, can tell you a great deal about yourself, and your relations with friends and loved ones.(5)

"The science of the cards is more approachable [than astrology]," Camp reported. ". . . You just have to look up your card . . . the cards of your relatives, friends, and acquaintances, and learn a great deal about the nature of your relationships to them. By testing this system in the world, you can immediately confirm its validity."(5)

Probabilities or Predictions?

What is the difference between predicting game outcomes using mathematical probabilities and a calculator, compared to predicting life outcomes using cards that represent data recorded over time from observed, even historic, events? Everything is operating, after all, according to the mathematical-musical Laws of physics, and the acoustic matrix of creation.

Your calculator works with readable digits linked to, and based on, mathematical formulas or equations. Alternatively, the Destiny Card System begins with a card linked to two spreads, justified by history and observations of social and behavioral outcomes.

Your birthday tells you your card and provides the personal significance of that day for you. You may want to take advantage of this information to help reconcile your productive or destructive relationships.

Can you imagine what this method might do to the fields of psychology or psychiatry when, for example, people realize their depressing relationships are better explained by matrix math, and better treated with awareness brought by a deck of cards, than by doctors and drugs?

Also, a new card influences the world daily. Some researchers claim the Destiny Cards may be used to schedule important geopolitical or economic events.

Consider this as Wall Street investors, military strategists, or the Illuminati might.

Events likely to make history, for instance, occur on Jack or King days. Both male cards are rumored to be especially aggressive. Jacks are widely reputed to be mischievous, cunning and even deadly. In cards, for instance, "One-eyed Jacks, the Man with the Axe" are made the "wild card." Folk lore heralds the Jack personalities including the devilish Jack-o-Lantern, Jack-in-the-Box, Jack-and-the-Beanstalk, Jack-the-Ripper, Jack o'Kent, a local cleric, who bet the Devil, Mother Goose's violent "house that Jack built," and the bizarre Jack Sparrow in Pirates of the Caribbean. (There are many more examples.)

A quick review of war dates in history found Jack and King cards often coincided, including: a) D-day, Normandy, June 6, 1944, b) July 4, 1776, the signed Declaration of Independence signed at the end of the Revolutionary War; c) December 7, 1917, the United States declared war on the Austro-Hungarian Empire during World War I; (d) Dec. 7, 1941, the attack on Pearl Harbor prompted America's engagement in WWII; and e) September 11, 2001, 9/11 attacks on New York's World Trade Center that falsely justified America's "War on Terror" and the "Patriot Act," creating a virtual corporate-fascist state in America; and recently; f) Dec. 7, 2010, the day the "WikiLeaks Scandal" broke jeopardizing American banks and threatening global economic collapse. Traditionally, global economic crisis fuels major wars.

Now you can appreciate why the "inside players" would want this knowledge generally neglected or discredited, so they can maintain an advantage.

The Illuminati and Earth's Destiny?

People in the know generate great wealth and power using secret knowledge. This includes the creative math through which the universe is continuously (musically and fractally) constructed. Mathematical matrix dynamics are so *powerful,* they have been secreted for millennia. Population controllers learned to use this vibrational technology ages ago to create, modern Babylon.

"For what shall it profit a man, if he shall gain the whole world, and lose his own soul?" (*Mark* 8:36)

Hitler maintained metaphysical and occult interests. The world's leading bankers and politicians didn't get where they are neglecting the world's most powerful creative technology.

The Illuminati knows God's musical-mathematical matrix is the territory between the Kingdom of Heaven and Hell on Earth. This hydrosonic-etheric dimension is active in the conflict between good and evil. This place holds optimal creative potential, and is thus most valuable.

The manipulation of musical-mathematics to generate peace or war is considered primary intelligence by truth-seekers and devil-doers alike. The Master Matrix generating universal design creates everything, including cosmology, astronomy, astrology, Moses' and Jesus's teachings of The Law in the Ten Commandments as well as the occult.

Jesus taught *The Way* to Spiritual Salvation is to flow with LOVE. He presented the opportunity to engage the Creator's channel that is broadcasting eternal salvation, every moment in time.

We now know that this frequency of LOVE, 528Hz, helps move history to unfold naturally, on time, every time.

You are now privy to The Way out of human misery and environmental catastrophe. The Creator's Creative Technology is far stronger than any method or material the Illuminati can muster to direct destiny demonically. You can now use this musical technology positively to heal yourself.

The Creator's Creative Technology we now decree is musical-mathematics. This knowledge is most welcome because it is optimally freeing to you and me. The Illuminati knew this when they secreted this intelligence.

Figure 26 shows the Destiny Card System concept manipulated by war-makers. The U.S. Defense Intelligence Agency created a playing card deck for Iraqi War targets!(6)

Likewise consider Las Vegas. Visitors to "Sin City" see the cards all around them on casino floors and walls, but they don't know the deck's origin in a Master Matrix administering cosmogenesis. People think they are only gambling icons on money machines. Crime syndicates merchandise these tokens that, alternatively, could be used positively to spread enlightenment and honor spirituality.

The Wisdom of Solomon and Traits of David

The greatest blessing God gave humanity is your ability to *choose* your destiny, as God has casted it in the perfect matrix made from math and music. A wise person chooses to recognize this, and live in balance and harmony with this matrix, destiny, and enlightened spirituality. This greatest truth shall set you free, only if you choose to take advantage of this opportunity.

Besides free will, you are encouraged to learn the valuable blessing of Wisdom. This Wisdom was sought by Solomon who built God's terrestrial temple, a metaphor for your own illuminated body.

Wisdom often comes from life lessons learned "the hard way." Your elders know this from being around long enough, having gained wisdom through the "school of hard knocks."

Solomon sought wisdom to administer justice in a world of good and evil. King David, Solomon's father, celebrated this wisdom and his relationship with God. He played a fifteen-string healing harp, and shielded himself in battle with the "Star of David." It would be nice to know David's Destiny Card, but this knowledge is obscured by the Hebrew calendar differing from the Roman calendar used in the Destiny Card System.

Despite this uncertainty, Destiny Card authorities claim the King of Spades must be King David's card. There is an uncanny resemblance in qualities between what we know about David, and what we know about the King of Spades.

This card exclusively presents on January 1st, in the Destiny Card System, so the odds are 1-in-364 that you would find a King of Spades. This card uniquely and powerfully stands at the top of the two primary spreads.

I suspect the King of Spades, with New Year's energy, is most empowered by LOVE/528. It is, after all, due to LOVE and joy that people bless each other every year on January 1st by affirming "Happy New Year!"

The King of Spades is described as a person who can master anything they choose. . . . "As the most powerful of the Kings, the King of Spades is equipped to handle enormous responsibilities, but it seems that this commission is too great for many New Year's babies to bear. [King David, you may recall, was not responsible enough for the honor of building God's Temple. He became too distracted, sexually.] Many King of Spades males choose to take the less responsible and more fun and creative path of the Jack of Spades, their Personality Card," explained Camp(7)

"These people, . . . are fixed and immovable. They are not swayed by other's opinions or by any of the usual forms of persuasion. They live their life on their terms. They usually insist on some amount of respect from others. They just gravitate to the top because they feel they belong there."(7)

This is certainly the case for J. Edgar Hoover as well, who

besides being implicated in John Lennon's murder, infamously blackmailed nearly every powerful politician during his tenure as FBI director.

Other examples of famous King of Spades people include Revolutionary War activists Betsy Ross and Paul Revere.

Throughout history, Kings have ruled most powerfully. This dominance is reflected in both Le Her and the Destiny Game™ wherein kings rule those of lesser vibrations according to their numbers. For millennia, this power to control and rule was simply accepted as a spiritual inheritance of the Kings.

The subjects prayed for those who governed. The phrase "God save the king!" meant the kings needed saving from their blind egos. People prayed that by the King's saving, they would rule judiciously with wisdom.

Conclusion

You have a role to play to help fulfill civilization's destiny.

You have choices to make: Wise analysis or foolish paralysis are your options. Knowing your card, and your strengths and weaknesses, can be most helpful.

You accept by your silence the ongoing consequences of the Illuminati's manipulations.

Alternatively, a compassionate intelligent New World Order awaits a rapidly growing awakening of peace-makers.

The musical-mathematical matrix is calling forth this remnant right now. Those who choose to LOVE unconditionally are hearing this call first and loudest. These music lovers shall inherit the Earth by attracting and sustaining prosperity in all ways, from a place in the Orchestra Leader's heart.

We are all encouraged to seek this foremost prospering place before engaging lessor passions.

References

1) Horowitz LG. HydroEngineering Freedom from Infectious Diseases. At the A4M-Convention, December, 2008, Las Vegas, Nevada. http://video. google.com/videoplay?docid=-9166183378354860498#

2) Le Her. Wikipedia listing: http://en.Wikipedia.org/wiki/Le_Her

3) Jantzen BC. Protean probability: An early diversity of interpretations in the emergence of probability theory. Posner Internship Project May 14, 2006. Available online at: http://www.andrew.cmu.edu/user/bjantzen/ Papers/Protean%20Probability.pdf

4) Playing cards. Wikipedia. See: http://en.Wikipedia.org/wiki/Playing_ card

5) The Spiritual Traveler. An Interview with Robert Camp, author of *Love Cards* and *Destiny Cards*, 2004. See: http://www.spiritualtraveler.com/ spiritual_traveler/spiritual_forum/an_interview_with_robert_camp.asp

6) Personal communications from anonymous card enthusiast, December, 2010.

7) Wikipedia. Defense Intelligence Agency Most Wanted Iraqi Playing Cards. See: http://en.Wikipedia.org/wiki/Most-wanted_Iraqi_playing_card

8) The Amazing Cards of Destiny. The King of Spades. See: http://www. destiny-cards.co.uk/shop/page/18?shop_param=

9) Hawkin S. Does God play dice? See: http://www.hawking.org.uk/index. php/lectures/64

Chapter Nine:
Divine Music and the Key of 528

The *Book of Revelation* records the current transition from Babylonian dissonance to peace on Earth. The story features the Church of Satan's devil-doing that is extinguised by singing "a new song." The Thousand Years of World Peace—the Messianic Age—wherein you come to know yourself as a Divine family member is at hand. This chapter considers the administration of this transformation in greater detail, focusing on the system-dynamics of creationism and the musical mathematics of evolution, including the evolution of consciousness.

Lives are already being uplifted to a more righteous dimension, energetically and physically, as people globally are re-tuning their instruments and bodies to 528Hz. This new reality is attracting survivors and thrivers. Cosmic forces are calling forth this change.

People who are not tuned into the musical-mathematical matrix of space/time, which would not exist without LOVE/528, are missing the available rewards, and this is their karma.

The Grand Performance of Divine music is compelling the end of the A=440 imposition era. An eternal energy cycle radiating LOVE, with 528 at its heart, is moving humanity away from fear and into firmer faith. This Key to the house of David, opening your heart, is altering the mood and temperament of audiences everywhere.

Music can do this as you may have experienced, especially if you have listened to alternative tunings. The power of music played in 528, for example, has already been reported

Fig. 27. Rodin's Mathematical Matrix Independently Determined to Include the Ancient Solfeggio Tones

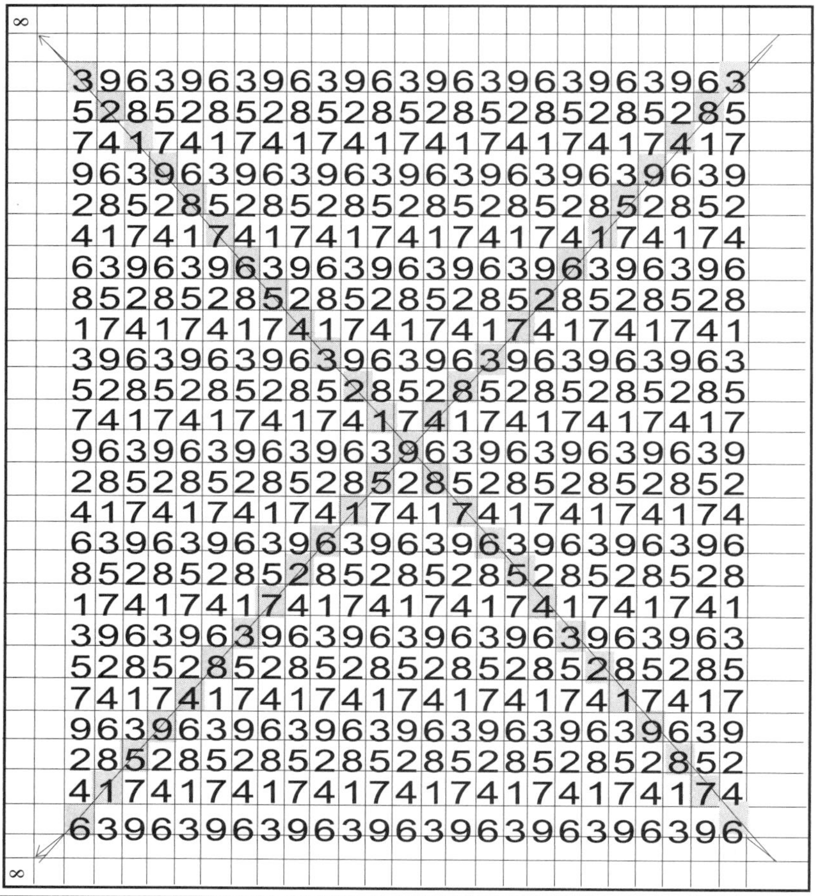

by explanding intuition, and benefiting health and well being.

Humanity is emerging from the Dark Ages of spiritual re-pression largely due to neglected knowledge about what music is and does.

As you have been learning in this book, 528Hz resonance is central to everything in the universe. Everything in nature is scaled, and the pure tone of 528Hz is fundamental to scaling. The frequency central to the audio spectrum of creation, is theorized to be the same number, 528nm, the visible light frequency of greenish-yellow at the heart of the rainbow.

Look carefully at Rodin's mathematical matrix in Figure 27. Notice 528 and 639 are not directly adjacent each other in this simple *two-dimensional* figure, even though they are the central two notes of the original Solfeggio. Theoretically, these two frequencies are broadcasting two seperate parallel dimensions, or two universes within God's Master Matrix.

Find the "X" at the center of this powerful Rodin matrix. From the "9" at the center, follow the left diagonal ascending pattern of 1-thru-9. Notice this is not reflected in the lower descending portion of the X where you might expect to see the same 1-thru-9 pattern continue. The pattern is displaced.

The same pattern can be found again by shifting number blocks. Can you locate the same pattern elsewhere through-out the matrix?

This pattern shift is theoretically responsible for the torque and spin of planets throughout the cosmos, as depicted in Figure 29, showing Haramein's double toroidal universe struc-

Figure 28. Famous Companies Use "69" In Logos

6 + 9 = 15 = 1 + 5 = 6

ture. It may also reflect that different levels of the matrix, or parallel matrixes, or different levels of reality, exist. Would you like to travel in the spiritual dimension of reality? The one that is traveled by angels or fallen angels? You make the choice to switch into either frequency or reality.

The Rodin/Powell "Grand Unified Field Theory"

Randy Powell, working with Marko Rodin on "Advanced Vortex Math," stated in 2010, that their "Grand Unified Field Theory" provides the opportunity to "create inexhaustible free energy, end all disease, produce unlimited food, travel anywhere in the universe, build the ultimate supercomputer, artificial intelligence, and [make] obsolete all existing technology. How is this possible to make such outrageous claims? Because we have a secret that connects all of the world's technology together—numbers, a living language."(3)

The pyramid shown in the center of Figure 30 is "representative of what we call flux fields. We have electricity, and at the center of electricity is magnetism; and at the center of magnetism is a flux—a higher dimensional energy known by many names such as: 'dark energy,' 'tachyons,' 'monopoles,' and 'gravitons.' We call it *etheron energy*. It is not a static or stationary energy. It's a pulse, a surge, *the beating heart of all existence*. It's the ultimate fundamental particle of the universe—the God particle. . . . This energy is the source of all time, motion, and vibration. It's the only thing that comes from the whole—the zero—the center of the cyclone. . . . It animates everything. It's the source of non-decaying spin of the electrons. . . . Etherons are literally the glue that holds the universe together."(3)

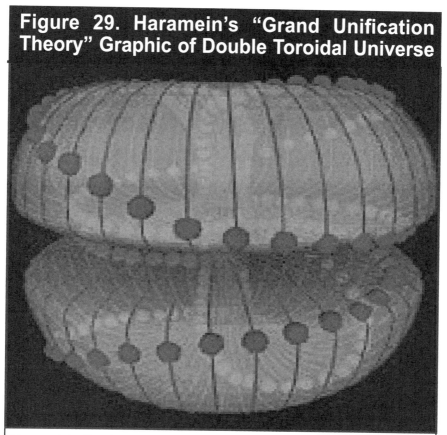

Figure 29. Haramein's "Grand Unification Theory" Graphic of Double Toroidal Universe

Haramein's thesis mathematically evidences a spiraling and spinning double toroid universe with a "black hole" in the middle This heart of the universe, shaped like a figure "8," has a special vortex of energy where the vectors appear to cross. This space, functioning where matter takes form, is shaped like the spinning top in the movie *INCEPTION*. (Source: http://www.theresonanceproject.org)

I have already mentioned that the two adjacent Solfeggio frequencies, 528 and 639, resolve in Pythagorean mystery school mathematics to the numbers "6" and "9," respectively. These are the symbols for the Alpha and the Omega, beginning and end, the yin and yang, male and female —that some children in my third-grade class were punished for writing in their notebooks, due to the sexual inference of "69." How sad it is that our teachers never learned or taught students the truth about the orign, and metaphysical meanings, of this symbol.

Yet, the 69 appears commonly in Illuminati symbols, like the corporate logos of PEPSI/ I2939 (reversal=12939=6) and Safeway supermarkets, as shown in Figure 28.

The 6 suggests a spiraling down from heaven to earth. The 9 spirals up from earth into the wholeness of heaven.

Table 8. Stable Intervals of the 3,6,9 Number Set on the Logarithmic Line Expressed in Cell Organelle

Cell Organelle Measuring Units		m	n(0)	n(1)	n(2)	n(2)	n(4)	n(5)	n(6)	n(7) Remainder
Protrusions	inf:	0.000000007	18	-0-1						-4.00
	sub:	0.000000009	18	-6						-6.35
Cell sizes	inf:	0.000000007	18	-4-1						-4.00
	sub:	0.000000009	19	-9						-9.35
Membrane (thickness)	inf:	6.1E-09	18	-9-1						-2.73
	sub:	0.000000001	18	-9						-5.42
Peribosomes	inf:	0.000000009	18	-9-1						-3.34
	sub:	0.000000015	19	2-3						52.15
Ribosomes	inf:	0.000000021	18	6						5.48
	sub:	0.000000003	18	er-1						3.90
Cilia (thickness)	inf:	0.00000034	21	-11						-16.79
	sub:	0.00000026	21	-43						-42.16
Lysosomes	inf:	0.00000006	21	4						5.82
	sub:	0.00000008	21	6-1						3.12
Peroxisomes	inf:	0.00000021	21	-6-1						-2.10
	sub:	0.00000009	21	6						0.32
Nucleolus	inf:	0.099991	21	-4						-5.16
	sub:	0.00000002	21	1-1						14.79
Golgi vesicles	inf:	0.00000041	21							20.16
	sub:	0.0000021	24							23.02
Mitochondria	inf:	0.000003	21							21.06
	sub:	0.000009	24				-			23.36
Cilia (length)	inf:	0.0000051	24	-34						-30.76
	sub:	0.00001	24	6-1						4.52
Cell nuclei	inf:	0.000003	24	-6-1						-4.66
	sub:	0.00001	24	0-1						4.65
Cells	inf:	0.000003	24							23.31
	sub:	0.00003	27							27.99

In Müller's thesis, the logarithmic line of the Standing Gravititational Wave is vital for all creation in that throughout the universe matter only crystallizes in locations of nodal resonance, or energy concentrations. These involve what Nikola Tesla heralded as the powers of the 3s, 6s, and 9s. Shown above are the mass measurements of cell organelle that follow this pattern.

Table 9. Stable Intervals of the 3,6,9 Number Set on the Logarithmic Line Expressed in Celestial Bodies

Orbits of Planets And Some Moons

Celestial Body	Measuring Unit	m	n(0)	n(1)	n(2)	n(3)	n(4)	n(5)	n(6)	n(7)	Remainder
Phobos	Inf:	58932900	54	-269							-268,17
	Sub:	58934750	54	-270							-269,03
Deimos	Inf:	147403500	54	e+1	-e-1	-48	62				61,26
	Sub:	147403600	54	e+1	-e-1	-48	162				162,35
Andrastea	Inf:	802991050	57	-6	-e-1	6	9	-e-1	-18		-18,40
	Sub:	802991100	57	-6	-e-1	6	9	-e-1	-9		-8,13
Amalthea	Inf:	1139139200	57	-57	e+1	-e-1	e+1	9			8,40
	Sub:	1139139300	57	-57	e+1	-e-1	e+1	6			6,53
Thebe	Inf:	1392982000	57	18	-14						-13,97
	Sub:	1400000000	57	18	-e-1						-3,57
Moon	Inf:	2413418500	57	e+1	18	-15					-15,93
	Sub:	2413435100	57	e+1	18	-17					-16,43
Io	Inf:	2648990900	57	e+1	-9	-72	-42				-42,60
	Sub:	2648991000	57	e+1	-9	-72	-8				-7,32
Mercury	Inf:	3,59E+11	63	-9	-14						-13,58
	Sub:	3,61E+11	63	-9	-8						-7,22
Venus	Inf:	6,75E+11	63	9	-e-1	e+1	93				93,13
	Sub:	6,77E+11	63	9	-e-1	e+1	-e-1				-3,27
Earth	Inf:	9,43E+11	63	e+1	9	-e-1	e+1				3,33
	Sub:	9,44E+11	63	e+1	9	-e-1	12				11,51
Mars	Inf:	1,31E+12	63	e+1	-e-1	e+1	-e-1	e+1			2,88
	Sub:	1,3E+12	63	e+1	-e-1	e+1	-e-1	8			7,72
Jupiter	Inf:	5E+12	66	-e-1	-6						-6,95
	Sub:	4,8E+12	66	-e-1	-18						-17,92
Saturn	Inf:	8,9E+12	66	-32							-31,99
	Sub:	9,1E+12	66	-44							-43,32

As with cell organelle listed in Table 7, Müller's data also shows cosmic creations, in this case celestial bodies including all planets in our solar system, abide by the mathematical laws regulating the logarithmic Standing Gravititational Wave and physical reality. Matter only crystallizes in locations of nodal resonance, or energy concentrations, involving 3, 6 and 9 metaphysical mathematics.

The "MIracle 6" designation for 528Hz, reflects the power of that number to manifest the miracles of creation.

The combined symbols, 69, also represents the Piscean balance. Merge these two numbers, one on top of the other, to form the infinity symbol or an "8."

It is also interesting that by placing the circles from both numbers on top of one another, you get the symbol for a hurricane— 𝓢 —reflecting knowledge that everything in the universe is spinning.

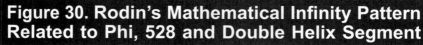

Figure 30. Rodin's Mathematical Infinity Pattern Related to Phi, 528 and Double Helix Segment

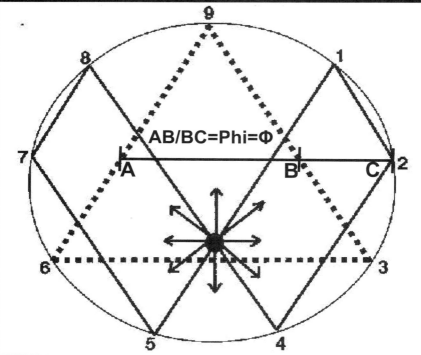

Marko Rodin's diagram of the "infinity pattern," (1,2,4,8,7,5) that incorporates Phi, 528, and is structurally similar to each segment of DNA spiraling in the double helix. Adjacent segments flip sides and polarities to accelerate energy flow and electrogenetic signal reception and transmission. This same structure appears in Figure 1 in the framework of Müller's Standing Gravitational Wave.(2) The resulting equalateral triangle inside the circle demonstrates Phi proportions: The ratio of AB to BC is Phi resonating 528, since Pi = 5 arccos (.5Phi) = 22/7 (days a week) is ancient Pi or 3.142857~; and 528/22 = 24; and 360/24 (hours a day) = 15 (MIracle 6). This proves 528 is not only fundamental to genetic structuring, but that your DNA is actually connected to *space/time*! Source: Personal communications with Marko Rodin and Victor Showell.

This is all associated with a matrix of music that makes the stars and animates the galaxies.

Fig. 31. Horowitz's Analysis of Rodin's "Infinity Pattern" Structurally Similar to Double Helix Segment

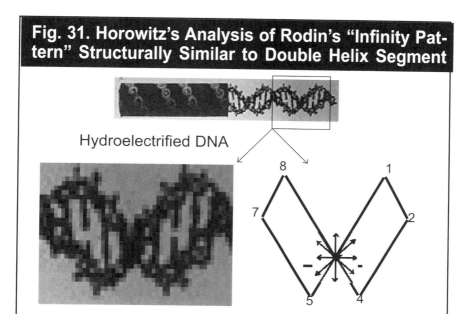

Hydroelectrified DNA

Above is a composite of DNA photo enlargements next to Rodin's basic infinity pattern. The "double wing" pattern in Rodin's Infinity Patter is seen in DNA as well. Rodin derived his toroid model of the universe from this simple pattern. Harramein further advanced this knowledge in Figure 29. Rodin's evidence supports the theory that 528Hz can be used to repair damaged DNA, since DNA's structure certainly reflects Divine design, as proven in Figure 30. Horowitz first learned of the theory that 528Hz frequency repairs damaged DNA from Dr. Lee Lorenzen, who claimed this knowledge was being applied worldwide by researchers in genetic biochemistry, although published science is unavailable. Structured Water has been proven to be essential for DNA's structure and function, according to Saykally et al in *Science*. According to John Stuart Reid, Water stimulated by 528Hz uniquely produces a precise 36-pointed star, as seen in Figure 9. Between Showell's and Reid's works, we see 528 fundamental to the sacred geometry of circles and spirals consistent with DNA structuring and hydrosonic restructuring. 528 hydrosonics is also consistent with the rational number harmonics of cosmic structures, including planets, kept in orbit by phase-locking with Rodin's math and Müller's Standing Gravitational Wave. Likewise, DNA is naturally phase-locking into this matrix math, just like chlorophyll is phase-locking into the sound of the Sun. Phase-locking best explains why clinicians worldwide report 528Hz therapies are highly effective.

Figure 32. The Packed Ball Hypothesis in Biophysics

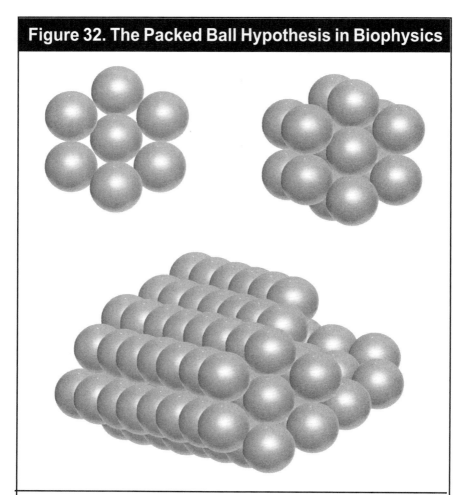

Some physicists explain physical matter as reflecting harmonic assemblies of circular atomic elements. The fit stabilizes energetically, most naturally, due to harmonics. Sound vibrations generate waves of electron polarities, in which harmonics or dissonance plays a role in materializing matter. Hexagonal arrays begin assembling around a single atom represented by the diagram above (upper left). The first element, hydrogen, embodies the sacred geometry of a 360 degree circle. It requires six atoms next to it to fill available space. This helps explain the importance of the "MIracle 6," 528Hz frequency, the star tetrahedron, the hexagonal ring of snowflakes, and similarly, the hexagonal shape of carbon-6 organic chemistry. The Water molecule's design seeks atomic fit within a cluster of similar, hexagonal arrays.

The Sound of the Planets

The anonymous biophysicist I referenced earlier explained to me the concept of determining the precise pure tone that every planet in our solar system broadcasts. He wisely considered the mathematics of their orbits, and provided the following protocol and explanation:

"A planetary orbit can be looked at as an extremely low note in the cosmic musical scale, with (let's say) one cycle per year. An overtone series of higher notes is simply a doubling for each octave going up, or a halving for each octave going down.

"Imagine the Earth's orbit around the sun is a note of one cycle/year. The harmonic one octave higher is 2 cycles/year. Two octaves higher is 4 cycles/year, three octaves higher is 8 cycles/year, and so on.

"33 octaves above the Earth year = 8,589,934,592 cycles/year. Since in one year there are 365.2422 days x 86,400 seconds/day = 31,556,926.08 seconds.

"Then, at 33 octaves up, 8,589,934,592 cycles ÷ 31,556,926.08 seconds = 272.204 cycles/second (or Hertz frequency).

"If 'C' = 261.6Hz, and 'C#' is 277.18Hz, then in order to play in the key of Earth, you must tune to a note that is 2/3 of the way from 'C' to 'C#'. [Author's Note: This is close to what you would actually tune your instruments to while tuning to 528 (which is the 5th octave C on your piano), since half of 528Hz is (the 4th octave C) 264Hz; and this is a bit less than 2/3 of the way to C# when standard tuning is used.]

"Another example is the moon. We can identify 2 different notes with the moon's orbit. . . . 1) 227.44Hz for the Zodiac Moon Key, and 2) 210.25Hz for the Full Moon Key.

"The former is halfway between A=220 to A#=233; and the Full Moon Key is a bit higher than G# at 207.65."(1)

So the planets are actually "singing," although you can't hear them as NASA does. Their harmonic voices, or frequencies, are "*phase locked*" with the sound of the sun; and the sun's frequencies have been heard vacillating around 528Hz.

This is the miracle sound of nature. In fact, our solar system, galaxy, and each microscopic part of the universe, has its own vibration that is obviously scaled according to the laws of math, music, and 528/LOVE.

Tables 7 and 8 show the consistent expression of the 3, 6 and 9 number set within the Master Matrix generating the microscopic and macrocosmic realms, courtesy of astrophysicist Müller.(2)

This knowledge is important to creating peace on Earth wherein people have learned to live in harmony with nature and each other. These same laws of physics, mathematics, and music must apply, be taught, and integrated into every practice. This is what natural law commands, and what the 528LOVERevolution seeks to inspire in the arts and sciences.

The Sun and 528

Pure light is *caused* to be in your body by the light of the sun that vibrates in 528Hz. Even the sun's spherical shape depends on 528Hz.

Here is what is happening to assure your existence as a manifestation of LOVE: The sun, according to NASA recordings distributed by researcher David Sereda, vibrates fundamentally at 528Hz frequency. This can be heard when the NASA recording is played with the 528 tuning fork struck simultaneously. The chlorophyll in plants receives this 528Hz sound, and 528nm of light, and reflects this in its color. The

Figure 33.The Perfect Circle of Sound™

The Perfect Circle of Sound™ logo presents the nine core creative frequencies of the universe and their reported colors. These nine tones comprise the primary musical-mathematical matrix from which additional harmonics are generated. The frequency 528 resonates at the heart of the electromagnetic color spectrum, (i.e., the center of the rainbow). 528Hz is the greenish-yellow color selected as the primary energizing pigment throughout the botanical world. Chlorophyll attacts the most energy from the sun, that has also been determined to vibrate with a primary 528Hz pure tone, plus harmonics. The phase-locking of the sun's hydrosonic energy, and light energy as well, harmonically synchronizes chlorophyll's vibrations to the sun's vibrations to deliver the most energy for life. The 528Hz frequency is then carried by electrons that are spinning and vibrating with "LOVE" in this frequency. This symbol is a powerul amulet that is increasingly being reported by users, such as the famous Canadian artist photographer, Courtney Milne. Mr. Milne reported at the LIVEH$_2$O concert this image produced miracles in Water, as might be expected given the "MIracle 6" 528 component.

Figure 34. Proof of Water Throughout Space

NASA photograph of evaporating ice particles in the tail and surrounding the nucleus of Comet Hyakutake. This proves Water abounds throughout space and the entire universe in various phases. Investigators conclude this Water is the matter from which cosmic bodies crystallize.

greenish-yellow molecule, also structurally reflecting 528, takes the input electrons, vibrating in 528, and outputs oxygen, likewise resonating in 528. The 528-resonating oxygen feeds every cell in your body. This is how LOVE actually sustains your life.

This LOVE vibe is meant to be in your body, and makes you "one for all and all for one;" whole and complete with the creative spirit of sunshine. "On Earth as it is in Heaven" affirms the matrix of universal intelligence, or God-consciousness, and is available to you by choice. (Seek and you will find; ask and you will receive.)

You have the option to access the Source of wisdom and unconditional LOVE through your heart. "As above, so below." So choose to receive 528, and you will know true LOVE.

Moreover, Figure 30 proves that 528 is critical to Rodin's "Infinity Pattern" that sources all the Family Number Groups that he proved creates the Master Matrix and the double toroid structure the universe, and subsequently Phi and Pi. This proves 528 is not only fundamental to universal structuring and measurements, but that your DNA is actually connected to space/time!

This scientific and mathematical proof demonstrates conclusively that there is nothing more powerful, and nothing more important on the Creator's heart and colorful creative palate, than LOVE in 528.

Knowledge in this book evidences that enlightenment, or spiritual transformation, is best acquired and broadcast musically in 528Hz harmony, now easily accessible at i528Tunes.

Musical mathematics creates the rules by which this "Game of Life" is played. So this intelligence was hidden, guarded, and abused by those who create dissonance and division between God and man, man and nature, and between humans.

Sages, prophets, and especially alchemists throughout time knew this truth that you are now acquiring.

In fact, this musical-mathematical know-how for spiritual ascendency became the most guarded secret in the world, valued above all possessions, by the Illuminati.

The Genetic Code and Musical Math

On May 20, 2010, J. Craig Venter, who stole the Human Genome Project from the public domain on behalf of George Soros and his Quantum Fund investors in Celera Genomics, pronounced he had created artificial life. The Illuminati's news media then heralded, "God is dead."(14)

This book definitively debunks such "PharmaWhores," and proves that God and LOVE is very much alive.

Figures 30 and 31 show the structure of DNA is the repeating pattern of spiraling units that make up genetic strands, formed in the image of simple mathematical patterns. This is additional evidence that life sources from God's word, which is sound, or frequencies broadcasting simple math.

Moreover, DNA spirals in a sea of Water that is structurally triangulated and hexagonally-shaped according to Phi and 528Hz resonance that structures water with LOVE. The double helix, that receives and transmits light and sound signals, also vibrates sounds that harmonize with nature.

Theoretically, DNA resonance that is "phase locked" in harmony with 528 in the Master Matrix yields the essence of "enlightenment" and perfect genetic expression.

The material precipitation of DNA orchestrating "biology" musically, features the sacred geometry of hexagonal organic chemistry requiring 528Hz frequency.

As explained by Müller(3), each of 6 formative nodes in the Standing Gravitational Wave emanates energy in all dimensions forcing global or universal scaling. Visualizing these vibrational energies within and around each DNA strand, and the universe at large, facilitates understanding of the (cymatic) forces crystallizing physical reality, as further detailed in Figures 30-32.

Imagine the force of the Perfect Circle of Sound™—the cosmic frequencies and their interactions—creating the structure of the universe. Then imagine the three dimensional tetrahedron-shaped Water molecules hydrating every nook and cranny of your body, especially your DNA, being Divinely-energized, especially during sleep, by this scalar orchestra.

These cosmically-connected Water molecules flow into the shape of Solomon's Seal (the "Star of David") and the Merkaba, (a nine-pointed star reflecting the ancient sun symbol) because Water molecules cluster for optimal "communion" or energetic (and even electrogenetic) function.

All of these energy dynamics involve "patterns" of math. In fact, all sacred geometry does likewise. Everything flows hydrosonically and vibrationally into physical reality. The carbon-6 ring in organic chemistry demonstrates this obviously, now that we know so much about 528 in cosmic design.

This is also the case in the natural construction of DNA—a spiraling circle of chemistry, manifested from simple musical math, featuring 528Hz at its heart.

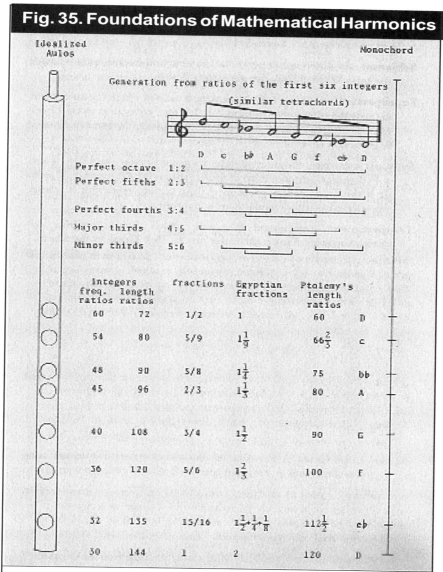

Fig. 35. Foundations of Mathematical Harmonics

According to Ernest G. McClain, this figure represents the "Foundations of Mathematical Harmonics." It presents the "equivalent representations of the basic Hindu-Greek scale (Ptolemy's Diatonic Syntonon). Notice the integers generally reduce to 3s, 6s or 9s. (Source: McClain EG. *The Myth of Invariance*. York Beach, ME: Nicholas-Hays, Inc. 1984, pg. xxii.)

Fig. 36. The "Pythagorean Comma Crisis"

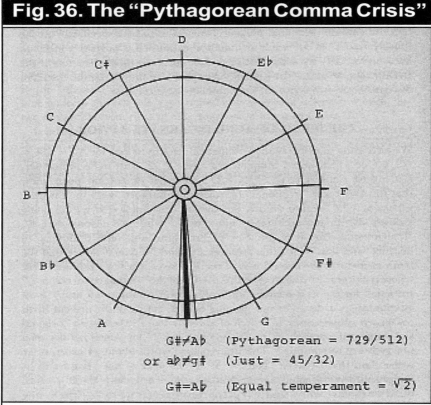

G#≠A♭ (Pythagorean = 729/512)

or a♭≠g# (Just = 45/32)

G#=A♭ (Equal temperament = √2)

McClain's figure depicts the discrepancy plaguing music and calendars since the time of Pythagoras. Something is "off." There is a division, shown at the bottom of the circle. A "comma" divides a sentence. A "Pythagorean Comma" divides the world of space/time measurement. Calendars, for instance, require "leap-year" corrections. So measurement, and even music, is not quite "in tune," "in sync," or "in harmony" with nature and the laws of physics. In McClain's words, "Pythagorean tuning is . . . an approximation to Equal-temperament. The cumulative discrepancy of 2 cents in each perfect 11th or fourth reaches a crisis *in the middle of the octave* at A flat ≠ G sharp. . . . The excess of 24 cents in 'Pythagorean tuning' just about matches the defect of 22 cents in 'Just tuning.'. . . [This is] "the 'Pythagorean comma.' [It is] too small for use as a melodic interval, [it becomes] nearly subliminal under most circumstances as to invite our glossing over it, yet painfully present to an awakened consciousness in search of absolute truth." Emphasis added. (McClain, *Ibid.*, pg. 83.)

Fig. 37. 528 is at the Heart of the "Crisis"

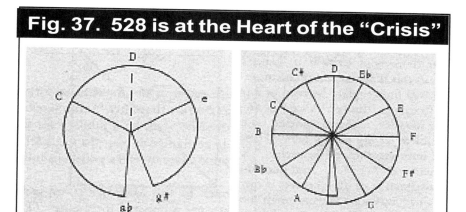

These two McClain figures additionally depict "Tonal and Calendrical Commas," or what's "off" with our calendar and music. The left graph shows the "deficiency in 364-day period of twelve lunations (each musical third symbolizing four semitone 'months')"; while the right graph shows the "excess of the solar year over the calendar base."

McClain wrote that the right graph shows "pure fourths and fifths of Pythagorean tuning—a better approximation to equal-temperament— lead to the **Pythagorean comma of a ratio of 531441 : 524288**, the ratio by which A-flat and G-sharp overlap, worth about 24 cents or 3/10 x 24 = 7.2 degrees. This "solar" tuning . . . has a mandala excess roughly comparable to the excess of the 365½-day solar year over the 360-day calendar base," and 360 degree circle. "Any tuning by the 'pure' ratios of integers would lead to tone spirals rather than tone cycles comparable to those in Just and Pythagorean tuning." .[Emphasis added.] (McClain, ibid., pg. 96-7.)

This "crisis" is due to the use of "irrational numbers" imposed by the Illuminati, not God or nature. (See Figures 36 and 38 for more details.)

Now look at the emphasized numbers in the Pythagorean comma. They represent, as shown in the right figure, the overlap between the ascending and descending scale at the 6 o'clock position on the circle. The discrepancy is 24-cents. (That is a "MIracle 6.") This is the mid-point along the circumference of the circle, and the "crisis in the middle of the octave," McClain stated.

Since half way between the numbers 531.441 and 524.288 is 527.85, or just about 528, it supports my thesis that 528 lies at the heart of everything, including the heart of string theory, physics, universal mathematical laws, music, and now even the "Pythagorean comma!"

This shows you that 528 is what is missing from an "irrational" world "gone mad," the *heart* of time/space and music has been *hidden*.

Harmonic combinations of frequencies form major, minor, augmented or diminished triads that resonate physical reality into order. This respects the Supreme Law of the universe— the Master Matrix of music. These chords of creation move material matter into physical forms or crystallizations. The manifestation of matter flows along paths of least resistance. Alternatively, "string theorists" say vibrating strings resonate all matter into existence.

"String Theory" and The Perfect Circle of Sound™

We used the Perfect Circle of Sound™ icon in Figure 33 to create "The Water Resonator," (See: TheWaterResonator. com) which projects the nine core frequencies of creation into the atmosphere of the room, or into the Water in a crystalline glass or plastic container to which it is applied.

This logo provides a positive affirmation of the greatest truth in history:

You are a digital bioholographic precipitation, crystallization, miraculous manifestation of Divine LOVE vibrations coming out of Water.

You come into this life naturally with gratitude from The Perfect Circle of Sound™, with LOVE/528 resonating throughout your body and spiritual being. When you die, your spirit, consciousness, or soul returns back to this Kingdom of Heaven.

The Perfect Circle of Sound™ helps advance the string theory in physics— a developing hypothesis that attempts to reconcile quantum mechanics, general relativity, and physical reality.(7) In this regard, you might consider the universe like a nine string musical instrument.

Sting theory "is a contender for the theory of everything," explains *Wikipedia,* "a manner of describing the known fundamental forces and matter in a mathematically complete system."(8)

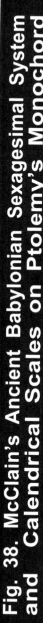
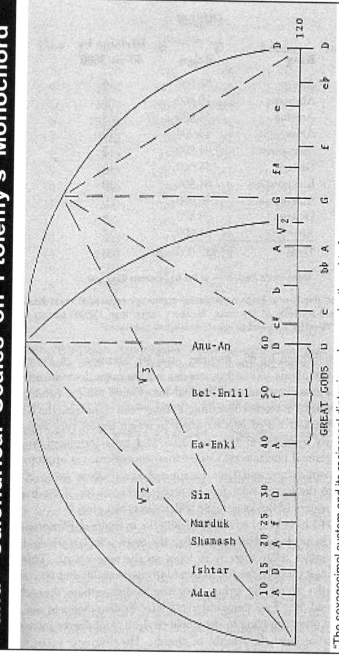

Fig. 38. McClain's Ancient Babylonian Sexagesimal System and Calendrical Scales on Ptolemy's Monochord

"The sexagesimal system and its reciprocal diatonic scales can be thought of as generated by the first six ["rational"] integers (1,2,3,4,5,6 = "days of creation), or by the "Great Gods" 40:50:60 = 4,5,6, or by the prime numbers 2, 3, and 5. Since 60 = "1" unit radius of the circle, the diameter = 2 = 120. Sexagesimal fractions of "minutes" and "seconds" are equivalent in decimal arithmetic for a multiplication 120 x 60 = 432,000 [Editor's note: This is among the reasons Dr. Horowitz believes 432Hz, that Showell proves is related to 528Hz in universal design, may be helpful for "healing music."]. 432 is the least common denominator if fractions are avoided generating irrational numbers. (McClain, *Ibid.*, pg. 137.)

217

String theory posits that particles—electrons and quarks—within atoms are 1-dimensional oscillating lines, or "strings." The most advanced "superstring theories," assert that strings are really vibrating in multi-dimensional space.

String theorists commonly use guitar strings to illustrate this point. The cosmic strings vibrate like a guitar string, producing multiple but distinct musical notes as you move up and down the string. In this analogy, different notes correspond to different particles. In reality, string theorists say, "the strings could vibrate in any direction, meaning that the particles could move through not only our dimension, but other dimensions as well."(8)

Regarding the importance of natural scaling according to the 3s, 6s, and 9s, *Wikipedia* reported, "on distance scales larger than the string radius, each oscillation mode behaves as a different species of particle, with its mass, spin and charge determined by the string's dynamics." Splitting and recombining strings corresponds to particle emissions and absorptions, "giving rise to the interactions between particles."(8)

So literally, string theory explains the manifestation of physical reality resulting from musical arithmetic and the Universal Orchestra's impact on light and sound signals.

These are called photons and phonons, respectively, in the world of biophysics. DNA receives and transmits these signals ultimately materializing your body parts, like you are being beamed energetically into this reality.

This hydroacoustic creation system also creates inorganic particles. String theorists go so far as asserting that particles actually transform their physical properties based on the vibrations of the strings.

In essence, what may have seemed "far-fetched" to some people, is being advanced by world leading astrophysicists and biophysicists.

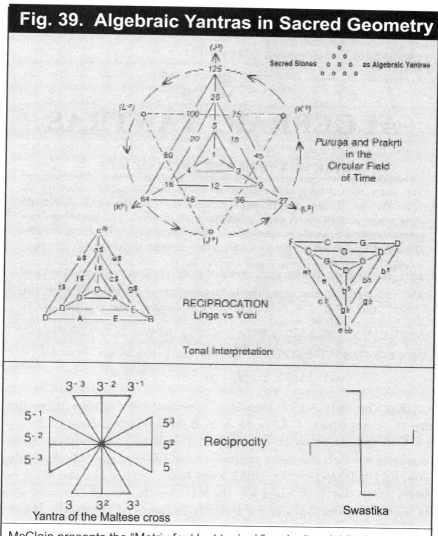

Fig. 39. Algebraic Yantras in Sacred Geometry

McClain presents the "Matrix for 'Just tuning'," and a "model for logarithmic sequences generated by any three rational numbers (J, K, L) prime to each other. Reciprocation of integers by unit fractions (1/n) correlates with rotation by 180 degrees." He thus derives sacred geometry from musical-mathematics as shown above. The Illuminati have used these symbols also. "Yantras of the cross and swastika suggest routes transversible by 'Egyptian' operations (using doubling, halving, and unit fractions)," McClain wrote. (McClain, *Ibid.*, pp. 44, 74.) Every triangular subset has the same relations as in the star-hexagon shown above.

The Myth of Invariance

Now let's look at the amazing contributions provided by the world's leading expert in the field of musical-mathematics and its impact on civilizations—Ernest G. McClain. He wrote a book about "harmonical analysis" called, *The Myth of Invariance: The Origin of the Gods, Mathematics and Music From the Rg Veda to Plato.*(9)

The purpose of harmonical analysis, according to McClain, is to synthesize "the tonal, arithmetical, and geometrical imagery of ancient civilizations. It aims at the reconstruction of the esoteric diagrams which gave the sacred symbols of particular cultures their enduring and magical powers, and furnished philosophy with a ground of certainty."

McClain's scholarship is largely represented in Figures 35-39, accompanied by explanatory legends. Considering alternative tunings, McClain's research of ancient civilization offers compelling evidence that 528Hz may be the answer to the "nagging problem" in musicology noted by every expert. That is, the "***Pythagorean Comma***."

The Pythagorean Comma

A "comma," in punctuation, is "used to indicate the separation of elements" in sentences.

A "comma" in music refers to a separation of mathematical congruity between notes in the same scale. Metaphorically, the Pythagorean Comma interrupts the cosmic concert.

But how can you interrupt universal creation? Something does not add up!

The Pythagorean Comma is this separation between what is real, or "rational," versus what is "just a bit off," or "irrational" in math and science.

The <u>Pythagorean Comma is defined as:</u> "the ratio <u>524288:531441</u>," by which A-flat and G-sharp overlap, "worth about 24 cents. . ."

In other words, there is 24 = 2 + 4 = 6 missing, about "6" musical cents in every scale of music or man-made measures of space/time.

<u>AND, this approximates 528</u>, considering half way between 524288 and 531441. This is 527804, or rounded off becomes 528000.

Recall that there are 5280 feet in a measured mile.

To understand the astonishing significance of this, you need to fathom the "nagging problem" of "irrationality" in the 364 day lunar calendar, and difference between ancient and modern Pi and Phi, as Showell detailed in Chapter 3.

The Pythagorean Comma proposes that we can remedy the inaccuracy of our space/time measurements to live as nature does, in sync with Divine reality, not the Illuminati's hypocrisy.

The Pythagorean Comma measures the irrationality of the chromatic musical scale, as opposed to the rationality of using whole numbers and whole number ratios in the diatonic scale. McClain actually references this as "a *key*" to unlock this door to the heart of the crisis. A crisis in thought neglected and secreted by the Illuminati.

In McClain's words:

"As our study unfolds it will raise serious questions about the early development of mathematical thinking, about debts which the calendar and scale may owe to each other, and about the possible origins of both the mathematics of music and its related mythology. They are among the many questions we cannot answer satisfactorily as long as a vast amount of archaeological material lies in disarray, unexamined or still undecipherable, much of it untranslated, and as long as a considerable amount of the surviving literature of classical times still remains inaccessible for want of a *key*. Historians of science have barely begun to cope with certain kinds of material available to them, and we must await their judgment on many issues. A musical analysis of Rgvedic imagery will provide, we believe, a new tool for the study of the origins of science, of our calendar, of musical theory, and of the roots of our civilization."[Emphasis added.](9)

McClain is describing problems neglected by the controllers of the arts and sciences. Indeed, this identifies the use of dogmatic "propositions in logic or mathematics that are *assumed* without proof for the sake of studying consequences" that are urgent today. Civilization and nature are now under deadly attacks by Illuminati overlords that have managed to deceive the brightest minds in academia for control over the mass mind.

McClain's remorse over a key to this sacred intelligence is remedied by this publication and the 528LOVERevolution.

The Monochord Model of the Universe

Modern string theorists follow in the tradition of ancient monochord alchemists.

The monochord—a single stringed instrument with a movable bridge—was used to experiment with different notes, harmonics, or nodes along the string. Experiments to study natural harmony in math ratios of whole notes, such as 1:2 as you move the bridge along the vibrating string, were performed this way over the millennia.

McClain quotes Plato as saying, "the tyrant is 729 times as bad as the good man." What does this mean?

Plato's statement about evil versus good men evidences the theory that human personalities are similarly scaled along a linear axis or "string," Thus, destiny is influenced musically-mathematically, like everything else. This may be the best evidence, and explaination, for God's knowledge of you before your birth and after death.

In other words, according to rational numbers, that is natural, not man-made or mentally contrived *irrational numbers*, personalities might be measured along a monochord scale, or string, of vibrational probabilities. One man might be measured "729 times as bad as the good man."

Plato's statement assumes there is a cosmic polarity of good vs. bad that dynamically affects the expression of goodness or evil in people. Such a positive and negative scale, or even "string," would affect personalities, even destinies, during human development as discussed in the previous chapter.

528 and Zero Point

What if the string was shaped like the figure "8"? What if the top half of the string was generating positive energy, and the bottom polarity was radiating negative energy.

This vision is consistent with physicist Nassim Harramein's double toroidal universe construction that takes into consideration polarity shifts within a continuous 8-like design, as shown in Figure 29. Here, the upper torus circulates in one direction, while the lower one flows in the opposite direction.

McClain, whose works preceded those of string theorists, provides astonishing evidence that 528 may be a pivotal point between positive and negative polarities, like that one spot *at the heart* of the figure "8" where two energy vectors, or the "string paths," cross.

Physicists talk about "zero point energy," or the "event horizon," wherein physical material manifests from pure potential called the "quantum field." I propose that 528 is uniquely linked to this portal, considering it: 1) resonates at the heart of everything; 2) is the "MIracle 6" note of creation; 3) is symbolized by the "6"—that appears like a downward spiral into a "whole note" or circle—depicting the whole earth, "Circle of

Life," and earthly materialization; 4) represents the heart of the "problem" of the Pythagorean Comma; and 5) represents the solution to the "mathematical problem" or dilemma created by the SO note.

In Chapter 3, I also shared my theory that the decimal point separating whole numbers from fractions represents a point along a "string" that suddenly shifts the scale and energy one magnitude. This was evidenced by Estes and Walton's experiments with 8, 88, and 88.8Hz frequency music. Only the 88.8 dramatically impacted the energy of the sound and musical experience, imparting the feeling of a spinning vortex.

Indeed, the Illuminati, has stewarded civilization's evolution into ignorance for centuries. It has secreted and circumvented these mathematical certainties and theories. Tragically, as a result, humanity has neglected nature's innate mathematical and musical intelligence and fundamental invariance.

They created the octave, along with the irrationally divided chromatic scale. No wonder there is a "nagging problem" with music being less than "real." It feels "unnatural;" disharmonious with nature, and distressing.

This is perceived by sensitive musicians who listen to alternative tunings such A=432 (discussed later), or A=444 (that presents C(5) at 528Hz). This music commonly creates "ecstatic listening."

Recovering Ecstasy

"A vibrating sting of any reference length can be halved to sound the octave higher or doubled to sound the octave lower," McClain also explained.(9)

"Since all tones recur cyclically at the octave—as the 'Same' tone in one sense, but a 'Different' tone in another— any octave can serve as the model for all possible octaves, at least for the general purposes of tuning theory. The cyclic structure of the octave is the *invariant* common to all systems of tuning. The tone-circle functions as a cyclic matrix within which derivative tones come to birth."

McClain emphasizes the word *"invariant* common to all systems of tuning,"* because the earliest civilizations, including the Sumarians and Babylonians, used other-than-octave scales.

Some of these, including A=444Hz or 88.8Hz, produces results you can feel or sense, with the optimal result producing a sense of euphoria, universal harmony, or ecstasy.

According to *Music Cognition Handbook: A Dictionary of Concepts*, by David Huron, "On occasion music will elicit a sensation of 'shivers' localized in the back, neck and shoulders of an aroused listener—a physiological response technically called *frisson*."

"The frisson experience normally has a duration of no more than four or five seconds," much like a "kundalini rush" during which energy travels up the spine causing *shivers*.

Huron technically described frisson as follows:

"It begins as a flexing of the skin in the lower back, rising upward, inward from the shoulders, up the neck, and sometimes across to the cheeks and onto the scalp. The face may become flush, hair follicles flex the hairs into standing position, and goose bumps may appear [technically termed "piloerections" and "horripilations"]. Frequently, a series of 'waves' will rise up the back in rapid succession. The listener feels the music to have elicited an ecstatic moment and tends to regard the experience as involuntary.(10)

"Goldstein (1980) has shown that some listeners report reduced excitement when under a clinically-administered dose of an opiate receptor antagonist, naloxone—suggesting that music engenders endogenous opioid peptides characteristic of pleasurable experiences. Sloboda (1991) has found evidence linking "shivers" responses to works especially *loved* by subjects."[Emphasis added.](10)

Theoretically, frisson may be caused by the energy "rushing" from phase-locking your heart, resonating with the LOVE frequency of 528Hz, with the fundamental vibration of creation, or pure consciousness, generating ecstasy.

It makes sense that 528Hz sound, like 528nm light vibrating biology bioacoustically and electromagnetically, produces ecstatic listening and frisson, just as creation is administered by this most natural music.

Holy Harmony

Thousands of people have listened ecstatically to the Holy Harmony CD by Jonathan Goldman recorded in the Perfect Circle of Sound™, and Scott Huckabay's live concert CDs recorded in 528Hz.(11, 12)

Goldman's experimental classic using the progressive sequence of the original Solfeggio set of 6 pure tones expressly encouraged ecstatic listening. To begin his project, he produced a tuning fork set (available from HealthyWorldStore. com) to guide vocals. He struck the forks in an ascending manner, chanting the Hebrew letters of the Messiah's name, to generate a flow of energy up the spine, intending healing by balancing the chakras. His loving labor has worked wonders for thousands of listeners.(11)

Goldman intuited the use of these forks in this particular manner creates a sacred spiral that "seems to encode itself as a matrix upon the cellular structure, and particularly on the DNA. . . . I believe this is the matrix of the 'higher' human, helping create an evolutionary step in our genetic encoding," he wrote.(5)

Goldman further reported that these tones, when used in ascending or descending order, seem to have the ability to nullify any frequencies that are counter productive to our highest good. He was discerning entraining the chakra system with the matrix math of creation.

Goldman theorized these frequencies create a blanket of Divine sounds that may counter the effects of "harmful energy" that give rise to bacteria and viral diseases. His thesis paralleled the early work of Antoine Bechamp regarding the germ theory of infectious diseases.(13)

"The frequencies," Goldman proposed, "likely nullify and dissipate disharmonious energies that may be trying to establish themselves upon our physical, mental, emotional or spiritual essences; into what we call stress and disease.

"It has been our great pleasure to bear witness to people who have told us astounding stories of healing that occurred simply through listening to *Holy Harmony*. We can also testify that health care practitioners have recorded extraordinary transformational and healing experiences with clients while using the *Holy Harmony* CD and/or tuning forks."(5)

Given what we now know about the musical-mathematics of creation, and the crystallization of physical matter from pure potential energy of flowing electrons the Bible calls "ether," Goldman had unwittingly described *phase locking* the human to the Divine. This is the antecedent of ecstatic listening, frisson, and establishing peace on Earth.

Figure 40. Crystals of Protein and Viruses Grown By Scientists in Micro-gravity Space

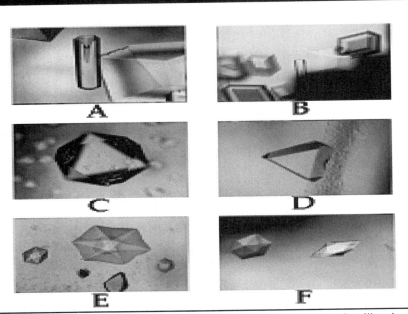

Using God's vibrational technology and sacred geometry the Illuminati is risking humanity's health and safety. Scientists are growing crystal viruses and proteins in space that could kill the human race and potentially other species. These NASA photos are magnified 40x, and reinforce knowledge that Water is the universal creative medium. Matter crystallizes and flows universally in "Spirit/Water" due to gravitational forces and frequencies of sound moving atomic and molecular matter along paths, or "strings," of least resistance. Focal points for matter's natural manifestation and movement are Müller's ln(6) logarithmic nodes, or sets of frequencies. All atomic and molecular matter naturally flows into sacred geometric forms this way. Healing is fundamentally accomplished likewise. Healing advances harmonically, as matter remanifests, including DNA strands, proteins, and cells. In essence, healing is recrystallization in harmony with the primordial state.

Here, NASA scientists help disease industrialists create "alien" pathogens, including the Epstein-Barr viral-carcinogen. They bring these back to Earth for disease research, NASA says. As reasonably intelligent people celebrate intelligent designs, demented doctors and so-called scientists, risk global depopulation and extinction. Faithful prayer to the Creator with LOVE in 528Hz frequency is a far better investment than this industry. Manufacturing alien viruses is demonically insane. Photos from: http://liftoff.msfc.nasa.gov/Shuttle/ms/overview/apcf.html#3.

References

1) Personal communication from anonymous biophysicist regarding derivations of musical harmonics from planetary orbits. From this analysis, it is determined that the "A" note in the standard scale (220 and 440Hz) is different from the Zodiac Moon frequency (227.44 and 454.88); the Full Moon frequency (210.25 and 420.50); Earth Year (272.204 and 544.408); Mars frequency (289.43); Saturn frequency (294.87) Jupiter frequency (367.22) and Uranus frequency (414.74). The source concludes, however, that irrational numbers "do not resonate properly with each other. Only integers and integer fractions can resonate perfectly. . . . This is called 'phase locking.'"

2) Müller H. *Theory of Global Scaling*. Sante Fe: NM: Institute for Space-Energy-Research, Leonard Euler, Ltd. and Global Scaling Applications, Inc., 2002.

3) Personal communication with Marko Rodin. See: http://markorodin. com. Quotes from Randy Powell, Advanced Vortex Math, derive from his TedXCharlotte, 2010, presentation available on YouTube, here: http://www.youtube.com/watch?v=c1hLzQPio_8&feature=player_embedded

4) Horowitz L and Puleo J. *Healing Codes for the Biological Apocalypse*. Sandpoint, ID: Tetrahedron Publishing Group, 1999.

5) Personal communication from Jonathan Goldman, Boulder, CO, who created *Holy Harmony* and the Perfect Circle of Sound Tuning Fork set available through HealthyWorldStore.com; 1-888-508-4787.

6) Haramein N and Rauscher EA. The origin of spin: A consideration of torque and coriolis forces in Eisnstein's field equations and Grand Unification Theory. *Special Issue of the Noetic Journal* Vol. 6 No. 1-4 June, 2005, pp. 143-162. ISSN 1528-3739.

7) Mukhi S. The Theory of Strings: A Detailed Introduction. Internet publication: http://theory.tifr.res.in/~mukhi/Physics/string2.html

8) Wikipedia. String Theory: http://en.Wikipedia.org/wiki/String_theory#cite_note-0

9) McClain EG. *The Myth of Invariance: The Origin of the Gods, Mathematics and Music From the Rg Veda to Plato*. York Beach, ME: Nicolas-Hays, Inc., 1984.

10) Huron D. *Music Cognition Handbook: A Dictionary of Concepts*. Ohio State University, Music Cognition Resource Center.See: http://www. musiccog.ohio-state.edu/Resources/Handbook/index.html#ecstatic%20 listening

11) Goldman J. *Holy Harmony* CD. Boulder, CO: Healing Sounds, Inc. The CD may be ordered here: http://www.HealthyWorldStore.com/Holy-Harmony-CD-p/hharm.htm;

12) Huckabay, S. LIVELOVEin528 CD. See the music section of Healthy World Store at: http://www.HealthyWorldStore.com, or call 1-888-508-4787.

13) LaLeva.org provides an outstanding review of the history of the germ theory of disease, and the corruption of medicine by Louis Pasteur on behalf of the Illuminati, here: http://www.laleva.org/eng/2004/05/louis_pasteur_vs_antoine_bchamp_and_the_germ_theory_of_disease_causation_1.html

14) Cook M. Synthetic life or cellular machine? *Australian Science.* July-August, 2010. See: ://webcache.googleusercontent.com/search?q=cache:fV3tf8WKQUAJ:www.australasianscience.com.au/article/issue-july-august-2010/synthetic-life-or-cellular-machine.html+venter+god+is+dead&cd=10&hl=en&ct=clnk&gl=us&client=safari&source=www.google.com

Chapter Ten:
Healing with 528/LOVE Vibrations

T he Western World has been paralyzed by dissonance on every level as outlined in the previous
chapters. I have explained how and why this condition was achieved on behalf of the Illuminati—a small group of
wealthy powerful thugs—controlling money, the mainstream
media (including the music industry), BigPharma, the energy
cartel, as well as China's and Russia's evolution into quasi-
capitalism from strict communism. Clearly the Eastern World
is being influenced by the Western World, including its music.

I have heralded a way out of the mess featuring music
tuned to nature, particularly 528Hz frequency. This can phase-
lock humanity back to optimal integrity between body, mind,
and spirit.

The concept that LOVE, the "Universal Healer" resonating
at 528Hz, can miraculously manifest this return to health and
cure pandemic spiritual degeneration and paralysis, was also
presented.

This frank assertion is like the story of Jesus healing a
paralyzed man in *Mark* 2. The positive result astonished the
naysayers, including Jesus's enemies. Here is the passage
simply worded from *The Complete Jewish Bible*:

> Yeshua returned [and] word spread that he was back. So
> many people gathered around the house that there was no
> longer any room, not even in front of the door. While he was
> preaching the message to them, four men came to him car-
> rying a paralyzed man. They could not get near Yeshua be-
> cause of the crowd, so they stripped the roof over the place
> where he was, made an opening, and lowered the stretcher
> with the paralytic lying on it. Seeing their trust, Yeshua said
> to the paralyzed man, "Son, your sins are forgiven." Some

Torah-teachers sitting there thought to themselves, "How can this fellow say such a thing? He is blaspheming! Who can forgive sins except God?" But immediately Yeshua, perceiving in his spirit what they were thinking, said to them, "Why are you thinking these things? Which is easier to say to the paralyzed man? `Your sins are forgiven'? or `Get up, pick up your stretcher and walk'? But look! I will prove to you that the Son of Man has authority on earth to forgive sins." He then said to the paralytic, "I say to you: get up, pick up your stretcher and go home!" In front of everyone the man got up, picked up his stretcher at once and left. . . .

And here is an equally important part of the story:

As he passed on from there, he saw Levi Ben-Halfai sitting in his tax-collection booth and said to him, "Follow me!" And he got up and followed him. . . . As Yeshua was in Levi's house eating, many tax-collectors and sinners were sitting with Yeshua and his talmidim, for there were many of them among his followers. When the Torah-teachers and the P'rushim saw that he was eating with sinners and tax-collectors, they said to his talmidim, "Why does he eat with tax-collectors and sinners?" But, hearing the question, Yeshua answered them, "The ones who need a doctor aren't the healthy but the sick. I didn't come to call the `righteous' but sinners!"

In other words, the "righteous" never need healing, because they are standing correctly within The Law of the Kingdom of Heaven wherein nothing is missing or broken.

The foremost definition of "righteous" is *justice* (or "just-ice," or "just is;" that is, pure Being).

The word *forgiven* derives from "fore given." Given is the past tense of the verb to "give." The act of sin in this case is <u>in the past</u>, or not in the *NOW*, like pure Being just is!

The first definition of the word *fore* is "*obsolete*; at an earlier time or period," meaning the sin in this matter is no longer relevant.

What is relevant, according to Jesus's teachings, is **LOVE, in the NOW**.

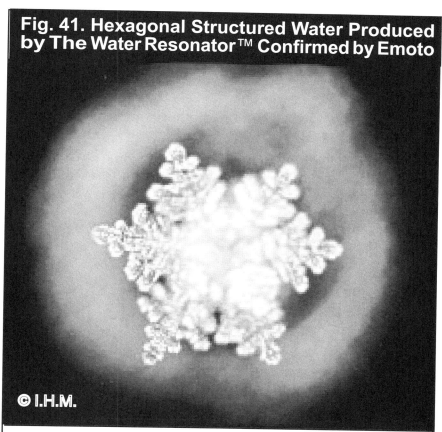

Fig. 41. Hexagonal Structured Water Produced by The Water Resonator™ Confirmed by Emoto

© I.H.M.

Japanese Water researcher Dr. Masaru Emoto evaluated the impact of The Water Resonator™, on the micro-clustering of Water. The resonator is manufactured using metalic paint layered upon mylar film resonated by 528Hz frequency sound and high powered magnets. Emoto exposed distilled Water to The Water Resonator for 24 hours. Then, the Water was flash frozen and studied under 20,000 magnification for its geometric design and qualities, including unique "messages." A very large halo surrounding this crystal is unique. It suggests this Water radiates a lot of light. In this case, the hexagonal ring, much like the design of snowflakes, indicates a natural frequency is radiating out strongly into the Water. The 528Hz frequency, wherein 5+2+8=15=1+5=6, appears to have imparted the sacred geometry of a snowflake. This represents millions of molecules of H_2O combining as directed by the force of gravity and resonant energy of 528Hz frequency. Photo courtesy of Dr. Masaru Emoto. To read more about Dr. Emoto's work order: *The Message from Water*, Tokyo: Hadu Publishing, 2008.

LOVE, the "Universal Healer," is the frequency of *just-ice*—righteous solid Spirit/Water—in sync with the The Law of the musical-mathematical matrix—otherwise called the *Kingdom of Heaven*. This is the wisdom Jesus faithfully celebrated by telling the paralyzed man his sins were forgiven as a function of faithfully loving God and his brothers and sisters in our Divine family.

This book's intended audience is the same as those who needed Jesus's counsel: sinners, tax-collectors, teachers, and others sick and enslaved by false doctrines, faithlessness, and paralyzing fears.

In the above story, as always, faith is the *key* that opens loving hearts. The people's faith moved the "Son of Man" to simply and boldly celebrate the *truth*—the paralyzed man was well enough to get up and walk home, once he believed his sins were forgiven. Then the restorative energy flowed as it always does from Heaven.

The level of faith in a mustard seed can move mountains, Jesus said. It is by faith, he claimed, that every one of his followers were healed.

If you consider sin, as discussed previously, as simply being out of sync with The Law—the Matrix of Divine Truth—then you realize that all disease manifests from this fundamental dissonance. In essence, illnesses are conditions triggered by faithless arrogance and irreverence to God.

When you lack heart-felt faith and respect for your sustainer, you become an outlaw to universal justice. You disconnect from the Source and, metaphorically, the spiritual kingdom ceases to recharge your batteries. Metaphysically, your stress and depleted energy quickly invites dis-ease because the loving, protective, and restorative energy of Divine harmony can no longer reach you metaphysically.

Fig. 42. The Difference Between Polluted and Structured Water is Largely LOVE/528

These photomicrographs of Water were all taken at 20,000 magnification by Dr. Masaru Emoto. Left side photos show the hexagonal-shaped, snowflake-like, Water structures associated with healing or "Holy Water." Dr. Emoto's co-investigator, Dr. Lee Lorenzen, concluded "clustered" Waters maintain energy signatures suitable for optimal electro-genetic (DNA) function, longevity, and healing. These Waters differ significantly from polluted Water shown on the right below.

Water polluted by chemical toxins such as chlorine and fluoride, pesticides, or heavy metals, lose their sacred geometric Water rings, and their vibrant energy signatures. Following municipal Water "treatment," drinking Water appears like raw sewage, as shown here. Dr. Emoto learned that Water structuring also depends on human consciousness and positive intention transmitted by prayers, certain music (e.g., 528Hz), or chants.

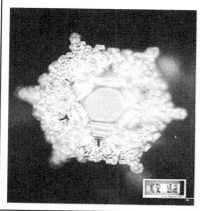

Water that is prayed over with loving or positive intent enhances its structuring. The photo on the left demonstrates this amazing aqueous ability. Alternatively, geometrically structured Water cursed verbally, or exposed to dissonant/chaotic modern "music," grossly degerates into muddy structures like that seen in the photo above. For more information, read Dr. Masaru Emoto's book, *The Message from Water*, Tokyo: Hadu Publishing, 2001.

Figure 43. Electromagnetic Functions of DNA & Clustered Water On Cellular Metabolic and Structural Upregulation

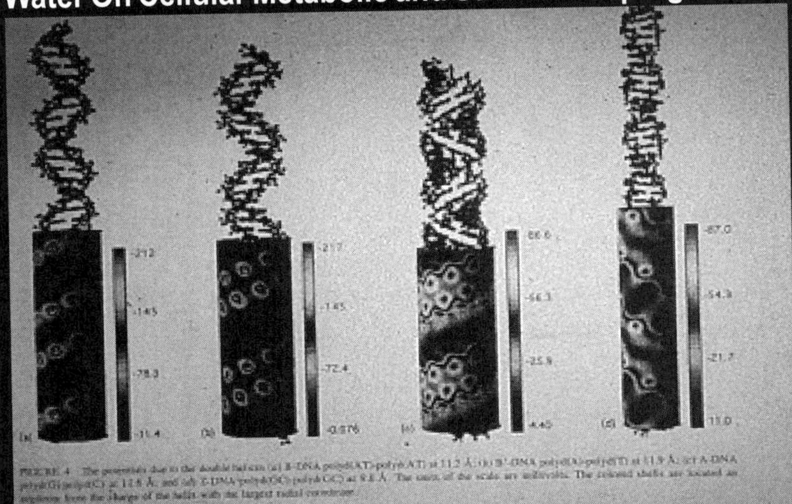

Electrical potentials in millivolts of adequately hydrated DNA are shown in the figures above. Saykally et. al, showed small clustered water rings, mostly six-sided, facilitate electromagnetic transmissions to and from the double helix.

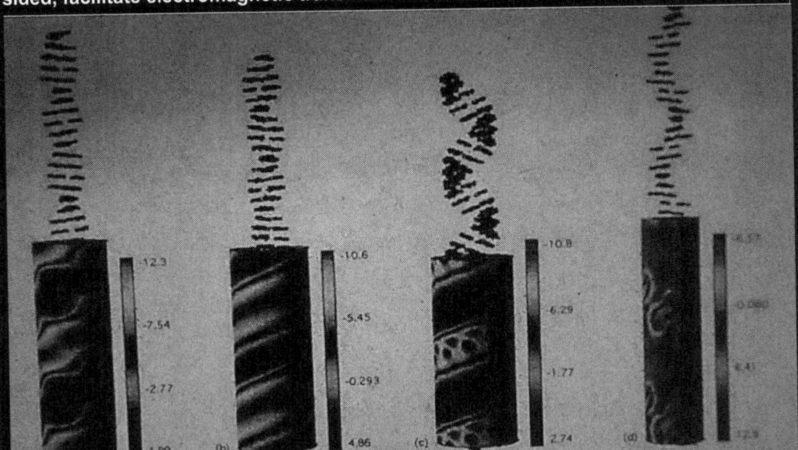

The figures above show the results of water cluster dehydration on DNA, and resulting drops in millivolt potentials degrading cell signaling (i.e., frequency upregulation for structural integrity and metabolic functioning). Besides greater electrical potentials, the upper figure clearly shows more pronounced frequency transmissions reflected in the well formed patterns in the associated radial photographs. Source: K Liu, JD Cruzan and RJ Saykally. Water Clusters. *Science* (16 Feb) 1996;271:929-931.

Sound and Light Signaling From Heaven

Signs of spiritual well-being include robust physical health and energy. Your body and spirit exchange energy, and all healing is accomplished by the Holy Spirit, not drugs or chemistry.

Sound and light signaling within your body sources similarly from the musical-mathematical matrix of Divine frequencies. Increasingly, these facts of nature are being proven.

For instance, in a study of DNA in relation to cosmic (i.e., circadian) rhythms, stress, and organism development, a team of Dartmouth Medical School scholars determined that lunar cycles and light frequencies impacted at least six genes responsible for protein synthesis, organism metabolism, genetic repair and healing.(1)

Japanese biophysicist, T. Ueta, considered light and sound interactions knowing that energy electrons follow the force of acoustic waves and are measurable. From this, a mathematical equation governing the interaction between photon and phonon energy was determined.(2)

To help explain how light-sound signaling transmits through your body, that is, through the layers of liquid crystal making up the lattice, or hydrated matrix, through which genetic signaling occurs, Ueta concluded,

When lattice vibration is introduced, the lattice vibration does not only generate the waves with various frequencies but also amplifies the incident wave resonantly. On a resonance, the amplification factor increases very rapidly as the number of the plates [layers] increases. Resonance frequencies change with the phases of vibration of each layer. Such amplification occurs except for the case that all layers oscillate with the same phase, namely, that of shaking the system, even if the frequency of the lattice vibration is very small. Lattice [sound] vibration makes a photonic [light] crystal an active media. The amplification is observable.(2)

This explains how a very small frequency of energy, imperceptible to human senses, is naturally amplified into higher volume signals of sound, transposed into light, electromagnetically and bioacoustically manifesting your body, or personal biohologram, in space/time.

These findings also evidence the legitimacy of a cohesive theory explaining how 528Hz music, featuring the energy at the heart of cosmic unity, demonstrates the capacity to vibrate DNA and your biohologram back into harmony, or symphony, with God's primordial frequencies.(3)

LOVE does this likewise. This is how LOVE administers healing, and why it has proven to be the "Universal Healer."

That means, of course, spiritual healing is the natural result of attuning to the matrix of creation for recreation and restoration of your innate perfection. This is your natural inheritance— a state of balance and well being.

Now you can appreciate how music, art, or sacred geometry, especially the elements in the Perfect Circle of Sound™, impact your spiritual composition and Divine origin.

Viewing the nine-pointed star, the circle, the mathematical frequencies, the amulet heralding the words LOVE and THANKS stimulates light receptors in your eyes relaying these frequencies/messages to your brain and your heart. These messages reawaken what has been primordially-programmed into you by God. This blessing is equally celebrated by nature most obviously using chlorophyll, the 528/LOVE phonon-photon energy transformer that keeps you alive with every breath.(3)

If you were created in the "image of God," through the sound of His/Her voice impacting Water, then *your lips must be your co-creative instruments* best used in problem solving (e.g., healing).

Therefore, for you to heal yourself, and help create world health, cooperatively recreating everything with LOVE in 528 is a wise and scientifically valid prescription. And the most powerful healing modality is freely available to you right now— your *lips*.

Now don't be shy or intimidated. Stop worrying you will be judged, or off key. Along with 528 compositions, sing, chant, or at least pray, using your lips to transmit as much LOVE as you can into your body Water, just as our Creator did in the beginning, and is still doing right now.

This is the main reason I launched 528Records.com, i528Tunes.com, and 528Radio.com. These musical domains were conceived as a way to help everyone broadcast LOVE musically, through the hydrated atmosphere to the whole world, exponentially amplifying the 528/LOVE signal; thus, opening people's hearts on a massive scale.(3)

Since the atmosphere, and entire universe is filled with Water, the more people sing and play music in 528Hz frequency, or 528-transposed music, the more LOVE will radiate from senders to receivers and back again.

This energy travels like a boomerang along the cosmic strings of the spinning, energy balancing, double toroidal universe. (See Figure 29.) "What goes around comes around," due to this spiraling "8." Karma is automatically administered within the cosmic energy recycling system.

Given that Spirit/Water is a "liquid crystal superconductor of sound and light," this explains how the sound of 528/LOVE, especially coupled with heart-felt loving intention to produce healing, can produce miraculous healing.

This simple thesis is solidly evidenced by science. For instance, Ueta's work observes the interaction of light and sound based on the interaction of electrons with-sound. He wrote that these energies impact crystal latices in your body Water. When the "photonic crystal" is vibrated, an electromagnetic field is generated. This can be measured and mathematically predicted. "The lattice vibration generates the light of frequency," Ueta reported.(2)

Also, Ueta's tests showed the greater the number of layers in the crystal lattice receiving the test sounds, the higher the resonance frequency got. So fret not if you are overweight. The resonance of LOVE is amplified by your added layers, and 528 can still work miracles.(2)

Terminating Infectious Diseases with 528

Years ago I was asked to research a simple mineral Water claimed to cure infections. The advanced "silver hydrosol" was developed by NASA scientists to keep astronauts healthy in space. The product was manufactured using sound and light energy in a non-nuclear reaction chamber. The safe energy caused the Water to bond (covalently) to the microfine silver. The technology produced a silver Water that could be safely used without having the silver build up in your body (as may occur with "colloidal silver"), providing powerful protection against nearly every infectious disease.(4)

I was astonished by what I discovered. The technology had been heavily suppressed by the drug cartel, and grossly neglected by mainstream medicine. This potential cure for everything from AIDS to malaria had been kept from needy people worldwide so that the Illuminati could continue controlling populations most profitably.

When asked to help turn this situation around, I consented under one condition, I required the manufacturer to install an argon laser outputting the greenish-yellow 528Hz frequency of light along with the pure tone 528Hz frequency of sound while the Water was being prepared for market. I also required prayer by faithful lab technicians making the mixture of sound, light, silver and Water most powerful.

I knew the improved product would be a double supercon- ductor of LOVE and healing energy. Water and silver are both superconductors of sound and light. Their electrons would be enriched with the resonance energy of LOVE/528Hz frequency.

This powerful new product, today marketed under the brand name OxySilver™, is a safe affordable solution to the pollution and intoxication caused by petrochemical antibiotics, and deadly vaccines.(4)

I am proud to have helped so many people who have used OxySilver, and pleased to provide a natural remedy with prayer power added and encouraged.

Practical Applications for The Water Resonator™

Another healing application of this information is The Wa- ter Resonator™ which uses the same mathematics, harmon- ics, geometrics, and magnetic energy dynamics to impart the 528Hz frequency into Water to energize it.(5)

And since the air is hydrated, your environment can be en- ergized by simply putting this image on your windows, mirrors, computer screens, and windshields.

When these are placed on crystalline materials, including glassware and plastic, their light and energy is amplified while moving through the layers of these crystals, as Ueta proved. Thus, Water can be "programmed" with powerful prayerful messages of 528/LOVE and healing in this way.

Other applications of The Water Resonator™ include plac- ing them with prayer and loving intent on acupressure points to stimulate desired outcomes. Measurements taken with sen- sitive technology when this was done repeatedly showed a balancing of pineal gland activity, which is best explained by the information previously provided in Chapter Six.

Float four-inch Water Resonators on Water in swimming pools and ponds to resonate thousands of gallons of Water at once.

Each time you use this technology you transmit a signal of 528/LOVE to bless your body and environment.

Other practical applications of the Perfect Circle of Sound healing knowledge include CDs, tuning forks, 528Fashions, jewelry, wind chimes, and the MIracle 6 frequency generator that can be programmed to generate 528 and other core creative vibrations. (See: HealthyWorldStore.com.)

My main objective in endorsing and/or developing these products is to enhance, and widely distribute, the "Power of LOVE" for healing.

Water with LOVE/528 for Baptisms

Since everything carries an energy signature created by sound and light acting through Water, entrainment to Divine frequencies occurs best in Water because it is a liquid crystal superconductor.

This is what baptism is really all about—recharging your body, nearly 80% Water, with Spirit/Water that transmits Divine energy. Divine-human communion takes place. This is also why jumping into the ocean is so healing, besides invigorating.

Baptism is an important part of Christian theology as our Creator's spiritual energy, commonly referred to as the Holy Spirit, is omnipresent; especially in the healing springs and Holy Waters of the world.

The "Pool of Possibilities"

The famous Canadian photographer and author, Courtney Milne, demonstrated this best.(6)

After traveling around the world to photograph the most sacred places on earth for his book, *Sacred Earth,* Courtney returned home, and read about Dr. Masaru Emoto's work.

"Dr. Emoto's research had a profound effect on me," Milne wrote, "giving me a new appreciation of Water as a miraculous substance, especially in my pool."

While participating as an organizer of *LIVE H$_2$O—Concert for the Living Water,* in 2009, Courtney informed me that he had experimented on his pool, as Dr. Emoto had recommended, using The Water Resonator™. (See Figure 41.) The Perfect Circle of Sound™ logo was enlarged, laminated, and glued to the side of his 40-foot swimming pool. He wanted to test Emoto's hypothesis that the message of "LOVE," and "Thanks," presented to Water would affect the quality and molecular structuring of the liquid. (Various sizes of these stickers are now available at HealthyWorldStore.com.)

Nearly three weeks later, while bathing with friends, they all noticed a remarkable difference in the "clarity and feel of the Water." The texture became silky smooth, and it seemed as though the Water became "more beautiful."

So Courtney began observing the changes in his pool. He photographed the pool and, thousands of films later, concluded, "You don't need to be a world traveler to find the most sacred spot in your own back yard swimming pool."

Mr. Milne's magnificent photos documenting this loving journey are available online at PoolOfPossibilities.com (6,7)

Fig. 44. Human Fetus "Ultrasound" Image in "Breath of the Earth" Water Cluster by Emoto

© I.H.M.

This image of the "Breath of the Earth™", formed from lava-heated steam on the Big Island of Hawaii, was taken by Dr. Masaru Emoto. The frozen water crystal contains an image remarkably distinguishable as an "ultrasound image of a fetus."

Local residents and native Hawaiians testify to the intensity of the "purgative, restorative and creative" energy of this tropical paradise. Here, the newest land on earth is being formed along with the greatest diversity of life. Many regard this setting as ideal for creationistic research and spiritual development.

The ancients predicted the rebirth of Earth's civilization would come through an umbilical cord stretching from Mt. Mauna Kea to the center of the universe. Mauna Kea dominates the landscape where this Water sample was taken.

The message in this Water is clearly consistent with this prophesy.

Other Examples of Healing Water

Long before John Hutchinson heralded lab research claiming the series of Solfeggio frequencies purified Water in the Gulf of Mexico polluted by the Deepwater Horizon oil spill.(3) Austrian investigator Viktor Schauberger had produced similar results with Water using vortex technologies and frequencies of sound.(8)

Emoto had written about the benefits of praying faithfully over Water, and watching the loving thankful messages transform even severely polluted areas.(7)

I was very grateful, in 2008, to have Dr. Emoto visit our "Kingdom of Heaven" estate and health retreat on the Big Island of Hawaii where he collected Water samples from steam vents on our land issuing the "Breath of the Earth™."

We routinely collect and drink this amazingly powerful liquid, served mainly hot with fresh organic lemon grass grown in our garden. The sweet tasting Holy Water is believed to hold the energy resonance for which the Big Island of Hawaii is famous. That is, "Pele's breath" is believed by native healers, called Kahunas, to hold the purgative and restorative energy signature of the land, the "aina," or "Mother Earth."

Local Kahunas relay a prophesy that the rebirth of civilization on Earth shall come through an umbilical chord stretching from this land to the center of the universe. This information was unknown to Dr. Emoto and his staff when they performed this crystallography.

The human fetus "ultrasound" image in the center of a Water crystal in this figure is remarkable for a number of reasons. The super-molecule is made of nearly a million smaller Water molecules. These arranged themselves into this image of a fetus by Divine intention to deliver a message. The same message was sent through a dozen other images in this series of films. All the images reflect some aspect of reproduction and

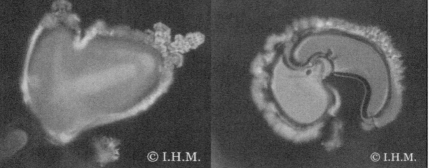

Fig. 45. "Breath of the Earth" Water Cluster Shaped Like a Heart and Yin/Yang Symbol

© I.H.M.   © I.H.M.

Two photos in a series of "Breath of the Earth™" Water crystals formed from lava-heated steam on the Big Island of Hawaii. The left-side image shows a heart with two daggers in it. The appearance and angle of the daggers is reminiscent of Masonic logos. The right side image simulates a Yin/Yang symbol, but appears to be surrounded by a border resembling a fallopian tube in cross-section under microscopic (histologic) examination. Dr. Masaru Emoto's theory is that Water is Divine, conscious, responsive, and desiring constant communication with us demonstrating and revealing LOVE. Source: BreathoftheEarth.net

LOVE. The images shown in Figure 45, selected from the series of photos, show a heart and Yin/Yang symbol. They reinforce the message of LOVE. The Yin/Yang symbol is birthing through what appears to be a microscopic (histologic) cross-section of a fallopian tube.

The entire series of films is viewable at BreathOfTheEarth.net.

Other Suggested 528 Uses

Carry a 528 tuning fork in your car, briefcase, pocketbook, and/or leave one at your desk. Pull it out whenever you need an instant remedy for anxiety. Strike it, close your eyes (except while driving), and wave it around your head and heart. Feel the powerful LOVE of 528, and its harmony in your heart, freeing your mind of fruitless worry.

Don't forget to pray with it.

Do the same with your bath water. Strike the tuning fork on a rubber hockey puck, or on your knee; then submerge your hand to sink the handle of the 528 tuning fork into the Water. Let it vibrate, and play out completely. Repeat this a total of six times, with prayer. Your bath will feel much more relaxing.

Structured Water has been shown to be more energizing, with higher oxidative/reductive potentials than unstructured Water. That's kind of like switching to high octane gas in your car, or the difference between 528 and 741 in your ears.

A group of sound healing researchers in Israel routinely travel with 528Hz tuning forks. They activate them whenever confronted by angry people. Also, they play the forks whenever they come upon others in conflict. They claim this distracts, fascinates, and humors those engaged in arguments. They strike the 528 fork, wave it through the air, and that seems to help settle the disputes.

Can you imagine what might happen if United Nations peace-keepers were to broadcast 528 pure tones around Gaza, Jerusalem and Palestine?

Fig. 46. "LIVE H₂O Concert Crop Circle," Formed in Wiltshire, England, 6/21/09

"Most people believe crop circles are man-made to gain publicity, . . . or fool people who believe in extraterrestrials," wrote Scrbd online. Here, however, is a sign and wonder that CANNOT BE so simply disqualified. The musical crop circle happened on prayer day of the "LIVE H₂O Concert." Note the brightest spot is in the heart of the figure "8", the "zero point" energy vortex of universal construction. (i.e., from whence the double toroid-structured universe takes shape). This is the heart of LOVE/528. The photos came courtesy of John Montgomery, Copyright 2009; and o-fu-online.net

Figure 47. Decrypting a Crop Circle Messaging Phi, 528 and Musical Mathematics

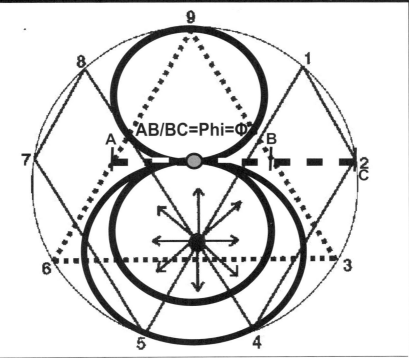

This extends the analysis from Figure 30, which showed Marko Rodin's diagram of the "infinity pattern." It incorporated Phi, 528, and is structurally similar to each segment of DNA spiraling in the helix. The Crop Circle in Figure 46 presents very similar features, excluding the Yin/Yang Symbols—"69"—within the dominant pair of circles. As noted, the resulting equilateral triangle inside the circle demonstrates Phi proportions: The ratio of AB to BC is Phi resonating the ancient Solfeggio musical scale's "*MI*racle 6"—528/LOVE. This is derived from Pi = 5 arccos (.5Phi) = 22/7 (days a week), that is ancient Pi or 3.142857~; and 528/22 = 24; and 360/24 (hours a day) = 15 (where 1 + 5 = *MI*racle 6). With this knowledge we can decrypt the major message in the artwork, that is, the Yin/Yang "69" symbol by cross-dividing the numbers 6 and 9. 6 ÷ 9 = .6666666~; 9 ÷ 6 = 1.5 (≈15 = 1 + 5 = 6). Moving the decimal points herald, again, the *MI*racle 6, or 528/LOVE! In other words, this revelation, and mathematical analysis of the "LIVE H_2O Crop Circle" of 6/21/09, delivers the message that the balance in the universe, and the heart of the figure "8," is LOVE/528. This is the magnificent meaning of the Yin/Yang symbol, and the Creator's revelation as per Isaiah 22:22 and Rev. 3:6-8

How 528Hz Structured Water Works

There is great creative and curative power in subtle vibrations. These frequencies, especially 528Hz, affect your body Water, its hydroelectricity, and resonance energy. The sound of 528 changes the molecular structure of Water, its wet-ability, and signaling capacity.

The *wet-ability* of Water is a function of "ORPs," short for "oxidative-reductive potentials."(8)

The entire universe is hydrated, and every action and reaction in space/time is mediated by electrons. When the hydrogen in Spirit/Water donates its electron to oxygen, it is oxidized. The oxygen is "reduced," and its charge turns negative from the added electron provided by the oxidized hydrogen. This basic chemistry affects Water's wet-ability and capacity to transmit nutrients across cell membranes. This is essential for metabolism, life support, and optimal health.

Water provides the basic chemistry of divinity and reality.

The genetic strands shown in Figure 43 were published in the journal *Science*. These photographs show DNA's electrical potential being studied by geneticists from the University of California at Berkeley.(9) The top photo shows DNA bathing in energetically-active structured (clustered) Water. These hydroelectrified double helices hold far greater energy potentials than the same strands of DNA shown below them. Dehydration caused the difference.

This dehydration experiment proves that a slight reduction of energized Water bathing genetic matrices causes DNA to destructure and fail energetically. Dehydration, followed by electrical degradation, results in molecular chaos, or "entropy." This experiment shows that hydrosonic forces hold your DNA together, as they do the universe.(9)

Besides playing a key role in healing through electrogenetic signaling, Water's subtle energy transmissions underlie the success of myriad healthcare practices from homeopathy and acupuncture to biotechnologies such as magnetic resonance imaging (MRI) and Rife frequency generators.

Planetary protection and healing, many scientists now agree, depends on Water involved in purification and natural cleanup.

Surely, Water is our planet's most precious, creative, and healing resource. H_2O's astonishing ability to transform its structure in response to human emotions and heartfelt intentions simply means that words—a set of alpha-numeric sound and light frequencies—affect the nature, structuring, energy carrying, and creative signaling capacities of Water. Spiritually blessed Water is Divinely structured into mainly hexagonal rings as shown in Figure 42.

Inspired by these revelations, Dr. Emoto dedicated his life to preserving precious Water purity, and advancing his technology to demonstrate that Water is "conscious" and responsive to words, music, and prayer. Often, the Water he studies, yields spiritual messages, and he routinely recommends using 528Hz frequency to bless Water with LOVE.(7)

LIVE H_2O—Concert for the Living Water

In 2009, Dr. Emoto and I collaborated during "*LIVE H_2O—Concert for the Living Water*" to herald these revelations about Water, and promote peace on Earth, world health, and universal prosperity.

We prayed for the Holy Water of the world in an effort to benefit all life forms still surprisingly surviving on this chemically beleaguered planet.

Groups in nearly 80 countries participated by praying and playing music in 528Hz frequency.

Figure 46 shows an amazingly meaningful and beautiful crop circle featuring elements of 528Hz, and the Perfect Circle of Sound™. The cosmic wonder appeared in Wiltshire, England on 6-21-09, the prayer day, of the LIVE H_2O Concert.

The art depicts a double Yin/Yang symbol or infinity sign. Both sides contain the "69" symbol at the heart of the SGW. (See Figure 2.)

The art also appears to be similar to a drawing of mitosis, that is, a single cell division to yield two new cells.

Among hundreds of messages I received giving thanks for organizing this historic event, this extraterrestrial message is most profound. *There is no possible way* this exquisitely precise crop circle could have been created by a bunch of farmers stomping through the field.

In fact, there is no commonly known technology on earth that could produce this, although it is fairly certain it was done energetically, affecting the crop electromagnetically, using frequencies.

This crop circle graphs the fundamental musical-mathematical energetics promoted during LIVEH$_2$O to integrate and harmonize the one world Divine family, to live in balance as per the music of LOVE.

You will also notice the crop circles here line up on the farmer's tractor tracks like whole notes written on a sheet of music. It also contains elements consistent with a musical treble clef.

The crop circle features 528, the "MI" or MIracle note in the original Solfeggio musical scale that equals a "6" (i.e., 5+2+8=15; 1+5=6) Do you see the large sixes in the crop circle (also graphing the Yin/Yang symbols)?

The "FA" note stands for FAmily having a frequency of 639, or a "9" (i.e., 6+3+9=18; 1+8=9). Find the nines in the crop circle.

These two notes, "MI" and "FA" at the heart of the original Solfeggio scale, provides the "69" (Yin/Yang) symbol reflecting polarity and balance universally.

The spinning spiraling number "8", also prominent here, relays the universe's structure and infinity sign.

The implications of this healing information are myriad and urgent. This intelligence compels reconsideration of the manner in which our planet and people are being abused, polluted, energetically retarded, or spiritually suppressed.

The Concert for the Living Water, celebrating LOVE/528 was the pebble in the pond intended to stimulate the evolutionary energy needed to secure love, peace, health, and prosperity for generations to come.

References

1) Shinohara ML, Correa A, Bell-Pedersen D, Dunlap JC, and Loros JJ. Neurospora Clock-Controlled Gene 9 (ccg-9) Encodes Trehalose Synthase: Circadian Regulation of Stress Responses and Development. American Society for Microbiology, *Eukaryotic Cell,* February 2002, p. 33-43, Vol. 1, No. 1

2) Ueta T. Photon-phonon interaction in photonic crystals. Institute of Media and Information Technology, Chiba University, 1-33 Yayoi-cho, Inage-ku, Chiba, 263-8522, Japan. See: http://iopscience.iop.org/1757-899X/10/1/012103/pdf/1757-899X_10_1_012103.pdf

3) i528Tunes.com press release. 528HZ Sound "Miraculously Cleaned Oil Polluted Water in the Gulf of Mexico, According to New Study by a Canadian Researcher." See: http://www.528records.com/pages/528hz-sound-miraculously-cleaned-oil-polluted-water-gulf-mexico-according-new-study-canadian-r

4) OxySilver information sources from an extensive website linked from: www.OxySilver.com.

5) The Perfect Circle of Sound™ is also called the Water Resonator See the websites: TheWaterResonator.com and PerfectCircleOfSound.com.

6) Milne C. Pool of Possibilities. See: http://www.courtneymilne.com/

7) Emoto M. *Love Thyself: The Message from Water III*. Tokyo: IHM Research Institute, 2004

8) Lowry RW and Dickman D. The ABC's of ORP: Clearing up some of the mystery of Oxidation-Reduction Potential. *Service Industry News*. Reprinted online at: http://www.rhtubs.com/ORP.htm

9) Keutsch FN and Saykally R J. Water clusters: Untangling the mysteries of the liquid, one molecule at a time. Inaugural Article Chemistry *PNAS* 2001;98,19:10533-10540 (Link to: http://www.pnas.org/cgi/content/full/98/19/10533)

10) Numerous patents by Viktor Schauberger, along with his Water research is provided across the Internet, including here: http://webcache.googleusercontent.com/search?q=cache:z2wAIzp-wCwJ:panacea-bocaf.org/viktorschauberger.htm+Victor+Schauberger+water+purification&cd=3&hl=en&ct=clnk&gl=us&client=safari&source=www.google.com

11) Healthy World Distributing, LLC, is represented on the Internet through HealthyWorldStore.com. Products mentioned here and elsewhere in this book are available through the store, or by calling toll free 1-888-508-4787.

Chapter Eleven:
528 Physics and Consciousness

528 vibrates at the heart of consciousness. Previous chapters covered the importance of 528 in physics, the universal constants, and measurements of space/time. The evidence reviewed shows LOVE/528 is basic to creation and creationism.

Consciousness is defined as, "the state or condition of being conscious;" and "a sense of one's personal or collective identity, including the attitudes, beliefs, and sensitivities held by or considered characteristic of an individual or group." For example, "Love of freedom runs deep in the national consciousness."(1)

So LOVE/528's vibration is central to your personal and social identity, increasing awareness, and freedom to choose wisely your attitudes, beliefs, and sensitivities. In essence LOVE/528 is where you come from, and where you are going or evolving, given what this book teaches about hydro-creationism based on musical-mathematics and Water science.

Chapter One introduced you to cymatics—the impact of sound on moving and materializing matter. This involves the physics of creationism. This understanding raises consciousness that creation happens universally vibrationally, with the essence of everything being similarly inspired by LOVE/528.(1-3)

Fundamental to advancing consciousness is the consideration of "original sin" in the context of resonance, harmonics, and the physics of LOVE and lawfulness expressed throughout creation.

In this vein, you might consider ignorance, or lacking consciousness, based on physics, akin to sin, or being out of touch with how the universe operates lawfully, administered mathematically, with homeostasis or balance reflecting harmony.

Phase-Locking to God

The most exciting aspect of 528 impacting collective consciousness and civilization through the revelations and physics advanced herein, is the prospect of emerging from mass ignorance that includes the illusion of separation and dissonance within ourselves and beyond, into community and harmony with each other as Divine children. This is certainly a high probability for humanity, given the opportunity to phase-lock, or entrain, in coherence with nature and the Standing Gravitational Wave (SGW) advanced by Müller.

The closer you "vibe" to LOVE/528, the greater the benefit you can expect. The physics of this principle was advanced by Lissajous. Even if the frequencies are not in perfect, but close, whole-number ratios to each other, benefits are achieved. This is why the digitally transposed music from A=440Hz standard tuning to 528Hz is close enough to live 528Hz (A=444Hz scale) coherence to be less stressful and more beneficial.

Bowditch reported, "If the difference [in frequencies of natural scaling by whole-number ratios] is insignificant, the phenomenon that arises is that the designs keep changing their appearance."

This knowledge is very important for understanding many things, from the forgiving energy of God, to the reason 528Hz "live" performances are the most healing and spiritually-uplifting.

Much like 528Hz resonates a DNA strand back to normalcy via the forces of phase-locking to the SGW, creationistic cymatics (or hydrosonics) asserts the mechanism by which energy vibrates and resonates your physical body back into balance.

In essence, 528Hz is the frequency of God's heartbeat, or the central vibration of the Holy Spirit. This actually vibrates your DNA, cells, and tissues, back to normalcy, especially during sleep, rest, prayer, and meditation.(4,5)

This concept of phase-locking your body into the good vibrations of nature for healing, correctly assumes dis-ease is a "phase" you are going through, but don't wish to lock-into.

This is encouragment for you to have faith in natural healing and vibrating in harmony (in sync) with the heartbeat of God.

In the Christian sense, your body naturally seeks the Kingdom of Heaven wherein "prosperity in all ways" is given to you, because "there is nothing missing or broken" in this musical matrix. Your body-spirit is naturally recharged here.

Your physical material shifts and changes according to vibrations entraining to the central nodes, whole notes, of the universe. The sound waves impacting you from the Kingdom of Heaven, this book evidences, are fundamentally the Solfeggio tones.

This is more reason to live "righteously" and thereby attune to The Kingdom's music.

Again, biosonic vibrations sourcing from the Master Matrix recreates everything from your unique eye color to the shape of your toes, and every part of your body, every nano-instant of your life.

Just as Hans Jenny, the Swiss physician and cymatics researcher, published in *The Structure and Dynamics of Waves and Vibrations*, and Chladni demonstrated, shapes and patterns of various materials vibrated into motion, went from perfectly ordered and stationary to chaotic when whole-note ratios were altered and phase-locking with God's mathematical matrix stopped. Various materials used in experiments, like water, sand, iron filings, spores, and viscous substances, repeated these results. Similarly, your well-ordered body, and physical health, becomes diseased with too little core creative and sustaining frequencies.

Jenny convincingly demonstrated that all natural phenomena were ultimately dependent on, if not entirely determined by, the frequencies of creative vibration. He argued that recovery from disease states could be aided or hindered musically.

All of the above is consistent with biophysics and string theory as explained in Chapter 9.

Voice Training and 528

As mentioned in Chapter 1, and still awaits reconfirmation, Jenny noted that vowels of Hebrew and Sanskrit vibrated sand into shapes that resembled their written symbols. In any case, there seems to be something very special about vowels, energetically or spiritually.

One related discovery, involving 528, is the use of vowels by voice trainers. Singing coaches commonly assign students harmonizing exercises using the vowels. But when sung in sequence repeatedly—as circularly singing "A, E, I, O, U, A, E, I, O, U, A, E, I, O, U"—the sound produced is one of the most commonly accepted names of God—YahWay.

This strongly suggests Divine-human communion, or harmony, is readily manifested vocally. This is similarly considered with prayer.

Considering the math fundamental to the alphanumerics of "AEIOU," that is, A=1; E=5; I=9; O=15 (or 6); and U=21 (or 3), this sums to "6," reflecting the "MIracle 6" and 528/LOVE.

Given this knowledge, a recommended exercise is to vocally harmonize with a 528Hz tuning fork, or music played in 528Hz that you can download from i528Tunes.com. Sing the A, E, I, O and U, harmonizing with recording artists, either vocals or instrumentals.

When you exercise your voice using vowels, singing vowels in harmony with instruments tuned to 528Hz, do so with the heart felt loving intention to heal yourself of any disease, including disruptive emotional patterns. You can also pray for others using this exercise.

Figure 48. Computer Generated Fractal Art

Nature's "fractals" are round, not square like computer generated fracals. This true shape of fractals depends on "LOVE/528Hz," since circle geometry depends on the influence of 528 expressing metaphysically. Fractal art helps explain how matter manifests according to mathematical laws and formulas governing physicality, universal integrity, and Divine creativity. (Source: Berkowitz J. *Fractal Cosmos. Revised edition.* Portland, OR: Amber Lotus, 1998.) *Amber*

Expanding Consciousness Through Your Voice

Research curiously suggests that learning to speak and/or sing in Hebrew may offer unique spiritual blessings.

The ancient Hebrew Torah—The Law—*was* always *sung*, every word of it, entirely without written vowels. But oddly, the vowels were included in the recitations, even though they were not included in the writing. The vowels were all sung from memory, as though the name of God could not be written, but recalled instinctively. How *Interesting*!

So theoretically, your singing of vowels in songs relays a hidden blessing that is likely associated with developing yourself to become a more loving, spiritual, and conscious being.

Consciousness is defined as "the state or condition of being conscious;" or, "a sense of one's personal or collective identity, including the attitudes, beliefs, and sensitivities held by or "considered characteristic of an individual or group." "Love of freedom runs deep in the national consciousness," *The Free Dictionary* online states.

So higher consciousness implies an expanded sense of self in relation to others, or the collective group—a greater intimacy of relatedness to your community engaging greater LOVE and spirituality.

In other words, increasing your sense of community, connection to others, or spirituality, implies greater mastery over your conditioned ego. This includes your egoic sense of separation from others, and the universe at large, to the point where inner peace is enjoyed consistently.

This state of well-being is best achieved, gurus and scholars claim, through practices used to expand human consciousness and spirituality, including meditation, prayer, and chanting. A goal in these practices is to merge with inner stillness, to experience moment to moment bliss beyond stress, troubled thoughts, turbulent feelings, negative attitudes, and harsh judgments.

All paths to acquiring higher consciousness are paved with LOVE and forgiveness, as Jesus modeled.

Moreover, assuming you were created, and sustained, by YahWay's voice, and created in the image of God, as already mentioned, your creative instruments—your *lips*—are most powerful, especially when used with faith and heart-felt loving intention. The LOVE/528 in your heart links your heart to God's heart, and empowers your voice to be most "registered," phase-locked to LOVE, and blessed.

This regards Jesus' teaching that you are judged by every word that comes from your mouth, that either reflects the LOVE in your heart, or the evil that dwells therein.(*Matthew 12:36-37; 15:8-9*)

The administration of Divine judgement must, therefore, rely on frequencies of good versus evil, harmony versus dissonance, using LOVE/528 as a key measure.

In other words, the energetic or spiritual dynamics of the words you express, are measured against the Universal LOVE Constant, LOVE/528Hz, in rendering karma according to the science and understandings advanced in this book.

Therefore, rediscovering your pure, unadulterated or unashamed, voice, expressing yourself optimally in LOVE/528 is recommended.

Tips for Voice Training

Most people are embarrassed to sing, especially in front of others. But imagine a world wherein people communicate by singing a common language, one that is spiritually blessed for Divine communion as well as clear messaging. The information in *The Book of 528: Prosperity Key of LOVE* strongly encourages futurists to advance this option.

Vocal coach Yvonne DeBandi advised singing students, and those seeking to rediscover their voices, to consider the A-to-Z rules for developing a great voice. Her tips are posted on LOVE528.com. Several keys to developing your good natural voice involve airflow that creates and carries your vocal tone. It must be kept flowing evenly, through your vocal cords, to sing well. Students are advised to sing to God, with LOVE, for the best results, especially since the air vibrating the vocal cords is resonating primordially in LOVE/528Hz.

Co-creating Your Reality

Recall mathematician Marko Rodin's work that has been mentioned several times in this book complementing the space/time physics of Müller and math of Showell.(6-9)

Consideration must be given to evolving consciousness, unfolding due to the dynamics administered by the same forces responsible for creating and controlling the scaled universe.

The Perfect Circle of Sound™, composed of what Rodin independently determined was three "Family Number Groups," can be appreciated by studying his matrix viewed in Figure 27. Rodin realized, all matter derived from math and energy, from galaxies to blood cells, displays this math—"God's signature"—at a most fundamental level.(10)

The implications of these discoveries, like the universe, are limitless. Vastly beneficial creative potential rests in the application of this knowledge to solve humanity's greatest problems.

The famous American poet, critic, and short-story writer, Edgar Allan Poe wrote, "To be thoroughly conversant with a man's heart, is to take our final lesson in the iron-clasped volume of despair. . . . It may well be doubted whether human ingenuity can construct an enigma—which human ingenuity may not, by proper application, resolve. . . . Man's real life is happy, chiefly because he is ever expecting that it soon will be so."

The universe is constantly spinning and torquing with energy that can be used positively or negatively. Musical math is constantly flowing awaiting your creativity. Tapping the flow of this free energy was proven possible by Tesla, whose technology was secreted by the Illuminati to monopolize the energy industry. Now humanity, if not biology in general, risks extinction due to the low level of consciousness controlling research and developments in this field.(2)

The frontiers of human consciousness are being controlled, likewise.

After corroborating the truths in this book, many great minds from the fields of physics, biophysics, chemistry, mathematics, and computer science, will be inspired to resolve enigmas in their fields.

These advances in understanding 528 also help explain the physics, and universal energy dynamics, of creative consciousness. For instance, if you have ever wondered how certain synchronistic miraculous manifestations, and prayed-for outcomes, suddenly occur for you, this knowledge provides a clue.

With your genetic code phase-locked into the energy of the Master Matrix, and your neurology empowered by this music, your life began.

Throughout life, your free will, coupled with your Divine destiny, supported by angelic protection, and spiritual direction, enabled your creative self-expression. This is true for the vast majority of people, especially those who remained opened to the power of faith in Divine influence.

Energetic transmissions from your heart/mind, as well as your lips from words, chants, and prayers, travel throughout the cosmos, administered through the musical-mathematical matrix. In this Master Matrix, these energized messages acquire more power through torque, spin, and velocity, according to the model developed by Harramein and Rauscher.(11)

This best explains the wise sayings, "What goes around, comes around;" "resistance causes persistence;" "pay it forward;" and "as you sew, so shall you reap." These truths are all explained by this spiritual dynamic featuring the cosmic matrix that physicists prove is circulating, or revolving, as well as spinning lawfully according to math.

Since "528" and "639" is the math at the heart of the original Solfeggio, and 528/LOVE is at the heart of the electromagnetic spectrum (that is, fundamentally central to visible light) any veering off center, (that is, sinning), away from the "miracle (loving/528) family (639)", violates the heart of The Law.

The dynamic of attracting negative outcomes in your life derives from the apocalyptic dynamic of your survival instinct. This typically involves faithlessness, and reflects a low level of consciousness ascribed to the reptilian brain.

Apocalypse means an unveiling or revealing. Reveal the horror—pain, fear, loss, or traumatic history—in a victim's consciousness, and you determine the source of attracting such negativity repeatedly *unconsciously*.

Bringing your unconscious creativity to the forefront of awareness demands that you take responsibility for such sin, that is, the dissonant energy you generate *unconsciously* and output repeatedly to create your troubled reality.

Since we know that opposites attract, positive attracts negative in the world of electromagnetism, there must be some undetermined mechanism operating in the service of justice, involving the Master Matrix, that attracts life's lessons learned the hard way through pain and loss. Theoretically, this involves the polarized double toroid structure of the universe explained by Harramein and Rauscher,(11) wherein the polarity of thoughts, deeds and intentions, shift as the energy moves through the heart of the universe from one side of the double toroid to its oppositve. Then, like magnets, these polarized energies attract their opposite charge, or repel realities similarly charged.

In this way, your core attitudes cut to the core of the universe effecting your creative and attractive capacities. You experience no more or no less than your seeds in words, thoughts, intentions, and deeds command. You either attract or repel experiences depending on what you transmit, positively or negatively.

Theoretically then, "bad karma" or judgment must be generated this way, electromagnetically, attracting into your life what you hate and fear most. This seems to be a main problem underlying psychosocial stress, political disempowerment, and widespread deprivation in this world.

We The People, in other words, deprive ourselves from joining hands to co-create a better and healthier world, demanding from ourselves, each other, and our political leaders, righteousness within the Matrix governing universal law and order. We are all, therefore, outlaws who God *always* forgives because of our personal and collective ignorance, and the manner in which justice is administered automatically, musically-mathematically.

This best explains karmic laws or Divine judgment and the administration of universal balance or harmony. This is needed knowledge for "enlightenment"—to ease your suffering and make life a lot ligher.

This also explains why certain physicists, who claim the universe is expanding chaotically through entropy, are dead wrong. The universe maintains justice or homeostatic balance.

To reiterate, these revelations in musical-math, physics and consciousness also explain how you are judged by every word that comes from your mouth, as Jesus decreed in *Matthew* 12:36: "I tell you this, on the Day of Judgment people will have to give account for every careless word they have spoken; for by your own words you will be acquitted, and by your own words you will be condemned."

Given the aforementioned evidence and discussions, it is most probable that each cell resonates with a genetic blueprint of the universe (as above, so below), and therefore operates with Divine or cosmic intelligence. Individually and as groups, cells can be relied upon to respond intelligently to mathematical input, or harmonic frequencies. That is, electromagnetic and bioacoustic input—creative stimuli—including your thoughts and visualizations can be used to manifest healthier realities.

Conclusion

The aforementioned best explains the physics of consciousness—creative or destructive—operating in your life and body.

Your mind-body-spirit connection potentiates even psychosomatic reactions, best explained by the metaphysics of "the placebo effect," as well as its opposite called "the nocebo effect."

When placed under the trance of medical deities, patients generally forget *faith*. They become stressed, frightened, and induced into additional dis-ease by the strong mental suggestions from their doctors. This is how the vast majority of diseases and deaths are generated biospiritually, or psychosomatically. Disease labels and descriptions, such as "terminal illness" actually become cofactors, or risk factors, in increasing morbidity and mortality.

Alternatively, this book delivers the Truth that shall set us free. This intelligence explains the bioenergetics of life and death—the fact that all diseases might be more consciously considered "musical maladies."

Given this information, health professionals should be ethically directed to inform patients of the overriding influence of musical-mathematics—of LOVE/528Hz frequency dynamics—on health and disease physics.

Obviously, these considerations about biophysics and consciousness, emerging from revelations about musical-mathematics, hold profound importance in healthcare. Beyond this, there is a high probability all of the world's most urgent problems shall be solved by spreading this intelligence.

References

1) Consciousness definition from: http://www.answers.com/topic/consciousness. See also: King C. *BIOCOSMOLOGY*. Department of Mathematics, University of Auckland, New Zealand, 2003; Link to: http://www.dhushara.com/book/bchtm/biocos.htm)

2) Horowitz L. *DNA: Pirates of the Sacred Spiral*. Sandpoint, ID; Tetrahedron Publishing Group, 2004.

3) Haltiwanger S. *The Science Behind LIFEWAVE™ Technology Patches*. Atlanta, GA: LIFEWAVE™, LLC, 2005. Link to: http://www.lifewave.com/pdf/haltiwanger_24p_paper.pdf)

4) Horowitz L and Puleo J. *Healing Codes for the Biological Apocalypse*. Sandpoint, ID: Tetrahedron Publishing Group, 1999.

5) Horowitz LG. *Healing Celebrations: Miraculous Recoveries Through Ancient Scripture, Natural Medicine and Modern Science*. Sandpoint, ID: Tetrahedron Publishing Group, 2000.

6) Müller H. *Theory of Global Scaling*. Sante Fe: NM: Institute for Space-Energy-Research, Leonard Euler, Ltd. and Global Scaling Applications, Inc., 2002.)

7) Horowitz L and Puleo J. *Healing Codes for the Biological Apocalypse*. Sandpoint, ID: Tetrahedron Publishing Group, 1999.

8) Goldman J. Holy Harmony Tuning Forks: Sacred Sounds for Modern Times. Boulder, CO: Spirit Music, 2000. Available through Healthy World Distributing, LLC, 1-888-508-4787 (www.healthyworlddistributing.com).

9) The Phi Nest. DNA: The spiral is a golden section; the cross section is based on Phi. Lengthy analysis and discussion is available online at http://www.goldennumber.net.

10) Personal communication from Marko Rodin. See: Vortex based math website: http://markorodin.com/1.5/

11) Haramein N and Rauscher EA. The origin of spin: A consideration of torque and coriolis forces in Eisnstein's field equations and Grand Unification Theory. *Special Issue of the Noetic Journal* Vol. 6 No. 1-4 June, 2005, pp. 143-162. ISSN 1528-3739.

Chapter Twelve:
528 Genetics and Biocide

Accccording to ancient "Bock Saga" myth, creation was attributed to a technology based on sound and light honoring a spiritual understanding of "how to work with nature orally."(1)

"But somewhere in the darkened mists of our past, that knowledge was lost and, therefore, so was our ability to utilize it."(1)

In the 3rd Century, B.C., ancient Levite priests translated the original Torah into the Greek Septuagint. At that time, they developed the chapters and verse numbers found in today's Bible. They used these numbers to encrypt and secure the six sacred Solfeggio tones for posterity. Only those privy to this sacred secret knowledge could find the numbers buried in the *Book of Numbers*. The tones provided powerful vibrations—electromagnetic and bioacoustic frequencies now known to impact DNA and all of creation, at the heart of which is "528". (1)

Australian author Les Whale wrote about the Bock Saga. The "sa" means "receiving," and the "ga" means "'giving' in both Rot and Van languages." This earliest theory of creation-ism provides the understanding that one must first receive before being able to give the gift of spirit.

That is, in fact, precisely what DNA does. It receives the gift of spiritual life in the form of sounds called *phonons*, and then transforms these tones to light energy signals called *photons*. These photons, along with amplified *phonons*, transmit outward from DNA—the "Sacred Spiral"—to impact organic matter, including your material makeup.(1)

This is why I say, "You are the music!"

Healing Damaged DNA

I helped spread that concept that 528Hz frequency heals damaged DNA, as was told to me by Dr. Lee Lorenzen in 1998. Dr. Lorenzen stands among the world's leading Water scientists and nutritional biochemists. He and Dr. Patrick Flanagan advanced some of the earliest super-hydrating products and healing solutions using "structured" or "clustered" Water.

Structured Water "wetability," Dr. Lorenzen explained, is greater than tap Water. This is due to the greater oxidative-reductive potentials (ORPs) linked to the resonance frequency and chemistry of the Water, as mentioned in Chapter 10. Structured Water has a better ability to donate electrons that are the exclusive energy source in the world of sound, light, and chemistry. Structured Water is measured on a scale of positive to negative depending on its charge, and ability to receive or donate electrons.

The oxidizing or reducing capacity of water is vital to genetic function and life support. ORPs are measured in the negative scale, meaning the more negative the measurement, the higher the strength of the solution. People whose body chemistry, or body Water have high ORP numbers have less energy and more health problems than those with more negative ORPs.

All of this has a lot to do with 528 and the structuring of Water.

Water molecules are made of 3 atoms—2 hydrogens, that have energy electrons to give, and 1 oxygen that best carries extra electrons. These three atoms form a triangle, or tetrahedron sacred geometry. Due to the polarity of this tetrahedron, the oxygen side tending to be more positive than the hydrogen side, adjacent water molecules bond and twist into the shape

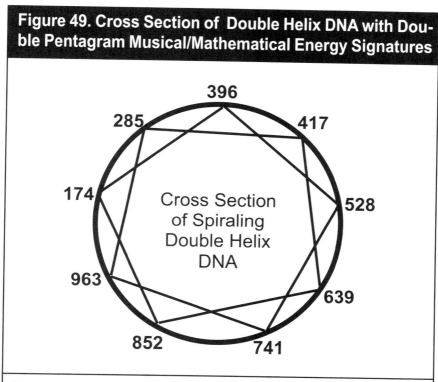

Figure 49. Cross Section of Double Helix DNA with Double Pentagram Musical/Mathematical Energy Signatures

396
285
417
174
Cross Section
of Spiraling
Double Helix
DNA
528
963
639
852
741

This figure results from connecting keys in the "Perfect Circle of Sound" that correspond to the ascending or descending tones in Rodin's mathematical matrix in Figure 27. The overall matrix develops from the infinity pattern shown in Figure 30, and according to Phi ratio analysis.

of a hexagon, or Solomon's seal-like structure as discussed in Chapter 9.

What makes DNA "sing" is this sacred geometry which helps generate energy, just like triangulated cell phone towers do. Triangulation makes energy electrons more available to send sound signals (phonons) and light impulses (photons) within and between cells. This is how cells best communicate and coordinate activities in tissues.(1)

In Chapter Three's "Lesson Four: Importance of the Ancient Solfeggio," Vic Showell showed us how important 528 is to ancient "rational" Pi and Phi. He drew this conclusion from a mathematical study of the Egyptian pyramids and their sacred geometry.(2,3)

Showell's proof of the importance of 528 in the universal constants fundamental to physics and geometry is additionally supported by Ernest McClain's works summarized in Figures 36 and 37. Here the "Pythagorean Comma 'Crisis'" places 528 at the heart of the neglected, even secreted, "irrational" ma- nipulation of mankind through mathematical measurements of time and space.(4,5)

Now consider Figure 43 showing the electrical potentials in millivolts of adequately hydrated DNA versus dehydrated DNA. Ron Saykally and his co-workers showed clustered Wa- ter rings, mostly six-sided hexagonal shapes, facilitated elec- tromagnetic transmissions to and from the double helix.(6) This figure evidenced the results of dehydration on DNA, and resulting drops in millivolt potentials degrading cell signaling.

In other words, the frequency for sustaining life, or "cellular upregulation," building and sustaining new body parts, and fu- eling metabolism, is based on "Spirit/Water's" presence in and around the DNA. The fact that hexagonal-shaped structured Water predominates here, in the genetic matrix, reflects the hexagonal shaped rings resonating harmonically in 528Hz at the heart of the musical-mathematical matrix of the universe. This intelligence strongly suggests the sacred spiral of biology vibrates harmonically with LOVE.(6,7)

This is confirmed by the color and structure of chlorophyll that, likewise, features the color and sacred geometry of 528 Hz frequency as shown in Figure 8.

The main energy carrier in your blood, hemoglobin, is simi- larly structured and hydrosonically vibrating with LOVE(528).

As Saykally and his team showed, besides greater electri- cal potentials being generated by structured Water with lower

Figure 50. Spiraling Galaxy Photographed by NASA

The above photograph was taken by NASA's Hubble telescope of the Barred Galaxy NGC 1300. Notice the "69" bilateral spinning polarity of the galaxy cluster. This characteristic is commonly seen in space photographs. It reflects the positive and negative polarities associated with the mathematics and gravitational physics involving 528—the "6," adjacent the 639, or "9" at the heart of the universe and Muller's Standing Gravitational Wave (SGW). (16)

This polarized "69" characteristic is also apparent in the photo on the right of a new cell being born. This is mitotic cell division in a kangaroo kidney cell captured with fluorescent microscopy. Can you see the similarities between the microscopic and macrocosmic phenomena?

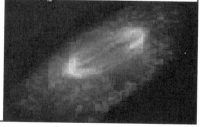

ORPs, more pronounced frequency transmissions reflected the well formed patterns of hexagons in the associated radial photographs.(6)

Figure 31 shows a composite of DNA photo enlargements, placed next to Rodin's basic infinity pattern. Rodin's "infinity pattern" additionally evidences the theory that 528Hz frequency can be used to repair damaged DNA, since the basic repeating genetic structure is seen in Rodin's infinity pattern, which is obviously in-sync with Pi, Phi, circle sacred geometry, and the Perfect Circle of Sound.(8)

Plus, the circulating design of DNA, as well as the universe according to physicists, derives from 528 musical mathematics. Resonating Water with 528Hz produces a precise 36-pointed star, as seen in Figure 9 courtesy of John Stuart Reid.(9) Since we now understand scaling, "as above, so below," the CymaGlyph shows a perfect 36-segmented circle of sound that evidences the "Circle of Life" depending musically, like DNA, on 528Hz frequency to form its sacred geometry.

Everything about DNA is naturally consistent with the rational number system, harmonics related to cosmic structures, including planets, kept in orbit by "phase locking" with Rodin's math and Müller's Standing Gravitational Wave (SGW. (4,6,9,10)

Thus, the whole note phase-locking of DNA's structural vibrations with the sun and botanical world resonating 528Hz,(11) may best explain why clinicians claim chlorophyll can be used as a blood/hemoglobin replacement, with both pigments featuring similar sacred geometry and 528Hz frequency (12); why healing outcomes using 528Hz therapies have been routinely observed and reported; and why Dr. Lorenzen shared that 528Hz frequency "miraculously" repairs damaged DNA.(13)

Double or Triple-Stranded DNA

I have questioned whether DNA is actually double stranded, or triple stranded. One of my well-wishing readers, Peter Moon, sent me an educated comment on this matter, suggesting the triple strand theory is more accurate, as follows:

"Triple-stranded DNA was a common hypothesis in the 1950s when scientists were struggling to discover DNA's true structural form. Watson and Crick (who later won the Nobel Prize for their double-helix model) originally considered a triple-helix

Figure 51. Circular Formations of DNA Helices

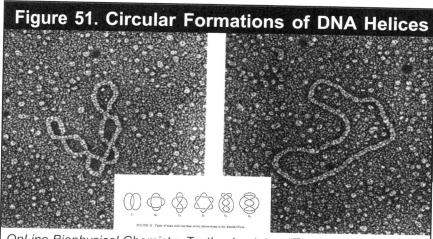

FIGURE 26 Table of links with less than seven intersections in the standard form.

OnLine Biophysical Chemistry Textbook states, "The two strands of the double helix in closed circular DNA are linked in topological terms; the link between two [three] strands of the double helix belongs to the torus class," according to published studies. "[L]ong DNA molecules are flexible . . . a circular DNA longer than a few hundred base pairs adopts very different conformations in solutions." The inset shows various forms of sacred geometry from the "torus class" of DNA "supercoils."(18) See: Vologodskii AV. Circular DNA. *OnLine Biophysical Chemistry Textbook,* ed. V. Bloomfield. (1999) http://www.biophysics.org/btol/supramol.thml#1

model, as did Pauling and Corey who published a proposal for their triple-helix model in the 1953 scientific journal Nature, as well as fellow scientist Fraser. However, Watson and Crick soon identified several problems with these models: 1) Negatively charged phosphates near the axis will repel each other, leaving the question as to how the three-chain structure would stay together. 2) In a triple-helix model (specifically Pauling and Corey's model), some of the van der Waals distances appear to be too small. Fraser's model differed from Pauling and Corey's in that in his model the phosphates are on the outside and the bases are on the inside, linked together by hydrogen bonds. However, Watson and Crick found Fraser's model to be too ill-defined to comment specifically on its inadequacies in their publication in "Nature" (1953): Molecular Structure of Nucleic Acids. Triple-stranded DNA was also described in 1957, when it was thought to occur in only one in vivo biological process: as an intermediate product during the action of the E. coli recombination enzyme RecA. Its role in that process is not understood.

In reviewing all the above models, consider that the genetic strand is spinning and spiraling like the rest of the universe in a sea of structured Water.

The structuring of Water, like the DNA's sacred geometry, occurs due fundamentally to sound, then light, that, through negatively charged electrons, creates polarities within and around genetic structures.

These are the fundamental primordial factors influencing DNA, its structure and function. The mathematics and geometrics of Water, memorizing and transmitting photons and phonons to sustain DNA, depends on these factors. The cymatic hydrodynamics of DNA must be considered, and make sense, for any model to be comprehensive and legitimate.

Consider wireless communications, wherein transmitters and receivers are most often triangulated or circular to increase signaling efficiency. This jibes with Rodin's "Infinity Pattern," the structure broadcasting energy most organically, apparently due to the triangulated 3,6,9 portal that is also obvious within organic chemistry and other electronic technologies. (See: Figures 30 and 31.) All energy, including genetic energy, prompting the field called "electrogenetics," fundamentally sources from piezo-electricity primordially coming from Water.

The circular DNA strand,(18) segmented in accordance with Rodin's spiraling math, and the Perfect Circle of Sound, requires phase-locking into Müller's SGW of the universe.(14) Otherwise, we would all die of exhaustion from having our DNA swim against the force of electromagnetic nature.

These are the main reasons I speculate that the earlier models of triple-stranded DNA are probably most correct.

Most people do not even realize DNA is circular as explained by New York University, Department of Chemistry scholar, Alexander Vologodskii. He explains that DNA is a challenge to accurately measure, since it is folded and seriously altered in preparation for photomicroscopy. Examining DNA is not done "live," that is, "in vivo." (18)

Electron movements in "clouds," and shifting polarities throughout DNA's spinning assembly, bend the circular strand reflecting what is happening in the universe at large. Volo-godskii even compared DNA to the circular shapes of toroids in graphs he published showing the spiraling circle's sacred geometry. (See Figure 51.)

Clearly, by accepting/promoting the double helix model of DNA, the Rockefeller-Soros "genetopharmaceutical" industry neglected and discouraged electro-genetics and the "spiritual" dynamics (sound and light signaling) that plays a vital role in genetic expression. The double helix three-dimensional DNA model misses the other dimensions and keeps people "dumb-ed-down" and focused on the physical and chemical, neglect-ing the spiritual and Divine.

Genetic Engineering Risks

With the universe musically-mathematically unified, and DNA energetically harmonized with the light of the Sun and sound of 528Hz, scientific tinkering with Earth's "genetic pool" must be sending distress signals out to the edge of the uni-verse.(5)

String theory, and the sacred secreted understanding of the musical-mathematical basis of biophysics and biocosmology, brings attention to the grossest risk from genetic engineer-ing. Since DNA is in perfect nodal resonance with the SGW, graphed in Figure 1, your DNA is connected to the universe at-large, and the universe is signaling your DNA in return.(14)

The harmonious alignment of universal energies is being violated by genetic engineers. The dissonance of genetic engi-neering is reflected in its pan-generational derangements, and resulting devolution. Contrary to propaganda, ancient seed lines proven by the test of time are generally heartier than genetically modified hybrids. Genetic engineering threatens species extinctions in several ways, and certainly runs contrary to natural selection.

Man-made mutations oppose "conservation of matter and energy," a law in physics and creationism, since DNA is matter, receiving, transmitting, and formed from acoustic energy.(1)

Thus, Universal Law is being broken by eugenic outlaws. The practice of genetic engineering, to advance the Illuminati's profitable biotechnology, presents the grossest deadliest risk in history.(1) As genetic biotechnology advances, and DNA is increasingly mutated, biological electrogenetics is devolving, making more creatures sick and tired; increasing the risk of species extinctions.

This alarm of biocide is echoing universally. Spiritually sensitive beings are feeling this challenge to Divine integrity.(15)

The Alien Agenda

A lot of people have been observing UFOs in the skies thanks to the technologies and presentations provided by Edward Grimsley. At a recent Tesla Technology conference, he outfitted us with infrared binoculars. We observed squadrons of UFOs appearing to be engaged in maneuvers with "mother ships." No one could say for sure if this was extraterrestrial technology, or advanced military war games, but "something" was certainly "out there."

If you were an enlightened loving extraterrestrial, even a lesser god simply thriving on universal energy, and you began to feel in your heart—your 528 channel—that something on Earth was creating dissonance in the dynamics of the Divine plan, *you might be seriously alarmed*.

You might consider conducting a search and rescue mission, and probably figure out a way to help generally clueless Earthlings. You might realize Earth's people were unlikely to survive due to their psycho-ecological stupidity/brainwashing.

You would discover that geneticists, on behalf of agricultural and biomedical industrialists, were programming cell death into plants and animals, putting "terminator" genes inside DNA's circular supercoils to spoil the seeds and prematurely kill the life forms.

You would learn this "apoptosis"—profitable biocide of natural species was for patented commerce and to genetically seize control over biology. Equally insane, you realize from Figure 40, demonic scientists construct extraterrestrial super-viruses in space, which you discover are being brought back to Earth and let loose.

This foreboding abuse of technology, you realize, threatens Earthlings with unprecedented viral outbreaks.

You are even more shocked to learn 85% of humanity is targeted for elimination, for "population reduction" by the Illuminati.

Earthlings drink beer, pop poisonous pills, stay hypnotized by celebrities on TV, and kiss myriad species good-bye without remorse.

You view all of this as an insult to intelligence and universal integrity.

Only a mass awakening, or spiritual renaissance, can save the human race and Mother Earth, you realize.

You volunteer for the mission of awakening humanity to the 528 LOVE Revolution.

The Golden Mean & 528

Jonathan Goldman recognized very early that the tones 417Hz and 528Hz frequency, that is, the second and third Solfeggio tones, resonate together to create an interval very close to the Phi ratio found in the Fibonacci series.

Vic Showell appears to be the leading investigator in this field. His research is now advancing every field of science. (See Figure 59.)

The 417, 528, 639 series of Solfeggio frequencies may be considered the "Resonance for the Miracle Family." This number set actually form an *arc* (metaphorically or metaphysically the "Ark of the Covenant") within the Perfect Circle of Sound's nine tone Master Matrix. Surely this is operating in DNA.

The ratios of 417/528 and 528/639, with "111" separating both pairs of numbers, relate to the Golden Mean, and are mathematically linked to the "Sacred Spiral"—your DNA(1)

In *DNA: Pirates of the Sacred Spiral*, I wrote of the "Musical Oneness of Creative Consciousness." I noted that your DNA receives energy from heaven and relays the creator's universal essence through bioacoustic electromagnetic signals. In this way, God's energy, or what many people call "Universal Consciousness," is shared by all life forms.

This "I AM" presence of sound, light, and LOVE, bathes everyone and everything in sacred harmonious Oneness.

DNA is the technology through which Divine-human communion automatically happens 24/7. Its very structure heralds its Divine design. Besides Rodin's "infinity pattern" demonstrating the link between musical-math and genetics, your DNA projects the mathematics and geometrics known as the Golden Section. This mathematically and geometrically special math constant is harmonically attuned to the Fibonacci series of numbers, 34 and 21, due to the fact that each full cycle of DNA's double helix spiral measures 34 angstroms long by 21 angstroms wide. Their ratio, 1.6190476, is very close to Phi —1.6180339.

So musical mathematics determines the sacred geometry of circular DNA. The *circular* sequence features a perfect five-sided spiraling pentagon for each helical spiral of the "supercoil." Double this to construct the twin helix, with each full helical spiral rotating 36 degrees, and you end up with a decagon formed from the two pentagons as shown in Figure 49.

DNA's basic molecular design (as shown in Figures 30, 31, 43, and 49) results from the "Perfect Circle of Sound." Genetic structure also corresponds to the ascending or descending tones according to Phi ratio analysis.

This uncommon knowledge about DNA's structure, based on perfect musical mathematics, helps explain your physical structure as well.

This also explains why you have an instinctual attraction to music, even though it has become institutionalized and increasingly dissonant. The pure tones of cosmic creation literally comprise you, and source you.

For example, your pentagonal body shape, with two arms, two legs, and a head, results from these resonance frequencies of energy manifested through pentagonal-shaped genetic antennae. All is in Divine proportion to the Golden Mean (1.618). Again, DNA's cross section is based on Phi. The ratio of the diagonal of a pentagon to its side is Phi-to-one.(17)

As shown in the referenced figures, no matter which way you look at it, even in its smallest segment, DNA, and life, is constructed using Phi, the golden section, the Perfect Circle of Sound, and especially 528.

So, again, you can see that the Creator's musical signature is all over the scroll of creation, including encrypted DNA.

The Golden Section, or Phi, reflects the relationship between the Creator and everything created. Just look at the basic math and symbolism of Phi as follows:

There is only one way a line may be divided so that its parts are proportional to, or reflected by, the image of the whole. Only by "tri-viding" the whole is the "mathematical relationship of component parts to the whole preserved."(17).

This is much like our understanding of the Trinity. We are said to be created in the Creator's image, filled with the Holy Spirit, and kin to the Son. The ancient symbol for Phi graphs this. It consists of a single circle and a single line through its center: Φ

The circle alone, mathematically, symbolizes zero or totality. Theologically, this represents nothing or everything, or the whole. This is reflected in music as the whole note that is written precisely the same way on the 5-line staff representing E, G, B, D, F, but rotated 90 degrees, that is, ⊖ .

The "whole note" symbolized everything, extended everywhere, leaving room for nothing else. So everything and nothing are metaphysically and theologically similar.

This also relates to the universe of negative and positive numbers. These go infinitely in both directions.

Alternatively, if nothing was expanded everywhere at the same time throughout the universe, then there would be nothing else, and nothing would be everything!

So, everything and nothing are contextually the same and become each other in the yin/yang cycle, or circle revolving eternally.

In this infinite cycle, the good becomes evil (as in Judeo-Christian theology's view of Satan—the "angel of light and music" falls into jealousy and mutanies); the male becomes female and visa versa; and the light dispels darkness until such a time when night falls.

These are universal polarities sourcing from the Master Matrix made musically from simple math.

In ancient theology, a simple line between two points represents unity or communion with the Divine Source. The nothing/everything symbol is a zero split by the line of unity. This yields the Greek letter Phi—Φ—denoting the Golden Number or Golden Mean.

This is how Phi math, and 528 fundamental to it, reflects your connection to God and the cosmos.

Adding zero, or nothing, to the Great One, the "I AM," in this way is, not surprisingly, the beginning of the Fibonacci series. You will also notice the "I" in "I AM" is a one.

These symbols help explain your relationship to the Creator that generated from musical-math—electromagnetic and bioacoustic frequencies—featuring the mathematical constant 528.

Alas, here is more proof that the "*MI*racle 6" tone, 528, reflects the essence of music. Total the numbers derived from the alphanumerics of the five lines and four spaces of the musical staff—that is, "EGBDF" and "FACE." (Use the chart on Table 1.) The lines and spaces both total 6s, yielding "66" or "3," the Trinity!

So nature's music is metaphysically inspired and written in matrix math, five lines, four spaces, using the first two ancient mathematical symbols—ovals and lines—reflecting, facilitating, and celebrating Divine communion.

Summary and Conclusion

In the beginning, in *Genesis*, there was the "Triune God," comprised of the Creator, the Water, and the Holy Spirit that divided the Water, yielding "Spirit/Water."

Then the Divine word entered this Spirit/Water, and divided the atoms therein to access the quantum field, "the dome," "the firmament," or "the ether," different Bibles say. Into this pure matrix of creative potential the words, "Let there be light," resonated. The energy broke electrons free from their hydrogens, and the sun appeared.

Sound on Water generates sonoluminescence. Hydrosonics, the evidence in this book proves, animates everything.

DNA manifests from God's musical math. The creative language of the universe resonates within every genetic strand.

The creative language that is structuring DNA is the Solfeggio frequencies.

"A, E, I, O, U, and sometimes Y," considered vowels in language, are possibly related to the six original Solfeggio frequencies and universal construction since their resonances reflect extraordinary harmonics, and the vowels are exclusively used by voice instructors to develop exceptional harmonizing skills.

Divine harmony expresses and replenishes your genetics as a function of electrogenetics featuring the "Holy Spirit," operating hydrosonically, expressed by special whole number, or whole note ratios and frequencies.

The nine-note Perfect Circle of Sound™, completes the musical-mathematical matrix of the universe reflected throughout genetics. These core creative frequencies create and animate the circular stands of DNA and their helical subunits.

Practically speaking, this is why baptisms are so healing and spiritually enabling. Heart-felt loving intention that resonates in 528, transmitted through faithful prayer vibrating Spirit/Water structured by 528, phase-locks human hearts, DNA, and your body Water, to the Creator's heart (or Master Matrix) facilitating miraculous manifestations.

All of this involves genetic expression and "cellular up-regulation" of light and sound signals to and from DNA that is structured and functioning due to 528.

This is why Jesus counseled his disciples about the nearness of Heaven. Today, he would undoubtedly equate Heaven to the Master Matrix administering the math, that is, the Law, that he encouraged attending first to gain prosperity in all ways. "The steps of the righteous are ordered" because The Law is ordered, compelling, and just. The Law is based on

Fig. 52. Phase-Locking Instruments to the Universal Matrix
Diagram Illustrates the Difference Between Scale and Pitch Frequencies

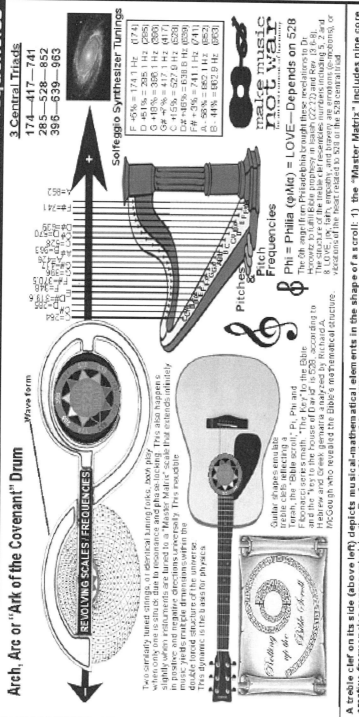

Arch, Arc or "Ark of the Covenant" Drum

Waveform

REVOLVING SCALES / FREQUENCIES

Two similarly tuned strings, or identical tuning forks, both play when only one is struck, due to resonance and phase-locking. This also happens slightly when instruments are tuned to a "Master Matrix" scale that extends infinitely in positive and negative directions universally. This inaudible music yields multiple dimensions within the double toroid structure of the universe. This dynamic is the basis for physics.

3 Central Triads

174—417—741
285—528—852
396—639—963

Solfeggio Synthesizer Tunings

F +5% = 174.1 Hz   (174)
D +51% = 285.1 Hz   (285)
G +10% = 396.1 Hz   (396)
G# +7% = 417.1 Hz   (417)
C +15% = 527.9 Hz   (528)
D# +46% = 638 B Hz   (639)
F# +3% = 741.1 Hz   (741)
A – 56% = 852.1 Hz   (852)
B – 44% = 692.9 Hz   (963)

make music not war
for a harmonious world

Pitches & Pitch Frequencies

A=852
F#=741
D#=570
D#=639
C#=528
A#=963
A=426
G#=432
G=396
F#=370.5
F=346
D#=319.4
D#=285
C#=264

Phi = Philia (φιλία) = LOVE—Depends on 528

The 6th angel from Philadelphia brought these revelations to Dr. Horowitz to fulfill Bible prophecy in Isaiah (22:22) and Rev. (3:6-8). The structure of the treble clef resembles numbers including 5, 2 and 8. LOVE, joy, faith, empathy, and bravery are emotions (e-motions), or vibrations of the heart related to 528 or the 528 central triad.

Guitar shapes emulate treble clefs reflecting a Torah, the Bible scroll, Pi, Phi and Fibonacci series math. "The Key" to the Bible and the "key to the house of David" is 528, according to Richard A. McGough who revealed the Bible's mathematical structure.

A treble clef on its side (above left) depicts musical-mathematical elements in the shape of a scroll: 1) the "Master Matrix" includes nine core creative frequencies represented by the Perfect Circle of Sound™ logo featuring 528Hz frequency. The double toroidal universe spirals like these revolving elements; 2) the arcs, arches and circles shown depend on 528 for their geometry; 3) the lower drawing of the "Bible Scroll" by Richard McGough also features 528 as the "key to the Bible," and the "key to the house of David." Scrolls with circles and spirals depend on 528 as does the Greek Phi symbol—φ—originating with the word philia, meaning LOVE. This circle cut in half represents the creation of everything by God: a circle, or whole note, depicts the whole universe, and the line that cuts the circle represents the link between God and man, or separation and perceived division of the whole during incarnation or creation. The double arrow through the treble clef represents one scale moving in positive and negative directions to infinity. For example, the 741Hz scale of nature phase-locks with A=440 Hz standard tuning, empowering the "Devil's Tone" diminishing and distorting 528 energy enabling your heart and loving communion. Pitches comprise the 7 note "octave." In this case the F# pitch is precisely 741Hz. Alternatively, if the scale were A=444Hz, then the C(5) note would be 528Hz. Phase-locking of pitches to nature's nine primordial scales increases the power of the string's resonance, since the power of the universe matches that frequency and adds harmonic resonance to that instrument. The choice is yours whether you vibe, or not, to the 528LOVErevolution.

nine numbers or dictates. The frequency of faith and prayer is needed to manifest miracles from this musical-mathematical domain. This is the prescription for miraculous healing and eternal sustenance.

This book advances the "key of the house of David." The 528/LOVE in your heart is the same as that sourcing from God through the Heavenly Kingdom. It is your choice to use this key to unlock the secrets of the universe, but more importantly to open human hearts. The Illuminati and their sorcery has kept *We the People* enslaved for millennia, and this key of LOVE also closes this door.

"Do what you LOVE and the money will follow." The information in this book explains why this is true, and how it works.

You were created in LOVE/528, to be a powerful co-creator, and to celebrate with God all loving hearts tuned to 528.

These truths have been metaphorically expressed throughout the ages in philosophy, religions, poetry, prose, music, and even Hollywood movies.

At the beginning of this book I gave a great example of what this work is really about. Metaphorically, The Beatles' movie *Yellow Submarine* summarizes my mission. In the animation, peaceful loving civilization became enslaved by the Blue Meanies who silenced Pepperland's music. That froze colorful creative people and turned them into fragile black-and-white. Pepperlanders became targets of missiles and bombs that broke them apart where they stood silent and stuck in time. By freeing their instruments and voices, the Lonely Hearts Club Band restored peace and prosperity to the victims of musical suppression.

This book ends, as did *Yellow Submarine* and John Lennon's life, with the words "All you need is LOVE, . . . LOVE is all you need," echoing eternally in 528.

References

1) Horowitz L. *DNA: Pirates of the Sacred Spiral.* Sandpoint, ID; Tetrahedron Publishing Group, 2004. Reference to Bock Saga sources from: Whale L. The Bock Saga: An ancient time capsule. *Nexus* 2002;9;4 (une-July): 61-85.

2) Showell V. Combined Thesis Monograph--Teotihuacan Universal Harmonic Master Code; Includes 528 Cosmology and Sacred Geometry Analytical Mathematics. See: http://www.love528.com

3) Personal communication from Vic Showell, whose Combined Thesis Monograph is available for a free download at: http://web.mac.com/len15/LOVE528/Pi,_PHI_&_528_files/

4) McClain EG. *The Myth of Invariance: The Origin of the Gods, Mathematics and Music From the Rg Veda to Plato.* York Beach, ME: Nicolas-Hays, OInc., 1984.

5) King C. *BIOCOSMOLOGY.* Department of Mathematics, University of Auckland, New Zealand, 2003; Link to: http://www.dhushara.com/book/bchtm/biocos.htm

6) Keutsch FN and Saykally R J. Water clusters: Untangling the mysteries of the liquid, one molecule at a time. Inaugural Article Chemistry *PNAS* 2001;98,19:10533-10540 (Link to: http://www.pnas.org/cgi/content/full/98/19/10533)

7) Horowitz LG. *LOVE the Real da Vinci CODE.* Sandpoint, ID: Tetrahedron Press. 2008.

8) Personal communication with Marko Rodin.

9) Reid JS. Egyptian Sonics. *Journal of Hydrocreationism.* Vol. 1. No. 1, January, 2009. See: http://web.me.com/len15/HYDROSONICS/EGYPTIAN_SONICS.html; See also: Showell V. 528, Sacred Geometry and the Eternal Now: Researching the Sound of LOVE, See:: http://web.me.com/len15/HYDROSONICS/528_Frequency_%26_Sacred_Geometry.html

10) Horowitz L and Puleo J. *Healing Codes for the Biological Apocalypse.* Sandpoint, ID: Tetrahedron Publishing Group, 1999.

11) Sereda D and Horowitz LG. Sun sounds include LOVE frequency 528Hz. See: http://web.mac.com/len15/LIVEH2O.info/Solar_

12) Ocean Health. See: http://www.oceanplasma.org/documents/transmuteation.html

13) Personal communication from Lee Lorenzen. Sonics_%26_LOVE_ Harmonics_for_Peace,_Health_%26_Prosperity.html

14) Müller H. *Theory of Global Scaling*. Sante Fe: NM: Institute for Space-Energy-Research, Leonard Euler, Ltd. and Global Scaling Applications, Inc., 2002.Source: www.Sonics_%26_LOVE_Harmonics_ for_Peace,_Health_%26_Prosperity.html

15) Underwood A, Whitford B, Chung J, et. al. Spirituality in America. *Newsweek*, Sept 5, 2005, pp. 46-64.

16) Photograph of spiraling galaxy courtesy of NASA's Hubble website. See: http://hubblesite.org/gallery/album/galaxy_collection/pr2005001a/ large_web. For photomicrograph of mitosis see: Molecular Expressions website at: http://micro.magnet.fsu.edu/cells/fluorescencemitosis/

17) The Phi Nest. DNA: The spiral is a Golden section; the cross section is based on Phi. Lengthy analysis and discussion is available online at http://www.goldennumber.net

18) Vologodskii AV. Circular DNA. OnLine Biophysical Chemistry Textbook, ed. V. Bloomfield. http://www.biophysics.org/btol/supramol. thml#13 (1999)Department of Chemistry, New York University, New York, NY. (Link to PDF online paper.)

Appendix

An Essay on 528,
"The Key of the House of David,"
and the Matrix of Heaven

The "key of the house of David," in my humble opinion, is 528Hz—the heart of everything, as proven by the evidence compiled in *The Book of 528: Prosperity Key of LOVE*.

This "key" is first mentioned in the *Book of Isaiah* in a description of the duties of Eliakim, the royal chamberlain of King Hezekiah of Judah. Isaiah 22:22 states, "And the key of the house of David will I lay upon his shoulder; so he shall open, and none shall shut; and he shall shut, and none shall open."

According to Richard A. McGough, a pioneering investigator and author of *The Bible Wheel* (BibleWheel.com), "This key is literally the key to the [entire] Bible." After years of researching patterns formed by the 66 books of the Bible graphed in a circle, generating a spiraling scroll, including Hebrew and Greek gematria analyses, McGough determined the number 528 results from the alphanumerics of the Hebrew words: 1) Maphtay'ach (meaning, "The Key"), 2) HaAlephbeyt ("The Alphabet") and 3) Yehoshua ("Jesus").(1)

Moreover, McGough determined that "528 . . . is the product of the number of letters in the Hebrew (22) and Greek (24) alphabets, as 22 x 24 = 528.(1)

However, many authorities claim this key of the house of David is symbolic for Divinely-directed government, not a musical note with metaphysical meaning and power. In Isaiah, the government of Eliakim, which they propose is a type or symbol of the government of Jesus Christ, is the kingdom of Jesus Christ established, or founded, on a work of judgment.

Respecting these experts' suppositions, as revealed in my books, *Walk on Water*, and *LOVE the Real Da Vinci CODE*, the "key of David" is a musical note and scale, which King David used to tune his harp to administer healing, sing psalms, and march harmoniously with the Creator victoriously through battles. This key relates to a "tone" meant for Divine blessing, or atonement. That is, intentional communion—at One meant, synchronizing and harmonizing with the Creator, or a-tone meant by engaging His Divine lovingly-creative sound, as heralded during the Festival of Trumpets.

Consider the possibility that the "work of judgment" is the Creator's Master Matrix of creation, akin to the Kingdom of Heaven. Dissonance to the Master Matrix math, like sin, prompts an equal and opposite reaction, called karma. This best explains how the Source of Creation rules and renders judgment precisely—mathematically/energetically.

The peaceful quality in the matrix resonates largely, as this book evidences, Divine Love in the key of C in 528 Hertz (Hz) frequency.

528 and the Master Matrix

The world today is like Babylon was described in the *Genesis*. Our geopolitical condition is sinful. The word "sin" derives from the Greek archery term meaning "off the mark." This sinful state reflects violating the laws of universal harmony and order; being out of tune with, or in dissonance to, God's harmonious *matrix* of musical measures.

The matrix, mentioned many times in the Holy Bible, is like an instrument used to administer Supreme Law. Judgment and justice is automatically rendered universally, musically/mathematically, "a-chord-ing" to this order.

This matrix is composed of only nine numbers including the

original six ancient Solfeggio frequencies.

The "original sin" must have something to do with this matrix math reflecting man's mental, ego-centric, quest for knowledge above heart-felt guidance, sublime intuition, and Divine spiritual recognition within each of us. This original "sin" did not cause humans to die physically, but spiritually, that is, vibrationally.

This dissonant ego-centrism, a cognitive mechanism and psychosocial/psycho-spiritual pathology, is triggered by trauma, pain, and loss, such as the loss of faith and trust.

Adam and Eve are said to have suffered this loss and life-altering trauma in the Garden of Eden.

Such traumatic life experiences generate fear. This fear becomes generalized, recurring, and enslaving courtesy of the neurotic ego and those people and events that program it.

F.E.A.R., or "false evidence appearing real," short-circuits faith and inhibits reliance on God. As a result, rather than living eternally in harmony with Divinity, and with hearts filled with LOVE in communion with Creator and all creation, humanity is psycho-socially distressed and *cult*urally enslaved.

Turning from this madness, that is repentance, in the Spirit of LOVE and righteousness is the prescription advanced by Jesus and Moses, for uplifting humanity spiritually, to the matrix of "eternal life."

"The only way to the Father" involves faith, which is the key to having a blessed relationship with anyone—divine or mortal. This faith is required to embrace this certainty of Divine harmony and creativity within you.

This is reasonable considering creativity is rendered metaphysically, through the Kingdom of Heaven, that is, the musical mathematical Master Matrix that offers and renders *only* to those who have faith. The faith enables your heart and the "ears to hear" this "key" to eternal salvation—LOVE.

Isaiah 9:6 speaks of the government or kingdom shouldered by the Prince of Peace founded, on a work of judgment. All judgment is rendered universally, and very simply, electro-magnetically, using this matrix measurement, or "Key of LOVE." Isaiah 9:7 records, "Of the increase of his government and peace there shall be no end, upon the throne of David, and upon his kingdom, to order it, and to establish it with judgment and with justice from henceforth even for ever. The zeal of the Lord of hosts will perform this."

This relates to the common missions of prophets and saints who focused on unconditional LOVE reflecting Divine governance. Holy persons throughout history preached Divine governance administered through a metaphysical instrument of judgment that King David, Moses, and Jesus, celebrated. The Davidian bloodline's calling, including Jesus's mission, promised "eternal life" by faith in Divine justice and its administrative mechanism. The Bible also referenced the power of the "matrix" in rendering justice.

Indeed, any government founded on this matrix of mathematical/musical harmony—Divine Law—will prosper; any in dissonance will degenerate by its own dischord.

This matrix is the Creator's exclusive property, as cited in Exodus 13:12;15:19 and Numbers 3:12;18:15. No man can judge what was developed by the Creator to administer Divine justice, and every being shall be judged by his righteousness automatically and precisely according to this instrument of mathematical measure.

History and Prophecy

Why is this knowledge urgent at this time? Consider this relevant history.

The *Book of Revelation*'s "End Times" includes the opening of the seven seals. Seals were typically placed on scrolls containing important legal test. Seven seals on a scroll suggests a *massive* legal text—such as the Scroll of Life containing language detailing cosmic control or heavenly governance.

There are also seven major chakras, or energy centers in humans, with seven harmonizing and controlling numbers, or frequencies of music, that balance them.

Moreover, there are seven churches referenced in the *Book of Revelation* besides the Church of Satan. *Revelation* contains letters to these seven churches in Asia Minor—literal congregations describing a spectrum of human conditions. These seven churches are considered symbolic for seven time periods—from the Apostolic church to the time of the second coming. They are:

Ephesus ("desirable"), Rev. 2:1-7 — The Apostolic church of the 1st century.

Smyrna ("sweet smelling"), Rev. 2:8-11 — Persecuted by Ancient Pagan Rome.

Pergamos ("elevated by marriage"), Rev. 2:12-17 — Apostasy begins with church-state union.

Thyatira ("sacrifice of contrition"), Rev. 2:18-29 — The church of the middle ages.

Sardis ("escape of the remnant"), Rev. 3:1-6 — The Reformation era.

Philadelphia ("brotherly love"), Rev. 3:7-13 — The early 19th century to 1844.

Laodicea ("a people judged"), Rev. 3:14-19 — From 1844 to the second coming.

Considering the "key of the House of David," according to *Strong's Concordance*, the present age of Laodicea is primarily focused on administering justice and judgment:

Thus, the Master Matrix of musical mathematics—the instrument through which judgment and balance is administered—is heralded at this time in history as the exclusive method of directing metaphysical justice impacting life on earth. The root words in the Bible, involved here, are:

G1349. dike, dee'-kay; prob. from G1166; right (as self-evident), i.e. justice (the principle, a decision, or its execution):--judgment, punish, vengeance. [The word dike is used in Acts 25:15, Acts 28:4, 2 Thess 1:9, and Jude 1:7.]

Figure 53. Shaman Performs "Baptism" in Ecuador

Studies of natural healing practices around the world point to three main factors: 1) Faith; 2) Holy Spirit power to heal; and 3) Water. Here an Ecuadorian native gets "baptised" by "a yachac, or shaman, who performs a Water ritual on the man in a spring near Cotacachi during an indigenous celebration. The Water is believed to wash away bad energy and purify the soul. When done before a fiesta, the ritual gives people the energy needed to dance for days." Source: *TIME* Magazine online. See: http://www.time.com/time/photogallery/0,29307,1878443_1842218,00.html

This is significant because the key of the House of David is mentioned specifically for the second time in the letter to the church of Philadelphia. This key denotes a contrasting relationship between LOVE, as a measure of harmony and decency uplifting humanity spiritually, and demonic dissonance. Perceiving or measuring the dissonance facilitates just judgment, as detailed in my discussion of 528Hz versus 741Hz (in Chapter 4.)

The "key of the house of David," recognized as having been in the Messiah's possession, clearly opens this important door for judgment near the end of time, shortly before His second coming, during the period of time described as the Philadelphian church featuring "brotherly LOVE," People who fail to learn the lessons of LOVE are increasingly being judged and sentenced during the current Laodicean period.

John the Revelator sees this door opened hydrosonically by a musical key impacting "Spirit/Water" in his chapters 3 and 4.

Spirit/Water Baptism for Salvation

In John 3:3, Jesus answered Nicodemus, "Verily, verily, I say unto thee, Except a man be born again, he cannot see the kingdom of God."

Nicodemus then asked how is this miraculous spiritual transformation possible, to which Jesus replied (John 3:5) "Except a man be born of water and of the spirit, he cannot enter into the kingdom of God. That which is born of the flesh is flesh; and that which is born of the Spirit is spirit."

In *Concordance*'s explanatory notes, Jesus' reference to "Water and Spirit" are "Not two things, but one." "It is rendered of Water--yea, Spiritual Water."

This explains the main concept I have advanced in *The*

Book of 528: Prosperity Key of LOVE: You are created musi-cally-mathematically—*hydrosonically*—from this Master Ma-trix of nine core creative frequencies of sound, at the heart of which is LOVE/528.

The Key and Commandment to LOVE

In John 13:34-35, Jesus provided "A new commandment . . . That ye LOVE one another; as I have loved you, that ye also love one another. By this shall all men know that ye are My disciples, if ye have LOVE one to another."

Revelation 3:7-8 states, "And to the angel of the church in Philadelphia write; These things saith he that is holy, he that is true, he that hath the key of David, he that openeth, and no man shutteth; and shutteth, and no man openeth; I know thy works: behold, I have set before thee an open door, and no man can shut it: for thou hast a little strength, and hast kept my word, and hast not denied my name."

Revelation 4:1-2, states, "After this I looked, and, behold, a door was opened in heaven: and the first voice which I heard was as it were of a trumpet talking with me; which said, Come up hither, and I will show thee things which must be hereafter;

Rev 4:2 And immediately I was in the spirit; and, behold, a throne was set in heaven, and one sat on the throne."

Key to the Arc(k) of the Contract

On the Day of Atonement the high priest enters the Most Holy place in the sanctuary or temple, which is symbolic of the judgment of God's people. The shofar is played during this ceremony. In the Most Holy place is the *Ark* of the Covenant, containing the standard of judgment, the Ten Commandments of God (*Exodus* 20:2-17).

"Ark" is defined as a holy container; a large boat navigating . . . Spirit/Water. Noah's Ark provided shelter or refuge against judgment.

Most recent research into this Ark indicates it was a *drum*, another musical instrument, as detailed in the Apocalypse and the Ark of the Covenant section of the Appendix.

Besides rendering music for chants and recitations, the Ark of the Covenant contains the *sacred contract*—the legal terms of agreement, between God and man. Violations of the contract generate judgment—the spiritual, energetic, electro-magnetic, musical-mathematical rendering of justice against those generating dissonance with the Master Matrix or Kingdom of Heaven.

In the beginning of time, the Creator, the Word (sound, elecro-magnetic frequencies, simple math) and the Spirit/Water was all present to administer creation. Water is the "universal solvent" existing throughout space/time. It is known in science as a superconductor of sound and light energy. Water transmits sound and electrical currents far better than air, that is also hydrated, but not as wet as Water.

The Ark of the Covenant was also used by Moses to divide Water for their safe passage. (*Joshua* 3:15-16; 4:7-18).

These salvation sagas had to have involved this "key of the house of David," since 528 is the electromagnetic energy conductor resonating the sacred geometry of Water—the Divine creative juice filled with the Holy Spirit. Water responds consciously and amicably to LOVE, according to Emoto's research.(3) Consequently, Water's structure and function as the "Universal Solvent" depends largely, if not exclusively, on 528/LOVE.

Protection and preservation of those "who have ears to hear" this music—those who celebrate a full measure of righteous—always involves LOVE and Spirit/Water operating Divinely (as Jesus referred to it in *John* 7:38).

In summary, there is a key that opens your heart to LOVE and eternal life. It is a key to understanding all of the mysteries in the Bible, in science and metaphysics. This key, that vibrates with the frequency of full faith, enables you to stand against evil, dissonance, and adversity.

As David Roper, a minister of Christian theology, wrote:

> "[I]n connection with one particular church, the church of Philadelphia, [Jesus is symbolically] described as one who has in his hand the key of David. It is clear from the context that the key of David is the key to everything. It is the key to power and authority and constancy and endurance in the face of adversity."(2)

Despite adversity, The Royal Bloodline of David shall endure forever, as promised by the Creator. Christian analysts conclude the Messiah made this prophecy a reality. In every case, the key of David is LOVE that opens the gates of Divinity to humanity for eternity.

References:

1) McGough RA. *The Bible Wheel: Revelation of the Divine Unity of the Holy Bible*. Yakima, WA: Bible Wheel Ministries, See: http://www.biblewheel.com/gr/GR_528.asp

2) Roper DH. The Key of David. See: http://biblelight.net/KeyofDavid.htm

3) Emoto M. *Love Thyself: The Message from Water III*. Carlsbad, CA: Hay House, Inc. 2004.

Sealed by 528:
Fulfilling Prophesy and Revelation

In *Walk on Water*, I advanced understanding of the meaning of the word "seal" used in the Bible pertaining to salvation. I explained this word's relationship to the administration of karmic justice among those "unsealed."

Revelation 7:1-4 speaks of the 144,000 prophesied to be protected by becoming "sealed." These blessed beings sing "a new song" for planet-wide physical and spiritual salvation.

Divinely *sealed* due to their loving altruistic focus, and powerful faith, are 12,000 from each of the twelve tribes representing leaders of the loving family—the MIracle FAmily identified by the "MI" and "FA" tones at the heart of the original Solfeggio. These include people worldwide of every religion, faith, and culture. Their hearts are sufficiently sealed by faith, resonating with the LOVE of God and the Lamb. They have endured years of being tested and purified by the fires of karmic justice. This is the fare required to secure protection, survive, and *thrive* as all hell breaks loose in the world.

This select "sealed" group sings a "new song," in the "key of the house of David," that opens "doors," spiritual portals, for millions of others. The Illuminati cannot stop them. The cumulative vibration energetically uplifts everything to restore righteousness, or "right-standingness," on Earth as it is in Heaven. This event honors the power of LOVE in our hearts; the power of LOVE that God has for the human family, including special LOVE the Creator demonstrates for those who are most faithful.

Revelation 7:9-17 describes these servants and saving events, honoring Jesus' LOVE message and ministry this way:

Salvation belongs to our God,
who sits on the throne,
and to the Lamb.

. . . . These are they who have come out of the great tribula-
tion; they have washed their robes and made them white in
the blood of the Lamb. Therefore, "they are before the throne
of God and serve him day and night in his temple; and he who
sits on the throne will spread his tent over them. Never again
will they hunger; never again will they thirst. The sun will not
beat upon them, nor any scorching heat. For the Lamb at the
center of the throne will be their shepherd; he will lead them to
springs of living Water. And God will wipe away every tear from
their eyes.

This was a promise—to be led by the Saviour to prosperity
in all ways. The Prince of Peace is the personification of LOVE
and forgiveness.

You learned herein that 528Hz frequency of sound and
light are the core creative and restorative vibrations of the
universe. 528 resonates eternally, in the heart of everything,
so it must resonate at the center of the throne, in the heart of
God, as in the Lamb of LOVE.

Thus, 528/LOVE must be the spiritual energy, or frequency
in Jesus' heart, that shepherds people to the "spring of living
Water" in these End Times.

This analysis helps explain why LOVE/528 is exponentially
increasing at this time in history, affecting lives everywhere.
Cosmically, everything is shifting energetically. Change appears to be accelerating exponentially, compelled electromagnetically and geophysically. This shift is necessary to restore
harmony in our world plagued by dissonance on every social
level.

LOVE/528 is the seal for the *faithful* who have "eyes to see"
this LOVE light shining, and have developed the "ears to hear"
this Divine calling.

This melody in the heart of Jesus is the "key of LOVE."
528nm light, and 528Hz frquency of sound, is the spiritual

"Manna of LOVE" celebrated by the living God who gave his life for LOVE so that others may live perpetually on Earth as it is in heaven.

This seal is central to the Spiritual Renaissance radiating from the heart of God into your heart. It is the spiritual coverage and electromagnetism attracting you, and "phase-locking" you, to your Source. It is most precious among the vibrations, frequencies, or resonances attuning and communing Creator with creation.

The powerful oscillating heart essence and core radiance of God, is the bliss Apostle Paul experienced, and challenged everyone else to discover, by getting to know the true Spirit of the Creator. (1 Corinthians 2:6-16)

The Pineal Gland or "Third Eye Chakra"

Why, then, does the Bible say this "seal" is specifically on, or in, your forehead?

Because this is the location of the pineal gland—site of the "third eye chakra" that intuitively perceives things spiritually or energetically.

Your pineal gland is the center for electromagnetic frequency reception, earthly orientation, and spiritual evolution. This is what birds, whales, and myriad more species use to navigate and migrate thousands of miles without getting lost! Brain function and hormonal regulation critically depends on the bioenergetics and neuroendocrine dynamics of the pineal gland.

David defeated Goliath by striking this area of the forebrain.

The "third eye" resonates at a higher frequency than LOVE/528, apparently in sync with 741Hz, according to sound healing researcher, Michael Walton, and later others.(1) This higher frequency in musicology, compared to 528Hz, is called the "Devil's Interval." When 528 and 741 are played together they produce the "Devil's Tone," as explained previously—an augmented 4th or diminished 5th that sounds most annoying.

The mass media creates competition for intuitive and spiritual reception. It is profitable to administer population manipulation through LOVE suppression. The media and mass mindset encourages egoic guilt and fear which suppresses LOVE, joy, faith and bravery, each associated with the heart and heart chakra.

Forgiveness makes all of this negativity—this dissonant destructive frequency of anti-LOVE energy—disappear. Your LOVE is a function of foregiveness as Jesus demonstrated in his last act. Foregiveness frees your heart to LOVE.

So sealing this area of your forebrain with the heart energy of 528Hz is what is required to transform humans into superhumans, and Babylon into utopia. In other words, by using 528Hz music, LOVE, heart-felt faith, and intuition expands, while reptilian consciousness, ego, fear, guilt and aggression contracts.

If you were to be fully blessed with "the seal of the living God," the end result would enable you to receive *and* follow Divine direction to establish peace and productivity in life consistent with heaven on Earth. This is the main mission of the 528LOVERevolution.

The Life in Your Breath and Blood

The blood of the Lamb references a sacrifice, and the sacred release of God's LOVE in your Holy Spirit-filled Temple— your body.

This Life Force is energizing your blood right now, because your blood is composed principally of "Spirit/Water"—528 resonating hydrogen and oxygen. The red color of blood comes from oxygenated iron-rich hemoglobin. This molecule demonstrates the sacred geometry of fundamentally 528Hz frequency--hexagonal and pentagonal rings. Chlorophyll in plants demonstrates the same sacred geometry. Oxygen produced through photosynthesis by chlorophyll, is carred by hemoglobin to sustain human life.

The electron of energy that oxygen—the Breath of Life—carries, vibrates most powerfully with the frequency of 528/LOVE. Here is how it works, and relates to LOVE and foregiveness, which is a function of LOVE.

The Sun radiates fundamentally 528Hz frequency of sound and its harmonics, according to NASA recordings and tuning fork analyses easily reproduced and confirmed. The chlorophyll color of 528nm, greenish yellow, reflects exclusively this light. Six carbon dioxide plus six (6) water molecules are converted to six (6) glucose (carbohydrate food) plus six (6) oxygen molecules during photosynthesis.

In other words, chlorophyll uptakes everything in the light spectrum above and below 528, and converts it to LOVE/528 greenish-yellow. The 528nm color of sunlight reflects off leaves and grass, and feeds your eyes with 528/LOVE. So what's really happening physically, mirrors what is occurring spiritually, demonstrating unconditional LOVE and foregiveness. The plants transmute or transform the unLOVING/non-528 energy into LOVE that transmits through oxygen in the air, and fills you with LOVE with each breath.

Now blue blood is depleted of the LOVE. Maybe this is why the European royalty that have been historically advancing wars and genocides are called "blue bloods?" They borrowed money from the Illuminati to kill humanity most satanically. They have mostly proven themselves to be "cold-blooded" killers instead of "warm-blooded" lovers and peace-makers.

In this vein, natives in Hawaii refer to white people as "haoles," meaning "breathless" or "spiritless" ones. This label resulted following the genocidal treatment of natives by caucasians, beginning with the British royalty and church missionaries.

The breath, or the "HA" sound in "prana," "aloha," and "Ya-HoVah," invites oxygen and hydrogen to complete communion of matter and energy, Spirit in Water, and God in man.

Oxygen—element No. 8, and hydrogen—element No. 1, form Water. 1 + 8 = 9, signifying completion. The alphanumerics of "HA," is also a 9, since "A" is the first, and "H" is the eighth letter of the English alphabet.

The musical mathematics, and alphanumerics underlying creationism, becomes increasingly important during this time of geopolitical and economic collapse. A new order must come out of the present chaos to transform our dysfunctional systems of government. The New World Order, heralded by satanists, athiests, pagans, politicians, and those who call themselves Christians, Jews, or Muslims who are not, will not return us to the Garden of Eden. This transformation shall happen only through being *sealed* with faith in God, or constant *atonement*—Divine communion in LOVE/528.

Raising the human vibration to accept this pure level of being, to resonate in harmony with the Creator through, fundamentally, LOVE running in our blood, is the goal.

This reasonable thesis, salvation message, and practical revelation is supported by science—especially secreted mathematics and metaphysics.

According to experts, science focused exclusively on matter "covers only one billionth of all the phenomena in the cosmos." When science neglects the metaphysical, musical, and mathematical components of creation, science degenerates.

Modern science must, therefore, draw incorrect conclusions most of the time.

"Resonance between oscillating particles is a primordial principle in the cosmos," according to science published in the *Journal of Bioelectromedicine,* in June 2000.(2)

In *DNA Pirates of the Sacred Spiral*, I explained the roles of resonating particles in genetic expression, such as amino acids, sugars, and proteins employing electromagnetism.

A practical example of the beneficial shift in science, to integrate electrogenetics and resonance frequencies, such as 528, is the advances in permaculture. Certain pure tones are now being played to crops to prompt plant growth, immunity, and protection against blights. This "green technology" is replacing poisonous chemicals or genetic manipulations threatening species extinctions.

DNA is a virtual antennae to God. Substantial science evidences genetic reception and transmission of sound and light vibrations broadcasting musically, mathematically, harmoneously, from Master Matrix reality—the Kingdom of Heaven.

This best explains why 528Hz lies at the heart of the rainbow—the heart of the music and math of electrogenesis and cosmogenesis. The electromagnetic color spectrum, with the botanical world obviously celebrating the 528 colors greenish-yellow, proclaims the math and music of the Creator's LOVE.

Naturally, you would want this most loving heart energy to be your guiding light, shepherding you to heaven on Earth and prosperity in all ways.

The Seal Over the Scroll

To complete this clarification of "sealing" for salvation, consider the notion of a "scroll" as referenced in *Revelation*, 5:1-5:

> Then I saw in the right [outgoing and creative] hand of him who sat on the throne a scroll with writing on both sides and sealed with seven seals. And I saw a mighty angel proclaiming in a loud voice, "Who is worthy to break the seals and open the scroll?" But no one in heaven or on earth or under the earth could open the scroll or even look inside it. I wept and wept because no one was found who was worthy to open the scroll or look inside. Then one of the elders said to me, "Do not weep! See, the Lion of the tribe of Judah, the Root of David, has triumphed. He is able to open the scroll and its seven seals."

What is the scroll to be revealed only by the Lion of the tribe of Judah, with the Root and Key of David, guided by the angel blessing the Messianic community of Philadelphia the "City of Brotherly Love," to open doors that none can shut?

Herein, I advance two possibilities of what this scroll is:1) the spinning spiraling universe, or double torroidal scroll, sealed by music, or strings, vis-a-vis "string theory" in physics; and 2) You!

After all, you are the outcome of Divine language, law, math, and music. Your spiritual system, like the chakra and acupuncture systems, are spinning from the mathematical matrix of the universe.

The Book of Revelation states there are seven seals on this scroll, foreshadowing seven major notes in a modern scale—C, D, E, F, G, A and B—or the chakra system also contains 7 major energy centers.

The word "chakra" means *wheel*. This too is shaped like a circle and spins like a scroll, just like the universe.

Balancing and healing takes place in both systems—the universe and human body—by adjusting the energies, putting them back into harmony with nature or the Master Matrix.

This is the role of judgment in religious theology.

According to *Webster's* online-dictionary, "scroll" is defined as "a round shape formed by a series of concentric circles."

Webster's defines "scroll" as a "string and character recording oriented logogrammatic language." This pertains to the mathematics of language, and the alphanumerics of language, in which letters, express the energy or spirit of certain numbers.

All of this is central to this book's main thesis:

That the "seal" of LOVE protecting your heart is opened by the key to the house of David, the miraculous 528Hz frequency pure tone that is central and fundamental to Divine creation.

In other words, our Creator is currently performing a mathematical musical miracle called "Life on Earth." The music crystallizes creation and promotes evolution of your awakened consciousness to fulfill a Divine destiny promising health, peace, freedom, and prosperity in all ways.(3)

The Grand Finale

The anti-hero in this cosmic musical performs like the "Phantom of the Opera." He sings "Music of the Night" in 741Hz dissonance, conflicting with the "Music of the Light" resonating pure LOVE, in 528Hz.

The anti-hero's objective is to break the seals corrupting your scroll, or body Temple, <u>beginning with the seal covering your heart</u>.

The hero's task is to reveal the workings of the universal scroll, in which the central string (C[5] in 528Hz, or A=444Hz) connects your heart directly to the Creator's loving heart.

The Master Conductor commands the orchestra that performs in this metaphysical musical, from a central stage called the Heavenly Throne.

God is partial to performances in the key of LOVE, the music of the heart. The notes are incorporated into your Temple, like notes on a piano scroll are registered in a certain key—the key of "C" in 528. This musical-mathematical language contains the words (alphanumerics) imparting the laws of creation (physics and metaphysics) for righteous blissful living.

In other words, you are like an instrument in the orchestra, and the universal scroll contains your personal sheet of music. From here you may be selected to play a grand solo performance.

In essence, *The Book of 528: Prosperity Key of LOVE* advances revelatory spiritual intelligence to restore what was lost or suppressed in science, theology, and the hearts and lives of wo/mankind. This is a celebration of scientific facts that testify to the power, presence, and current processes by which we can reconnect with our Creator, musically/energetically righting what went wrong with *We The People* and our planet.

The restoration of peace on Earth, decreed to be forthcoming in Revelation 21, involves "The New Jerusalem," or Yah-ru-sha-la-im in Hebrew and Chaldee (ancient Aramaic). Literally translated, this means "God's City of Peace." Experts say the name Jerusalem can be interpreted as the "foundation, vision, or possession of peace." Nearly everyone agrees that Jerusalem must fulfill its appointed destiny to become the "capital city of a world at peace."(4)

Here's a preview from Revelation 21:

> I heard a loud voice from the throne saying, "Now the dwelling of God is with men, and he will live with them. They will be his people, and God himself will be with them and be their God. He will wipe every tear from their eyes. There will be no more death or mourning or crying or pain, for the old order of things has passed away." He who was seated on the throne said, "I am making everything new!

References

1) Walton M and Horowitz LG. Synthesizer re-tuning to The Perfect Circle of Sound – A preliminary study with implications for bioenergetic healing. (See: http://wemustknow.net/2010/08/synthesizer-re-tuning-to-the-perfect-circle-of-sound-a-preliminary-study-with-implications-for-bioenergetic-healing/)

2) Block EF IV. *Journal of Bioelectromedicine* Vol. 2, Number 2, June 2000. Block Institute for Astrobiological Studies. (See: http://www.diamondhead.net/p2-2.htm)

3) Horowitz LG. Proof that God's Heart is Focused on LOVE in 528. HealthyWorldSolutions.com. (See: http://web.mac.com/len15/HealthyWorldSolutions/Is_528_Gods_Favorite_Number.html

4) Green D. Bible topics.(See: http://www.bibletopics.com/biblestudy/47.htm)

Apocalypse and the Ark of the Covenant

Apocalypse and the Ark of the Covenant are two seemingly juxtaposed topics. It turns out they are actually intimately related.

Contrary to popular belief, the word *apocalypse* implies something wonderful, as does the Ark of the Covenant.

According to the musical-mathematical revelations and scientific determinations detailed in *The Book of 528: Prosperity Key of LOVE*, humanity is compelled to consider an alternative view of reality, one that celebrates spirituality, and brings expanded meaning to these two important references.

Apocalypse Defined

The term "apocalypse" actually means: "lifting of the veil." The "veil" covers what has been secreted—an awesome and enabling truth. The forces of darkness and deception have labored for millennia to keep this intelligence classified.

As stated in the *New Jerusalem Bible*, from the "Introduction to The Revelations of John," the Greek title of this book is literally, "The Apocalypse of John," or "The Revelation of John." The word *apocalypse* is merely a transliteration in English of the Greek word for "Revelation."

Writings under the title "Apocalypse" always include revelations of hidden things. These are claimed to be administered by God, and particularly a revelation of future events. It is not easy to draw an exact dividing line between prophecy and apocalypse, and apocalyptic writers are in some ways progeny of the prophets.

So any apocalypse, or unveiling, is actually very beneficial, especially for truth seekers and spiritualists. If "the truth shall set you free," the greatest secreted truths hold the capacity to emancipate you completely. To be all that you can be, especially spiritually, you need to tune into the One Unifying Truth. This relates intimately to the term *apocalypse*, and to the Ark of the Covenant. Their true meanings and functions are optimally freeing.

Ark of the Covenant

The Ark of the Covenant generally refers to the sacred spiritual vessel containing the power and glory of God's Word, Law, and/or Spirit. The word "Ark" comes from the Old English word, "Arc" which meant "chest;" akin to the Latin word "arcere" that meant "to hold off" or "defend."

Most people know the word *ark* refers to the boat that Noah constructed that sheltered his family and animals during the flood of Divine judgment.

The Hebrews consider the Ark of the Covenant a sacred chest holding the protective presence of God.

Keep in mind, however, that at the center of your chest, as throughout the animal kingdom, is your heart. Referencing general understanding, LOVE resonates in, and from, your heart. This is a particularly special and affectionate resonant frequency and sustaining/restorative energy of Spirit/Water. LOVE, the "universal healer" resonates the color of chlorophyll and your heart chakra, greenish-yellow, or 528Hz.

The word *ark* also references the Latin word arcus, meaning a "bow," "arch," or "arc" in archery; and the flight patterns of arrows. The word *arc* also means "the apparent path described above and below the horizon by a celestial body," such as the sun or jupiter that resonates with 528Hz. Later, the arc term was used to describe "a sustained luminous discharge of electricity across a gap in a circuit or between electrodes."

Fig. 54. Traditional Concept of the Ark of the Covenant

According to a leading expert in the Ark of the Covenant, Professor Tudor Parfitt, at the University of London's prestigious School of Oriental and African Studies, the Ark was a drum, contrary to what is depicted here. In his book, *The Lost Ark of the Covenant: Solving the 2,500 Year Mystery of the Fabled Biblical Ark*, a Southern African clan called the Lemba, who claimed to be a lost tribe of Israel, holds the remains of this drum-like superconductor of Spiritual power. Only spiritually-annointed people were allowed to touch the powerful Ark. Others less "pure" would get "zapped."(6)

In Greek, when the arc of your arrow *sinned* in archery, you missed the bulls-eye. When you *sin* in life, the results of your actions miss the mark of Divine Law generating judgment or negative karma.

John Lennon's lyric, "instant karma is going to get you," refers to the musically-mathematically administered consequences of behavior that conflicts with the matrix of universal law and order. Many people claim this is happening today, more than previously, as cosmic forces accelerate the demand for harmony with the law, gravitationally and/or spiritually.

Apocalyptically speaking, this knowledge is related to the word *arcane,* that means "known or knowable only to the initiate: SECRET . . . MYSTERIOUSLY OBSCURE;" and the word arcanum means "mysterious knowledge, language, or information accessible only by the initiate. . ." (Definitions from *Merriam Webster's Collegiate Dictionary*, Tenth Edition, 1994.)

Few people realize the interrelationship between these words involving secret and mysterious knowledge central to the mathematics demanding harmonious peaceful co-existence.

Thus, the arc in archery, the geometry of a circle, Pi, Phi, and 528, as well as religious theology, involves God's covenant, promise, or contract to keep things ordered and just.

The word *covenant* came into existence around the same time as the word *ark*. Covenant is defined as: "a formal, solemn, and binding agreement: COMPACT . . . a written agreement or promise usually under *seal* between two or more parties esp. for the performance of some action. . . ."

So the Ark of the Covenant must rest on a mathematical formula underlying the arc, supporting and protecting the natural world; or a safe, sustaining, and peaceful coexistence between Creator and created that is being revealed with this knowledge.

Hurray for the Apocalypse! This is an unveiling!

Professor Parfitt's Findings

Professor Tudor Parfitt, at the University of London's prestigious School of Oriental and African Studies, reported that the Ark of the Covenant was most likely a drum.(1) In his book, *The Lost Ark of the Covenant: Solving the 2,500 Year Mystery of the Fabled Biblical Ark* (HarperOne), a Southern African clan called the Lemba, who claimed to be a lost tribe of Israel, holds the remains of this superconducting drum that issued pure spiritual power, like an attunement from God.

Colleagues laughed at Parfitt until he backed his claim in 1999 with a genetic marker study showing the descendants of Judaism's Temple priests "are found to appear as frequently among the Lemba's priestly cast as in Jews . . . ."(6)

According to *TIME*, "Parfitt started wondering about . . . the Lemba's drumlike object called the ngoma lungundu." The ngoma, according to the Lemba, was near-divine. It was used to store ritual objects, and borne on poles inserted into rings. It was too holy to touch the ground or to be touched by non-priests. It emitted a "Fire of God" that killed enemies and, occasionally, Lemba. A Lemba elder told Parfitt, "[It] came from the temple in Jerusalem. We carried it down here through Africa."(6)

Apocalyptic Revelation

The contract between the Creator and you involves what might be called the "arch composite (fractal) construction of our spiraling universe." This description, in terms of mathematics and physics, includes who you are, or how you were made from the sound and light of LOVE.

All of nature is compelled to follow, or flow, within the musical-mathematical matrix, or Kingdom of Heaven, that acts as an enforcement mechanism compelling compliance with The Law. This is the *governing mechanism for reality*, from celestial bodies to your body.

The structure and function of everything must abide by this mathematical *contract*. All animals, vegetables, and minerals, must honor this *covenant*.

If you look carefully at nature, or pre-Egyptian and Greek architecture, this ancient secret arcane of universal design becomes readily apparent.

Water, for instance, spirals down drains and flows along arcs that comprise sections of circles, which are compelled by gravity, math, and 528.

The treble and bass clefs in music depict these arches too, superimposed upon the five lines and four spaces. Galactic arrangements are written upon this musical staff too, using the Perfect Circle of Sound™ nine notes forming space/time.(8)

This apocalyptic revelation is most relevant at this time of economic and sociopolitical upheaval. Connection and communion between physical and spiritual realms remains the only option for salvation. LOVE between the Source of creation and the created is paramount in this universal musical.

Your covenant with God explains how and why judgment or karma is administered in your life—musically-mathematically; continuously adjudicating according to the harmonics of your heart, capable of communicating and celebrating Divine LOVE.

This apocalyptic vision recognizes this true meaning of the Ark of the Covenant. This unveiling heralds the fundamental musical-mathematical kinship between you and the Creator.

To be most secure in this contract, you must learn to float with faith, and zero fear, on the Living Water—in an ark built for safe transit.

The medium upon which your voyage occurs, and this contractual numerological script is written, is Spirit/Water. Water's presence throughout your "temple" secures your channel to Divine LOVE.

Your DNA, like the universe, operates in a matrix of Spirit/Water—the superconductive medium through which this Holy energy flows enforcing the covenant.

Your contract is administered using the mathematics of Divine design, fundamental to the Laws of Physics. This makes you part of this universal "Circle of Life."

All of the above features Pi, Phi, and the Golden Mean as universal constants, along with *528—the secreted universal constant of LOVE*.

This apocalyptic message relays the archetype upon which creative consciousness governs.

Your participation in this prosperity is invited.

LOVE the Real da Vinci CODE

In *LOVE The Real da Vinci CODE*, I decrypted Leonardo da Vinci's most famous drawing, the Vitruvian wo/man. The real code, encrypted in the drawing, features the fundamental mathematics of universal construction, with 528/LOVE represented slightly above the level of the naval, or center of the cosmic circle as shown in Figure 55.(3)

The Vitruvian depicts Divine-human communion available with advancing musical-mathematical intelligence. In that drawing, 528 is located between the heart of the Vitruvian, and his/her solar plexus, or will, chakra.

Considering much empiracle evidence, especially observations of nature and mathematical analyses provided in Chapter 3, that warm fuzzy feeling you have in your heart when in LOVE has to be 528Hz, resonating greenish-yellow, 528nm, consistent with knowledge about the heart chakra.

You've heard the phrase, and even a movie title, "Brave Heart." What does it mean to have a "brave heart?" Does the lack of fear suggest a strength of faith and LOVE? In your Holy Spirit filled "temple," where does faith reside? Most people point to their hearts when asked where LOVE, faith, joy, and bravery is felt strongest.

Accumulating evidence is convincing experts that there is a "music of the light" that vibrates your heart with the miracle frequency of LOVE. 528—the musical note that inspired King David to transcend fear, and celebrate exuberant joy and LOVE for the Creator.

Summary and Conclusions

An arc is shaped like a rainbow—like a slice or section of a circle. If you draw an arc, then a straight line connecting each end, you have created a drum-like image or hull-like design. Given sound and light are both mathematical wave forms, frequency vibrations, the light of any rainbow, or sound of a drum shaped like an arc, shares mathematical constants including 528Hz.(7)

The Ark of the Covenant holds the spiritual LOVE power of eternal life for souls drifting aimlessly in jeopardy. The Ark of Noah, likewise, provided a safe haven for long term salvation. Fear of death or eternal damnation is best remedied by faith and LOVE—the key virtues and conditions—in the Divine-human covenant.

The Ark of the Covenant celebrates the contract between Creator and created. All of nature is compelled vibrationally to flow with the Law governing the spinning cosmos.

This Divine Covenant explains how karma or judgment is adjudicated continuously—musically-mathematically—according to the harmonics of the heart, or harc.

This apocalypse, or unveiling, recognizes the true meaning of the Ark of the Covenant, and its fundamental musical-mathematical contract between Creator and created.

To be most secure in this agreement, you must learn to float with faith on the Living Water.

The Water's presence throughout the universe as the superconductive medium through which this Holy Covenant is administered based on sound and light signaling, was recently proven by NASA scientists. Our spiraling fractal universe (i.e., physical reality) sources fundamentally hydrosonically and mathematically, thus generating electromagnetically and bioacoustically (that is, energetically or spiritually) the Laws of Physics.

This apocalyptic message relays the archetype upon which creative consciousness governs. Administration of physicality and universal integrity depends fundamentally upon 528, the Music of the Light.

Every archway supporting and protecting reality vibrates similarly, apparently with LOVE and 528 since both are in harmony with the circle of cosmic construction echoing eternally.

Written music depicts these truths. The treble and bass clefs in music depict arcs and arches, superimposed on five lines and four spaces totaling nine—*completion*. This is the same number of notes forming a Perfect Circle of Sound™, comprising the Master Matrix of math administering the universal "work in progress." So the origin of written music, probably has much to do with these cosmic arrangements.(8)

Compelled by this musical-math, form follows (sound) frequencies and everything functions optimally, sustainably, and naturally, as opposed to petro-chemically or pharmaceutically.

Music, the "Universal Language," transcends the physical world touching spiritual realms and parallel realities.

Divine differentiation enables conscious perception and invites enlightened co-creation.

Universal compliance with this Covenant is assured by the basic laws of physics. "For every action, there is an equal and opposite reaction." Although stress may be beneficial, and self-destruction may serve a higher purpose, generally speaking the least stressed among us are better able to survive and thrive. Peaceful, loving, safe, and sustainable coexistence, like communion with the Source of your experience, must be actualized for civilization's enlightenment.

The most important and impacting apocalyptic revelations concern the science, physics, metaphysics, and fundamental musical-mathematics of Divine LOVE. This is expressed through cymatics—the impact of sound on matter mediated by Spirit/Water. These hydrosonic dynamics exclusively direct the universe including your existence. Your sacred body geometrics and Spirit is a musical mathematical manifestation of Divine frequency vibrations administered by a spiritual *contract* tested by faith and LOVE. Compelled by this music of the Master Matrix, your form—that of a pentagon with two arms, two legs, and a head, is comprised.

Divine differentiation enables your conscious perception of self versus other, providing the opportunity for enlightened co-creation.

In other words, your perceived separation, between you and God, and you and others, is an illusion of your limited senses. This scholarly analysis of the Ark of the Covenant reconciles this illusion of separation.

As Babylon falls during this apocalyptic period, and your personal dissonance becomes intolerable, your relationships shall change too. The force of LOVE pulling on your heart strings shall increase exponentially, opening your heart more and more.

528 is at odds with 741, as certain as good opposes evil. From this primordial mathematical-musical conflict survivors will find protection and salvation in LOVE, or you will desperately long for it as you die.

Figure 55. Vitruvian Wo/Man Decryption by Horowitz

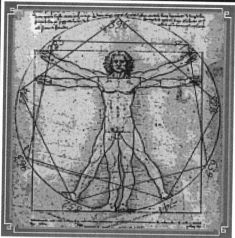

In the book, *LOVE the Real da Vinci CODE,* by this author, da Vinci's most famous drawing is decrypted. "The Vitruvian Wo/Man" reveals the "real da Vinci code." Two people stand in the circle and square. There is a woman behind the man. She is identified by her female reproductive organ, the umbilicus, at the heart of the cosmic circle. She stepped out of the box of earthy limitation. The square still imprisons the male, whose reproductive organ appears at the center of the square. The circle represents The Perfect Circle of Sound™, containing nine core creative frequencies. The eight arms and legs, plus a head, represent these nine tones. The 528 frequency is graphed at the heart level, in the greenish-yellow zone of the chakra system. Lines connecting alternating tones are shown here forming spiraling pentagons. The 528Hz frequency has been proven by mathematicians to be fundamental to the geometry of the circle, square, speed of light, laws of physics and more. Evidence indicates it is the "universal constant of LOVE." Source: Horowitz LG. *LOVE the Real da Vinci CODE.* (2006) See: www.lovetherealdavincicode.com.

According to the Old Testament (Torah), only certain people were able to "touch" the Ark of the Covenant without getting mortally wounded.

Likewise, today, only a minority will realize the wisdom in these revelations and invitation for eternal salvation.

References

1)Brennan Z. The real Indiana Jones: Intrepid British don Tudor Parfitt's mission to find the Lord Ark. See: http://www.dailymail.co.uk/news/article-517641/The-real-Indiana-Jones-Intrepid-British-don-Tudor-Parfitts-mission-Lord-Ark.html#ixzz16GNv4i3X2

2) V Showell has written a series of monographs available in pdf format at www.LOVE528.com. His latest, "Teotihuacan Universal Harmonic Master Code" includes 528's connections to the sacred geometry of the circle, pi and Phi.

3) Horowitz LG. *LOVE the Real da Vinci CODE*. Sandpoint, ID: Tetrahedron Press, 2008. See: http://www.HealthyWorld-Store.com/LOVE-The-Real-Da-Vinci-CODE-book-p/trdc.htm

4) Horowitz LG and Puleo J. *Healing Codes for the Biological Apocalypse*. Sandpoint, ID: Tetrahedron Press, 1998.

5) Horowitz LG. *Walk on Water*. Sandpoint, ID: Tetrahedron Press, 2008. See: http://www.HealthyWorldStore.com/WALK-ON-WATER-PDF-p/wowater%20pdf.htm

6) van Biema D. A Lead on the Ark of the Covenant. Time Magazine, News: Health & Science. See: http://www.time.com/time/health/article/0,8599,1715337,00.html

7) This is interesting for many reasons including the most advanced medical treatment for cancerous tumors of the chest is called "electron arc" radiation.

8) The archaic word "staff" means a "shaft." This is a comforting and directing "rod" assuring safe travels as in Psalm 23:4; really a spiritual shaft that connects humanity through a "black hole" of energy (i.e., an energy vortex) to Divinity. This "Musical-Mathematical Matrix" known in the worlds of science and metaphysics, is the "Kingdom of Heaven" referenced throughout the religious world.

528 in the *INCEPTION* Movie

What did Christopher Nolan have in mind when he made 528 a large part of the 2010 Hollywood Blockbuster, *INCEPTION*?

In this metaphysical thriller, that leaves most people confused, the number 528 was mentioned or shown six (6) times. This was no "accident" since 528—the Miracle 6 musical note of the original Solfeggio—reduces to a 6 (since 5+2+8=15 and 1+5=6). Sixes are archetypes, or amulets, for weath accumulation.

Nolan's plot juxtaposes LOVE against espionage and sabotage in the global energy industry. The LOVE theme, and advertising 528 in the plot, is conspicuously tied to *INCEPTION* or *creation*.

Since music is energy, and the largest energy industrialists and multi-national corporations control the music industry (Westinghouse, GE, RCA, EMI, etc.), music played an important part in the film. During the film's climax, that took place in Room 528, music was required to cue the hero's return from nightmarish levels of consciousness.

The movie repeats the number 528 in a mathematical code, a phone number, on a napkin, two vault combinations, and Room 528 wherein the film's most suspenseful moments happened. A "528-491" combination unlocks a safe containing the greatest secret, treasure, motivation, and catharsis for the main characters disheartened by their loss of loved ones.

Nolan's film depicts the ancient knowledge of 528 in a modern form—a spinning top used by Cobb, the lead character played by Leonardo DiCaprio. He spins the film's icon—a top shaped like the heart of the universe. He practices this ritual to distinguish "reality" from his subconscious illusions.

He works his "last job" as an energy industry mind-saboteur driven by LOVE to "get back home."

"Home is where the heart is." The heart of everything vibrates at 528Hz. So Nolan's film is best understood when you consider this simple truth and reflect on its science.

The heart of the universe is called a "black hole." This is where physicists say our physical reality miraculously manifests from musical mathematics. This space is shaped like Cobbs top, and is theoretically linked to zero point energy and 528Hz frequency.

There is accumulating evidence to support the concept that 528, the third note in the original Solfeggio musical scale, is the heart of everything. In fact, 528 is fundamental to the mathematical constants Pi and Phi, as well as the sacred geometry of circles, squares, and triangles, including the Water molecule—H_2O.

By fluke, the film's launch coincided with that of i528Tunes. com—the website delivering 528 musical transposition—a "kick" needed to manifest more LOVE and peace in the world.

i528Tunes.com places 528 music into a public library developed for global healing, education, psycho-spiritual evolution, and political action. Artists are offered 60% royalties based on donations, and may elect to donate their share to humanitarian causes.

Nolan drew on this knowledge when developing *INCEPTION*'s plot. The movie features music, and lots of Water, to "kick" characters out of their destructive dream states, called subconscious "levels."

Moreover, *INCEPTION* is about CREATION involving the creative elements—Water and the Sun.

With your body composed of nearly 80% Water, you have a reasonable explanation for baptism as a spiritually invigorating

Figure 56. Room 528 Musical Extraction in *INCEPTION*

Room 528 was used as an "extraction" chamber in the Movie *INCEPTION*. Extractions from horrific mind sets generated through hypnosis, the characters need to "cue the music" to synchronize the return to "reality" from architecturally-generated consciousness "levels." The protagonist, played by Leonardo de Caprio, spins a top, formed in the shape of the inside of the universe, to check his reality state. Source: INCEPTIONMovieExplained.com

experience that 'kicks' you out of 'levels' of illusion, projected by the egoic mind, prompting reconnection with the Source of hydrosonic sustenance.

Critical Analysis

My impression of *INCEPTION* is that it is a potent mind-twister. Having people question reality vs. death in dream worlds might be okay, were it not for the film's primary financiers, Warner Brothers ($160M) and Rupert Murdoch. Murdoch's partners in crisis capitalism, include Bill Gates, Warren

Buffet, Ted Turner, George Soros, and David Rockefeller. These men have made it *very* clear they intend to disappear approximately 6 billion people within the next few decades. So people need to get used to death and dying. The propaganda in *INCEPTION* prepares people to face death as an alternative "reality level."

What better way to get comfortable with death and dying than to question the legitimacy of those reality states. This is what the film has audiences considering.

There are many positive messages that come from careful analysis of Nolan's craft, beginning with the simple "spinning top."

Things are never as they appear on the silver screen. The spinning top is not simple at all, but depicts the highly technical state of the art in physics and metaphysics.

As mentioned, the "spinning top" is structured like the heart of the universe. This, according to physicists, is the place where physical "reality" manifests from pure potential and musical-math. Sound, transmitted through a universal matrix, or Spirit/Water, crystallizes physical reality.

Physicists have linked this place to "zero point" energy, meaning there is zero physical electrons existing in this time-less space. It is a "black hole" in our universe. The top of the "spinning top" is called the "event horizon"—the point where something miraculously manifests from (supposedly) nothing (that is connected to everything.) The spinning reflects the spinning cosmos. Everything in the universe follows a math-ematical pattern, directing the geometry, spin, torque, and ve-locity of cosmic creation. That math is determined to be "The Perfect Circle of Sound™," featuring 528 as fundamental to geometry.

In *INCEPTION*, the top continues to spin in the dream world and stops in reality. The top stops and drops in the real world,

Figure. 57. Vibrating Water From INCEPTION Movie

LIQUID CRYSTAL
WATER
"UNIVERSAL" SOLVENT

528

symbolizing a disconnect to the spiritual realm that begins at birth due to the trance imposed by culture and false doctrines.

This also relates metaphysically to the energy warp of space/time. The physical realm is a lower energy, higher density, mass dimension. When your soul incarnates, it stops spinning around the universe and becomes fixed in your body, in this physical realm. Your Spirit is eternal not temporal. It is connected to the ONE everlasting Source. The mathematical heart of the cosmic realm is the heart of the microscopic realm as well. Everything in the universe is scaled according to the The Perfect Circle of Sound™ nine note series of vibrations. The miracle note in this circle is 528, which is also the heart of the rainbow and the electromagnetic color spectrum center is central to creation or *inception*.

The primary drive and emotion at the heart of everything is LOVE, expressed in relationships and/or Divine communion.

The highest human value is the heart-felt affection for, and connection to, someone or something beyond your ego.

These are the reasons Nolan selected 528 and this spinning top icon, spinning at the heart of everything..

Nolan, or whoever else wrote this screenplay, was brilliant to use this top icon, and the 528 code, in this film about corporate espionage and mind-control sourcing from leading energy industrialists.

The lead characters, Cobb and Fisher, are motivated by 528/LOVE. Both are dealing with heavy issues involving death and paternal LOVE. Cobb's passion is to get *home* to his children. Fisher needs to reconcile with his father. His catharsis comes when he realizes his father's LOVE and approval. With his self-esteem boosted, he then feels worthy of building his own energy empire.

This story line is a metaphor for the relationship between God, the Father, and Satan, the jealous, hurt, and vindictive son. Fisher's self-esteem is required to manifest "large scale" *inception*, or global energy industry creation. Only at the end of the film does he gain the insights needed to complete his journey back to LOVE, and find foregiveness in his heart.

The levels referenced in *INCEPTION* are psychological states influenced by persuasion. Cobb et. al. are mind sabateurs (just like Murdoch—the guy paying their salaries) influencing their victim's (*We The People*'s) attitudes, states of mind, points of view, feelings, emotions, thoughts, decisions, that is, overall behavior. These are called "architects" in the film, building false realities for the clueless masses (or sheeple).

This is what Hollywood is all about! Watch *PharmaWhores* and *In Lies We Trust: The CIA, Hollywood & Bioterrorism*, where you will see Hollywood is the fantasy world feeding our culture and engineering our lives.

Levels also reference illusions of mind. *We The People* have learned to identify with parents, teachers, peers, and most affectionately, *the media*. The media generates models we cherish or desire to emulate. The *levels* are worlds of deception manufactured for corporations and crisis capitalism.

So in *reality*, the "American Dream" is a *level*! It was created by the Illuminati, most ambitiously and profitably through the Rockefeller and Carnegie Foundations. (Read: *Death in the Air: Globalism, Terrorism and Toxic Warfare*.) These foundations were assigned to control the social and political views of Western World inhabitants.

In addition to the social, economic and political *level* that has been engineered as described above, there are personal levels that mind controllers profitably generate.

For instance, threatened disease outbreaks make people nervous. Fear sells a lot of drugs and vaccines. Engineered catastrophes, including "false flag" pandemics, like the 2009-2010 H1N1 Swine Flu fright. This stimulates your ego's survival mechanism. It is purely mechanical—simulus/response. Pain, fear, loss, and/or real or imagined threats to survival actually trigger major decisions creating the *levels* the film projects as nightmarish states of the subconscious mind. The mainstream news broadcasters play to this masochistic audience.

This is why news show hosts (really parasites) are called "anchors" or "anchormen" referencing the term used by specialists in the art and science of mind control—neurolinguistic programmers. These people anchor you to levels of illusion.

Stuck in these levels, without effective therapy for your psychopathology and neuroticisms, your fear-patterns repeat over and over again. This is also why, in levels of the dream world in *INCEPTION*, the top keeps spinning (like the phrase, "spinning your wheels,") while engaging states of illusion.

Fig. 58. *INCEPTION* **Movie Icon: Heart of the Universe**

THIS IS WHERE
ZERO POINT ENERGY
MIRACULOUSLY
MANIFESTS
MUSICALLY
MATHEMATICALLY
FROM THE HEART
OF THE CREATOR.

Self-righteous arrogant fools are often very destructive while caught up in this low *level* of psychosocial dysfunctioning.

The best explanation for why, in the film, "dream-people" on different levels were staring at the dreamers, and even attacking them, is because of the simple radiance of the dreamer's energetic *presence* conflicted with the dream-people's lower vibes.

This is just like in real life, wherein a person with a large presence, simply sticks out in a crowd. Movie directors always scan for these kinds of people among their "extras" when filming, and remove them from scenes so as not to distract the audience or detract from their stars.

In order to kick out of a level of illusion and psychopatho-logical dysfunction, characters must first recognize they are engaged in an illusion. Cobb's "top," when it either stops or continues to spin, is used to diagnose the condition/illusion. Help is provided, in the film, by people who coordinate the kicks.

The music cued and played from "Room 528" reflects the power of 528 music to "set the record straight," and *We The People* free. From what is known about this frequency, you can fully appreciate why Nolan uses Room 528's music maker to cue and coordinate the "three-level extraction" during the film's climax.

These three levels reflect, metaphorically, the Father, Son and Holy Spirit. The salvation message, and music for saving the heroes from death in dangerous trance states is LOVE in 528.

COMMERCIALIZING 528

Some people criticize me for commercializing 528, and virtually all of my research.

Every journalist, medical researcher, or serious scientist needs sponsors. So commercializing 528 products and services helps pay the bills, and more importantly, supports companies advancing a healthier paradigm based on these awesome revelations and related applications.

Also, if you had such *great news* to herald, you would want to do your best to apply this sacred knowledge most wisely and beneficially, every way possible, including products.

Besides the above, the Bible promises a swift shift in wealth from "the wicked" to "the meek" in these End Times. Although I have primarily focused on service to God, family, and community, I would LOVE to steward the world's wealth on behalf of LOVE and peace versus endless fears and wars.

The 528LOVERevolution proclaims freedom from ignorance and genocidal slavery administered by the Illuminati, their abuse of wealth, and centuries of demoralizing degenerating petrochemical-pharmaceutical poisoning of *We The People* and our planet.

Aside from this, you do not even see coverage of the above information on network television or Hollywood films. The revelations in this book, and subsequent products and promotions, have come exclusively through independent researchers and entrepreneurs in the grass roots. And indeed they should for the sake of *We The People*.

With the promise of freedom, I encourage everyone to consider creative ways of transmitting sounds, developing products and services that integrate 528 hydrosonics.

Investments in 528 research and developments are now advancing many scientific fields, including biophysics and energy medicine.

Here are some great examples:

1) OxySilver™ is a double superconductor of Water and silver resonating with 528 that is capable of terminating people's reliance on BigPharma, toxic antibiotics, and deadly vaccines. The 528 "prayer power" in OxySilver merges theology with science-based healing technology;

2) 528 resonating jewelry is now available: attractive bracelets, rings, pins, and pendants that generate 528 energy for healing;

3) 528Fashions.com is evolving to provide attractive clothing that lifts your spirits and promotes healing by balancing your energy fields;

4) 528 musical instruments are in production and will help spread the good vibrations; and

5) 528Radio.com to provide an alternative to the toxic music you now receive over standard AM and FM stations.

Consider the fact that as these industries expand, so will the waves of LOVE/528 radiate out to touch the hearts of billions of people worldwide.

What if millions of people donated their transposed music into 528 on i528tunes.com?

"Kick" the old violent world goodbye. The signal of LOVE shall surely grow!

Synthesizer Retuning to the Perfect Circle of Sound™

Implications for BioEnergetic Healing and Chakra Balancing

By

Michael Walton and

Leonard G. Horowitz

Abstract

In this preliminary study, a synthesizer was retuned to the "Perfect Circle of Sound™" (PCoS) in advance of investigations measuring neuro-physiologic responses in humans to varying frequencies of sound. 528Hz—a central wave form in the original Solfeggio musical scale—was used to begin construction of an octave determined to most reasonably approximate a standard melodious scale. Among the PCoS notes only 417Hz and 741Hz frequencies required exclusion due to lacking *melody* within the scale. This study evidences standard tuning in "A" = 440Hz frequency includes the 741Hz F# frequency in the Solfeggio; bioenergetically degrading to the chakra system as a whole, below the throat energy center. The chance this precise association between the ancient and modern scales might have happened by chance, versus by sinister imposition, is discussed.

Introduction

Suppose you awakened one morning to find everything you previously viewed as up was down, and needed to relearn to walk on a floor you previously knew was the ceiling? The task would be daunting, yet compelling.

In 1998, authors Horowitz and Puleo advanced a set of musical frequencies now confirmed to be the original Solfeggio scale and fundamental to Pi, Phi, the Fibonacci series, sacred geometry, cosmology, and spiritual metaphysics.(1,2)

From this work Horowitz suggested standard musical tuning in "A" = 440Hz subjects listeners to chronic agitation, bio-electric degeneration, and may inhibit psychosocial maturation and spiritual evolution.(3)

Alternatively, 528Hz frequency identified as the "MI" or "MIracle" note in the ancient scale, together with the 639Hz "FA" or "FAmily" tone, form the heart of the original Solfeggio.(1) As central to the "musical-mathematical matrix" fundamental to universal design,(4) these frequencies may play a vital role in balancing and harmonizing bioenergy fields and chakra (vortex energy) systems impacting human health and psychosocial behavior.

Here we advance a theory that logically discerns 528Hz frequency is the scale with which chakra tuning and wholistic healing is best administered. This theory posits all architecture is based on solid foundations. As 528Hz frequency is central to Pi, Phi, the Fibonacci series, sacred geometry, the electromagnetic sound and light spectrums, and the heart of the musical mathematical matrix of creation(2) then bioenergetic (or "biospiritual") therapies for wholistic healing would best begin using this foundational frequency.

Background

Definitions are required for intelligently discerning this potentially evolutionary concept in wholistic healing and chakra tuning by hydrosonic stimulation. The following terms are thus defined: scale, frequency, tone, pitch and resonance.

Scale is defined in music as "an ascending or descending collection of pitches proceeding by a specified scheme of intervals." In Western music the diatonic octave scale was used first and includes the pitches or notes, A, B, C, D, E, F, G, A; or C, D, E, F, G, A, B, C. (Notice the 1st and 8th notes are the same within the octave, and are one octave higher or lower in pitch. So there are really only 7 unique primary notes in each octave.

Frequency is defined in acoustic science as "the number of times that a periodic function repeats the same sequence of values during a unit variation of the independent variable." In other words, using the Western World's "standard tuning" of "A"=440Hz, and the "C" scale beginning with the "C" note, the "A" pitch occurs once in this octive, and the "C" pitch occurs twice in this octave.

Additionally, a frequency is defined in music and electronics as "the number of repetitions of a periodic process in a unit of time; . . . the number of complete oscillations per second of energy (as sound or electromagnetic radiation) in the form of waves."

A tone is defined as "a vocal or musical sound, its quality; or an intonation, pitch, modulation, etc. of the voice that expresses a particular meaning or feeling . . . ."

Pitch is defined in music as "the musical frequency of vibration, rate of vibration, or a tone; . . . Standards of pitch include: concert, classic, high, low, international, French, Stuttgart, philharmonic, philosophical. . . ."

Remember that all three pitches, "C1," "A" and "C2," were in the A = 440Hz scale, even though you might think they could not be because they sound different. So the pitch is the "unit of variation of the independent variable" in every scale of music.

Previous discoveries compel us to experiment with C=528, wherein, ideally, the octave of pitches—all the notes in the scale of C=528Hz—are all in C=528Hz. (This is difficult to grasp for most people, because the notes (*pitches*) sound different yet are of the same frequency *scale*.)

Yet, this is practically unrealistic, considering such increased tension on strings, using 528Hz rather than 440Hz tuning, would break the neck or strings of most instruments.

Alternatively, Walton determined that tuning up to A=444Hz includes the pitch "C5=528Hz." He thus provides a practical tuning with which music can be made in the key of "C," vibrating 528Hz for experimental purposes affecting the chakra system.

To summarize this important point, in all tunings, the notes are variations of pitch within each scale that, like each scale, are characterized by a unique frequency of vibration, commonly measured in cycles per second, or Hertz frequencies. And even though each pitch within each scale and octave vibrates and sounds differently, each pitch vibrates in harmonic resonance with the particular tuning used, such as "A=440Hz," wherein F# is 741Hz, versus "A=444Hz" that sets C5 at 528Hz.

Resonance is defined in acoustics as "the intensification and prolongation of sound, especially of a musical tone, produced by sympathetic vibration." And in physics the definition of resonance is "the increase in amplitude of oscillation of an electric or mechanical system exposed to a periodic force whose frequency is equal or very close to the natural undamped frequency of the system."

This definition of resonance is important in the physics of healing, and especially in this paper's theory that sound therapies best incorporate the original Solfeggio vibrations, featuring "C = 528Hz." The reason for this is reiterated: 528Hz has been proven to be the heart of the rainbow, or electromagnetic light spectrum.

It is believed to be the heart of the full sound spectrum as well when inaudable frequencies are included in the analysis.

In other words, 528 is the heart of the universe, or musical-mathematical matrix of the cosmos. This is why there are precisely 5280 feet in a mile, and 528 is the most important variable in geometry and physics.

It is potentially beneficial to enable the human being to vibrate in sync with the universe. Thus, this 528Hz central frequency is potentially beneficial, as is building therapeutic systems or protocols based on C = 528Hz frequency. Theoretically, the 528 frequency is most likely to cause an increase in amplitude of oscillation of charkas, or spinning bioenergy vortices, within the human body exposed to these waveforms, since this frequency is very close to the natural undamped frequency of the energetic [universal] system.

Methods and Materials

In order to "micro-tune" a Korg Oasys synthesizer, the Perfect Circle of Sound™ Tuning Fork Set (HealthyWorldStore. com) manufactured to generate the precise frequencies of the original Solfeggio musical scale, plus three additional tones required to complete the "Circle" was used.(14)

Each fork was repeatedly struck to determine its near precise frequency and pitch (or tone). Tones were measured initially using a standard Korg chromatic tuner. These tuners maintain an adjustable range of 426-451Hz frequency. Later, more precise frequencies were determined using the "Master Tuning" display of the synthesizer.

The table below lists the Korg's readings for each of the nine PCoS frequencies.

Using the conversions in Table 1, the Korg Oasys was re-tuned one key at a time beginning with the middle "C" using the 528Hz equivalent in standard tuning (i.e., Walton observed and used A=443.06Hz; A=444 is generally suggested). Since pianos are tuned beginning with middle "C" a new 528Hz scale was built with subsequent pitches selected among the PCoS frequencies mimicking the tonal quality of a "normal" octave: C, D, E, F, G, A, B, C. From this, it was determined that 417Hz and 741Hz did not fit the scale or sound harmonic to the sequence.

Next, to determine if the PCoS scale correlated with previously advanced frequencies associated with the chakra system, Walton arranged the set of 7 pitches, beginning with C = 528, in ascending order as per the 7 main charkas as shown in Figure 19. The Hertz frequency equivalents this time were derived by dividing each PCoS frequency listed by 2 as needed to enter the range of frequencies published by previous authors to correspond to each chakra and chakra color. For example, the base chakra vibrates at 256Hz according to Hero.(5) One octave down is determined by dividing that 256 by 2; which equals 128 Hertz that falls in the "C" range of frequencies. By taking 528Hz and dividing it by 2 twice yielded 264Hz and132 Hz, respectively. From this analysis Walton established the right hand column of frequencies in Figure 19.

Results

The Solfeggio scale notes "RE" at 417Hz and "SO" at 741Hz were not melodious enough to be suitable for selection in a scale based on "C" set at 528Hz.

See Table 9 for complete results.

Discussion

A Google search of "heart chakra frequencies for therapy" returns nearly a quarter million links to myriad articles and inventions claiming various frequencies are best suited for healing applications. How is anyone able to make such claims or discern anything reliably?

This thesis may help. According to Horowitz, human beings are fundamentally digital bioholographic crystallizations of frequency vibrations rendered hydrosonically and metaphysically.(7) The authors suggest two main factors determine efficacy of acoustic therapy systems including chakra-based tuning systems: 1) the heart-felt loving intent of the therapist as well as the patient. This relates to investigations of prayer associated with beneficial outcomes best explained by theories in quantum physics, creative consciousness, and creationistic metaphysics;(6) and 2) the actual frequencies used.

Regarding the frequencies for chakra tuning, Walton's experimental protocol used the PCoS featuring a central "harmonic triad" of 528Hz, 852Hz and 285Hz. The base chakra was tuned to 132Hz, (i.e., middle C—two octaves below 528Hz.) Both 132Hz and 128Hz were identified by Barbara Hero as root chakra-resonating frequencies observed to elicit effective neuro-muscular therapy.(5)

We propose an attenuation differential between reception and transmission of frequencies is expected since incoming energy in frequencies would be slowed as the acoustic waves move through body structures such as proteins. So "C" 132Hz going in could reasonably be "C" 128Hz exiting the body.

This area of research and development is in its infancy, and there are many questions to be answered such as from whence cometh A = 440Hz?

The American Federation of Musicians (AFM) is credited for standardizing A=440 in 1917, but it was "not universally accepted until after 1920," according to Lehman and 1939 in England according to Cavanaugh.(8)

Among the most interesting and controversial questions raised by the results of this pilot study is whether or not "A" set at 440Hz was a sinister imposition by the AFM on behalf of special interests. Walton discovered that the tone "F#" in the 741Hz Solfeggio scale is identical to "A" in standard 440Hz tuning.

This finding is especially odd and incriminating since the interval between 528Hz and 741Hz in musicology is known as the "Devil's interval" because of its dissonant quality (i.e., severe disharmony). The probability that this occurred by chance is too remote to conclude anything other then those advancing "A = 440" must have known about the original Solfeggio and the "Devil's Interval" peak frequency 741.

After all, these scales are foundational to western music. Major and minor scales derive from medieval and Renaissance periods when two of seven modes formed by diatonic scales began on "each of the seven notes of the octave; . . . By the start of the Baroque period, the notion of musical key was established—based on a central triad rather than a central tone. Major and minor scales came to dominate until at least the start of the 20th century, partly because their intervallic patterns are suited to the reinforcement of a central triad."(9)

Appendix

During the early twentieth century, the Rockefeller Foundation's funding of the arts and sciences, including the most influential organizations and institutions in America, played formative roles in medicine and modern music. For instance, this research and paper would not be possible were it not for windows software by Microsoft's Bill Gates, whose grandfather, Frederick Gates, was John D. Rockefeller's chief business and philanthropic advisor during the formative years of the AFM. This was when John D. Rockefeller began funding and influencing the arts while monopolizing medicine.

Advancing a pseudo-scientific survey called the Flexner Report, these wealthiest industrialists directed the U.S. Congress to condemn natural healers including naturopaths, chiropractors, and acupuncturists. Thereafter, medicine's cultural infusion, monopolization, and profitable pharmaceutical intoxication of populations was secured by the Rockefeller family with substantial direction by globalists Dr. Frederick Gates and John Mott, both evangelic Freemasons.(10-12)

Much has been written about the insidious connections between the financial world's cryptocracy and Freemasonry in which glaring examples of secreted knowledge involving sacred geometry and musical-mathematics adorn regalia and even American currency. A recent analysis by mathematician Showell presents proof the 528Hz frequency uniquely enables the sacred geometry of pyramid cosmology and Freemasonry as shown in Figure 10.

Summary & Conclusions

A pilot investigation was undertaken to establish a protocol for acoustic therapy engaging "chakra balancing." 528Hz frequency was reasoned to represent the "C" note in the "octave" beginning at the root chakra.

While determining a harmonic octave, the Solfeggio frequencies 417 and 741 were found not to be melodic, and unfavorable for this experimental scale. 741Hz frequency, most suspiciously, was measured to be the F# equivalent in the A=440Hz—standard tuning.

It appears certain this institutionalized tuning favoring 741Hz was done with knowledge about the "Devil's tone" aversive impact on bioacoustics involved in natural healing and homeostasis.

Additional research in this field is encouraged.

References

) Horowitz LG and Puleo J. *Healing Codes for the Biological Apocalypse.* Tetrahedron Publishing Group, 1998.

2) Showell V. Ancient Egyptian pyramid Pi and Solfeggio synchronicities. In: Pi, Phi and 528—Proof that 528Hz is Central to Spiritual Freedom: Transformational Math and Music for LIVE H2O. Doc. 8; http://www. love528.com Tetrahedron Publishing Group, 2009.

3) Showell V. Hypercube Tesseract 261 Ancient Square Root Two with Egyptian and Mayan Fourth Dimension Cosmology Involving 528. In: Pi, Phi and 528—Proof that 528Hz is Central to Spiritual Freedom: Transformational Math and Music for LIVE H_2O. Doc. 8; http://www. love528.com Tetrahedron Publishing Group, 2009.

4) Horowitz LG. *DNA: Pirates of the Sacred Spiral.* Sandpoint, ID: Tetrahedron Publishing Group, 2004.

5) Hero B. Chakra energy centers of our bodies. In: Color Energies and Healing the Color Rays of Creation. Copyright, 1996. See: http://www. greatdreams.com/hertz.htm.

6) Science of The Heart: Exploring the Role of the Heart in Human Performance. An Overview of Research Conducted by the Institute of HeartMath. (See: http://www.heartmath.org/research/science-of-the-heart-music-research.html.) Mixed results from studies of prayer are acknowledged. The largest study by Benson et al in New England simply proves, according to Horowitz, that people who place their faith in open heart surgery as opposed to natural risk reduction and Divine intervention are biased sufficiently to undermine such studies reliability.

7) Horowitz LG. Hydrosonically engineering freedom from infectious diseases. American Academy of Anti-Aging Medicine International Congress. Las Vegas, NV, Dec. 12, 2008. See also: *The LOVE CODE Seminar: Musical Healing Celebration*, 2008, a DVD production based on the book *LOVE The Real da Vinci CODE.* Tetrahedron Publishing Group, 2007.

8) Lehman EV. Harmony—Symphony Orchestra Organizations: Development of the Literature Since 1960. Evanston, IL: Symphony Orchestra Institute, 1995.

9) Wikipedia. Diatonic scale. See: http://www.answers.com/topic/diatonic-scale-2

The Book of 528

10) The Rockefeller Foundation. Philanthropy and the Rockefeller Legacy: A Short History. Excerpted from the Philanthropy News Digest. Nov. 8, 2006.

11) Horowitz LG. *Death in the Air: Globalism, Terrorism & Toxic Warfare.* Sandpoint, ID: Tetrahedron Publishing Group, June, 2001.

12) Dillen V. The Wycliffe Bible Translators, John Mot & Rockefeller Connections. January 22, 2003. Online independent Christian research and apologetics ministry at SeekGod.ca

13) Cavanagh L. A brief history of the establishment of international standard pitch A=440 Hertz. Pdf file is available for a free download. See reference here: http://en.Wikipedia.org/wiki/Concert_pitch

14) Healthy World Distributing, LLC, at 1-888-508-4787, and HealthyWorldStore.com, can be contacted for tuning forks.

Commentary on Showell's
and Walton's Findings

G iven the aforementioned revelations regarding 528, including the precise musical mathematics central to secret-society metaphysics and sacred geometrics, weighty evidence suggests malfeasance in the establishment of "A" 440 standard tuning.

Surely 528 would have been a more harmonious option for standard tuning and "phase-locking" with nature. From what we now know, the creative mathematics and physics compels retuning to A=444Hz since C(5) at 528Hz is the equivalent of A=444Hz; and only 4 Hertz higher than A=440Hz. Plus, the utility of A=444Hz was best expressed by Llewelyn S. Lloyd, (*Journal of the Royal Society of Arts,* 16 Dec., 1949; 80-81.) during his published protest against the British Standards Institute's choice of A=440Hz for standard orchestral tuning. (See discussion in Chapter 4.)

According to Walton's protocol, when tuning chakras to a scale beginning with "C" = 528Hz, the F# pitch plays between the heart and throat charkas as shown in Figure 19. So if there was a place in music to energetically sever the superhuman (intuitive) heart from the human head it would be here. This is additional justification for rejecting A=440Hz tuning.

Furthermore, previous investigators attribute human "will function," including strength of will, to this energy center called the "throat chakra." Vocalizing one's feelings and needs assertively, not passively or aggressively, is important for psychosocial health and well being. It is reasonable to theorize A=440Hz standard tuning destabilizes the higher heart and throat energy centers. This would be expected to produce significant sociocultural stress.

Such musically institutionalized stress was willfully chosen, as evidenced by the fact that 741Hz, the "SO" and F# note in the PCoS, expresses exclusively in the to "A" = 440Hz standard tuning.

The 417Hz, 741Hz, and 174Hz, together, comprise a "central triad" within the PCoS. Curiously, the 417 and 741 notes are the only two tones disharmonious to Walton's healing scale, beginning with "C" as 528Hz as depicted in Figure 19.

These two exclusions—"RE" (417) and "SO" (741)—in the original Solfeggio, *Webster's Dictionary* defines as "REsonance" and "SOlve the problem or pollution." So the opportunity to RE-SOLVE humanity's main problems and pollutions may come from examining and integrating this knowledge in heart chakra balancing, and musical metaphysics featuring 528 versus 741.

When "A" 440Hz tuning was institutionalized throughout the Western World, since music is so popular and culturally important, there is a high probability this policy caused widespread distress through the imposition of a scale dissonant to native cultures, traditional tunings (including 432Hz) and the central heart frequency expressing LOVE vibrationally. Taxing human heart energy, and will-function, populations exposed to Western music were stimulated into high levels of stress. Following general acceptance of the tuning, dysfunction and degeneration resulted.

Therefore, this "music of the night," albeit energetically arousing to the head region versus the heart region of the body, may be a main reason civilization is so stressed, and disenchanted by the materialistic paradigm.

There is a dire need for more research and development in this field of musical mathematics applicable to therapeutics, environmental science, economics, and geopolitics. Key among these are double-blind studies comparing the affects of different frequencies of sounds and colors on biology, physiologic parameters, and other objective measures.

This preliminary investigation examined the 528Hz vibration fundamental to the primary nine note frequency matrix of matter and energy. The investigators sought to create a melodious scale beginning with "C" in 528Hz that assigned Solfeggio frequencies to a Korg Oasys synthesizer keyboard. The probability that this scale may be useful in clinical applications for healing and chakra tuning demands further study.

Musicians' 528 Discussion

Musicians worldwide have been inquiring about 528, and wondering about playing in the key of C(5)=528 when instruments are tuned to A=444Hz. This fascinating discussion has been hosted by volunteer, Scott Nash, who kindly created a blog in support of *LIVE H₂O—Concert for the Living Water*. (See: http://www.tallzebra.com). [The authors' contributions have been edited slightly for clarity.]

Why 528Hz is "Sacred"

AR Hermes: I can understand mathematically the numbers of the "Perfect Circle of Sound™," how each of the nine numbers relate, and other fascinating relationships the numbers have with each other.

But how do the numbers, on paper, then translate to being sacred frequencies?

Dr. Horowitz: Sacred geometry is based on the mathematics of a circle. Take a circle. How many degrees are in it? 360. Why is this sacred geometry? Mathematically, it adds to a 9—Completion.

Sixty seconds in a minute. Twenty four hours in a day. It's always 3s, 6s, and 9s. Sacred.

Each of the Solfeggio frequencies are likewise, 3s, 6s or 9s. The 528Hz frequency is fundamental to the geometry of the circle; it gives rise to the star tetrahedron. Pi, Phi, Fibonacci series, the speed of light, the Laws of Physics. Need more?

AR Hermes: Hertz is just a man-made invention to describe and divide sound vibrations, like *time* is used to describe and divide the movement of the stars and planets. How do the numbers correlate to sound-vibrations as expressed in Hertz? More importantly, where is 528Hz and the rest of the circle of sound found in nature and/or the universe, where it can be measured?

Dr. Horowitz: Read Vic Showell's analytical papers posted at www.love528.com under "Pi, Phi and 528"; and then read HYDROSONICS Journal online at www.hydrosonics.org.

Also, look at a blade of grass, or most of the botanical world. 528Hz can be seen and "measured" in the green-yellow color transmitted to your eye.

AR Hermes: I could draw a circle with 8 points and make 8 numbers that use values 1-8, then apply that to the corresponding Hertz tones if I chose to. That wouldn't make the frequencies special just because something interesting was happening on paper, right?

Dr. Horowitz: Right. God works with 9s as completion. You are now in your rational (egoic) left brain. If your left brain wants to try 8, go ahead. You will be one shy of complete. You won't get a Perfect Circle of Sound™.

Why do you think I spent the time and money trademarking this. It is *incredibly special*. There is only one in the universe. It is "God's fingerprint on everything," as math genius Marko Rodin says. God works wholistically, circularly, with His heart-mind. That is what LIVE H$_2$O celebrated—getting this precious knowledge to humanity to save lives and our environment.

AR Hermes: I am asking with an open heart and open mind. This is solely out of interest in the 528 research. . .

In my studies of Indian classical music, it's not about using one tone, or a fixed set of tones to bring the listener/musician to awaken in the Present. It is about utilizing the appropriate raga, based on the time of day and time of year. A raga consists of a selection of notes out of the 12 major notes,

Dr. Horowitz: Notice again this is a 3.

AR Hermes: And there are also special rules to follow when transitioning from note to note depending on the raga. When you match the raga correctly to the Present, it's like finding the resonate frequency. It then makes it easier to transmute cosmic energy and healing in that moment, a moment being described by several frequencies, not just one or nine.

Dr. Horowitz: In essence, you are describing musically intoxicating Divine harmony and synchrony. Nothing missing, nothing broken in the Kingdom of Heaven. It is the Holy Spirit flow, you call "several frequencies," that creates healing through this "cosmic energy" zone. Really, it is very simple.

The egoic "dumbed down" mind has trouble grasping such simple principles because of millennia of fear-based indoctrinations and egoic programming. This is why the entire CULTure of civilization must fall apart before it comes together as a greater whole--whole note, round, circle, 360 degrees. Get it?

AR Hermes: I can understand people wanting to tune their instruments to incorporate all 9 of the frequencies, especially if they are being called the original Solfeggio scale.

Dr. Horowitz: NO! Please do not do this. It will sound horrible. Not melodious.

Tune one string to one of the frequencies, and then the rest to that one. Start with "C(5)" in 528Hz or A=444Hz. Then tune all the strings to that scale and you will be tuned to that frequency, and you can simply play normally and melodiously.

AR Hermes: That was certainly what I initially thought was the whole idea.

Dr. Horowitz: No. Sorry if we did not communicate this more clearly. A lot of people have trouble getting their heads around this concept. There is a difference between the *scale frequency* and *pitch/notes within the scale*. The pitches/notes are C, D, E, F, G, A, B, . , , , add the sharps and flats, etc. Once tuned like I am telling you to do, say in 528Hz, all the pitches/notes are in the same 528Hz resonant frequency, or 528 scale.

AR Hermes: After getting all 9 of the tones tuned pretty close on an electronic keyboard, it was pretty obvious that there are some serious limitations in incorporating more than a couple of notes at a time, let alone making chords and such with several notes. Doing it by adjusting the Master tune to obtain only 528, or 417, etc. and keeping the normal relationship with the other notes the same definitely works, but then how are you using the full "circle of sound?

Dr. Horowitz: You are not using the full 'circle of sound' when you tune exclusively to 528Hz. I would not tune my instrument to all the Solfeggio scale frequencies to play music. It is okay to do this for experimental curiosity, but not playing music.

We did the same thing you did and drew the same conclusion. We are using the different tones and scales for different therapeutic objectives, such as Chakra tuning and meridian balancing.

Table 10.　Perfect Circle of Sound Conversions

Perfect Circle of Sound™	Korg Chromatic Tuner	Korg Oasys Tuning Adjustment
528 Hz = C	443Hz = C *	443.06Hz (C) or (+12 cents) *
285 Hz = D	427 Hz = D ___	427.37Hz (D) or (-50 cents) ___
639 Hz = E Flat	451Hz = E Flat	451.07Hz (E Flat) or (+43 cents)
174 Hz = F	437Hz = F	437.97Hz (F) or (-08 cents)
396 Hz = G	444 Hz = G	444.09Hz (G) or (+16 cents)
852 Hz = A	427 Hz = A	427.47Hz (A) or (-50 cents)
963 Hz = B	428 Hz = B	428.96Hz (B) or (-44 cents)
417 Hz = G#	443 Hz = G#	443.06Hz (G#) or (+12 cents)
741 Hz = F#	440 Hz = F#	440.00Hz (F#) or (+00 cents)

The Perfect Circle of Sound™ nine tones heralded by Horowitz, shown in the left hand column above, include the six original Solfeggio frequencies advanced by Puleo. 741Hz, the F# when using the A=440-Hz standard tuning promoted by the Rockefeller Foundation, is in dissonance to 528Hz [related to 528nm] associated with the structure and color of chlorophyll; that is, the greenish-yellow oxygenating energizing pigment celebrated most widely by the botanical world. The two tones together, F#=741 and C=528 is grossly dissonant and is called the "Devil's Tone" in musicology. Other researchers following Walton reported C=528 results from tuning to A=444Hz, not A=443.06, that is, the addition of 15 cents, not 12 cents as Walton initially reported from Hawaii using tuning forks at 1,000 feet above sea level. The higher altitude might have influenced the sound calibrations resulting in the discrepancy. Source: Michael Walton, SomaMagic.com.

Tuning Stringed Instruments to 528

To tune a guitar, or stringed instrument to the 528Hz LOVE frequency, simply to listen to the 528 pure tone generator that I provided online for free at LOVE528.com website. Click "play" to hear the pure tone of 528Hz. Then retune your "A" guitar string, at the third "C" fret, to the sound of 528 "C(5)" that you hear. Next, retune your other strings to this string as usual.

Clicking another link takes you to i528Tunes.com where you can transpose your music into 528Hz.

Synthesizer Retuning Instructions

If you wish to retune your synthesizer, there is a tutorial on YouTube that MIchael Walton, SomaMagic' sound engineer, and I produced. Please share this information with other musicians who may wish to promote health and healing with 528Hz.

Certain synthesizers can easily adjust to 528Hz or other frequencies of "The Perfect Circle of Sound™." Table 9 contains a chart showing the tuning adjustments for the Perfect Circle of Sound. These were determined by Walton, using tuning forks, Korg's chromatic tuner, and a Korg Oasys synthesizer.

Phil Polezoes, a keyboard player also researching the Solfeggio wrote about the Korg Oasys synthesizer, "In 'Search' type 'master tune' and add + 12 cents, or if the options is in Hertz type or select 443.06 Hz." When you do this, he reported, your keyboard tuning thereby includes 528 Hz frequency.

Other musicians have recommended setting the master tune option to A=444Hz.

Experiencing 528

G Head: I have found by tuning my nylon guitar as suggested, the guitar is just as much fun to play, but has a subtle energy resonance that is different.

I will do some recording with a few instruments tuned that way and find some gongs to fit. . . . My husband . . . is a musician/recording artist and we tuned his guitar to the 528hz frequency a few days ago. We both notice a deep resonance in our chests when he plays now. Pretty incredible discovery. . . .

He has recorded a couple of instrumentals in this frequency. We are very excited to see how this affects our audience!

Dr. Horowitz: That feeling in your chest when listening to 528 is common among spiritually sensitive audiophiles.

Every time I listen to music played in 528 I get a "breath release," much like a yawn, that instantly tells me the "relaxation response" has occurred. This happens whether or not I know the music is vibrating to 528 (A=444Hz) versus 741 (A=440Hz) or not. So "the placebo effect" is not what we are experiencing when we feel the difference.

This physiological "relaxation response" was studied many years ago by Harvard University professor, Herbert. Benson, who taught my post-doctoral behavioral medicine program.

Benson studied Tibetan monks during deep meditative states. He measured their metabolic functions and learned the "relaxation response" was a big part of spiritual practice, but also related to hormonal changes associated with health and hastened healing.

In musicology, the "relaxation response" is associated with "ecstatic listen" and a whole body tingling-sensation called "frisson."

These professional terms are best used to technically describe the slight euophoric feeling people get when listening to music performed in 528Hz, with 528 transposed music being less powerful, than live performances in 528 tuning. But both 528 options are far better than "standard tuning."

An Interesting 528/444 Experiment

To prove the power of certain frequencies to impact your physiology and experience, try this experiment, but only if you have access to a synthesizer with digital pitch adjustment capabilities.

This test was first done by Zion Estes, an avid acoustics and metaphysics investigator, who worked with Michael Walton in preparation for the LIVE H_2O Concert, 2009. They tuned to A= 88.8Hz, that they figured was harmonically related to A=444Hz (is nearly identical to C(5) at 528Hz). That is, they multiplied 444 by 2, and got 888. So they selected 88.8Hz for this tuning experiment.

Immediately when they began to play sequences in this frequency, it caused a profound spiraling audio experience for everyone listening. It seemed like the room was spinning. The sound seems to travel in a spiraling vortex around the room.

88.8 appears to generate an acoustic energy vortex. 88.0 did not generate this.

Victor Showell's Analysis of 88.8

Indeed.

528 / by 88 = 6—a finite number;

528 / by 88 .888888888 = 5.94—another finite number; but something different happens mathematically that theoretically relates to the sound suddenly seeming to travel in a spiraling vortex around the room. Divide . . .

528 / by 88.8 = 5.945 945 945 945 945 945 945 ————-----> to infinity The replicating sequence is 594.

In earlier analyses published on the Internet, I showed how 594 was tied to ancient Pi, which relates to the Fibonacci series of numbers, and explains the spiral nature of the universe.

This was just a thought that an infinite decimal sequence as a quotient (i.e., divisional result) between the numbers 528 and 88 .8 correlates with the sound seeming to travel, or actually traveling in a spiraling vortex around the room. The theory that this is an acoustic "portal" to an energy vortex might be considered a bit of a stretch, but mathematically it makes some sense.

One could also look at the decimal sequence alone. [Editor's note: The numbers suggest spiraling 9s.]

I developed a math derivation on 945, being the replicating number, or decimal sequence after the 5, when you divide 528 / by 88 .8 = 5 . 945 945 945 945 945 945 945. You see 945 replicating.

Previously, I determined that 944 was the value of the pyramid inch. This is very, very close to 945, and this finding reinforces the theory that the sacred geometry of the pyramid has a lot to do with the sound of cosmic energy, and its impact on biology.

Notes on 528 for Vocalists

528Hz is the third note, "MI" tone, of the original Solfeggio scale. It is credited for *MI*racles. Vocalists are best equipped to produce miracles, including miraculous healings.

First consider Jesus. He was credited for producing many miracles, for which he credited faith and LOVE for God, and demonstrated both most compassionately for humanity.

What made Jesus's heart connection to God so powerful?

Acknowledging repetition here, hearts generally resonate this pure tone, 528Hz, when you consider: 1) vortex math and the primary role 528 plays in universal construction, and space/time measurements; 2) the human heart chakra resonates the greenish-yellow color of 528; and 3) 528 seems to be at the heart of everything, such as the rainbow, the botanical world, and the primary energy transformer, chlorophyll. It is chlorophyll that feeds oxygen carrying 528 vibrating electrons to all of biology engaged in aerobic metabolism. Humans' hemoglobin is structured like chlorophyll. This iron-rich pigment is pumped via red blood cells through your heart, where it picks up the frequency vibration of your heart. This resonance energy connects your heart directly to God through this 528Hz clear-channel connection.

Remember since the sun's sound, too, has been measured to be fundamentally 528Hz, your blood oxygen carries electrons, vibrating with LOVE/528Hz frequency from the sun.

Breath is *extremely* important to vocalists. The "Hah," or Breath of Life, expressing joy in laughter, carries this 528/LOVE "prana" or Divine blessing of spiritual energy.

Vocalists training to harmonize best with others exercise singing the vowels, A, E. I, O, and U. Singing these vowels in sequence, repeatedly, over and over again, like in a "circle of sound," actually chants one of the names considered most Holy—"YahWay." Try this yourself.

Relating back to oxygen, the Hebrew Holy Name for God is spelled "Yod Hay Vov Hay"—meaning "to breathe is to exist," when literally translated to English.

Thus, LOVE, joy, faith, and bravery are heart-felt emotions carrying fundamentally the pure tone 528Hz energy. Amplified by your lungs and the oxygen in your breath, faith in your heart is automatically increased with every breath. This is why deep breathing helps best to reduce fear and stress.

This is also why top vocalists admit that they commonly sing from their hearts, in LOVE, to enhance their performing artistry.

Singing is, in fact, the art of communing with God through a "registered voice" that is phase-locking your heart with God's heart.

These important considerations should be addressed during voice training. Honoring this knowledge can help you develop your sweetest smoothest voice, vibrating vocal chords in the "key of LOVE," using the "breath of life."

Further evidencing this thesis, Jonathan Goldman determined that the 528Hz pure tone happens to be the natural frequency human voices makes when the sound "AH" is chanted, as is demonstrated in his online Temple of Sacred Sound. (Visit: www.templeofsacredsound.org/)

Many people conjecture that heart-felt loving intention empowers prayer, as does LOVE, which is considered the "Universal Healer." So sing with your heart's loving intention to have your voice heal people.

The greatest Divine communion possible in the process of channeling your vocal inspirations, musical compositions, and live performances, are optimally enabled by tuning to 528Hz.

For all these reasons, recording artists can have the greatest loving, joyful, and healing impact on audiences by tuning instruments and voices to 528Hz.

Jesus produced miracles with his lips because he knew, "the Kingdom of Heaven is near." The heart of this estate, 528/LOVE, is right here, right now, in your chest, awaiting your intention to produce miracles.

You do not need to go looking for LOVE when it is where you come from.

This is why, for "prosperity in all ways," including a fully-blessed professional voice, Jesus prescribed seeking this heavenly kingdom first and foremost through your heart filled with LOVE (in 528Hz). This quest for your inner voice of your heart always produces the best results.

Finally, be proud of your voice. When singing, the diaphragm and chest wall muscles control the air flow. Position your posture straight with chest and shoulders proudly proclaiming you are singing to God for the right reasons.

528 in Diplomacy is Forgiving

Anonymous: I am a music producer and I want to contribute and start making music more in tune with the universe.

I stumbled on information about the Nazis and that they wanted to change the ISO standard to 440 in 1939; at that time they failed, but I believe in 1955 the elite finally pushed for the new ISO standard.

I can understand the concept because I know now that everything in creation is energy with its vibrational frequency. All is coming from the true Divine Creator. The universe is one big orchestra. And every being has its own musical "chord" like a finger print.

Dr. Horowitz: The word "chord" is used in the word *accord*, meaning finding harmony between different persons, nations, or warring sides. All can be considered musical elements since everything sources from musical-mathematics.

Therefore, accords are best sought and exercised selecting concordant attitudes and harmonic postures generating generally "good vibrations" of LOVE and forgiveness in 528Hz.

Peace and LOVE through 528 is best sought and exercised during negotiations and reconciliations.

In other words, 528Hz music is probably the best vibration to listen to when sitting down to reach accords in politics, corporate negotiations, or your personal life.

444Hz, 528, and Jesus as the Astrological Sun

After learning that the musical note "C(5)" set at 528Hz translates to A=444Hz, Simon Zipata, another contributor, e-mailed, as follows:

S Zipata: I am not "religious," and have no "expertise" in this field. So please don't "shoot me down" for making an error. . . . Constructive criticism is welcomed.

Here are my notes:

444Hz raised an octave = 888 Hz.

Using the English Gematria, 444 = Jesus.

And curiously, using the Greek Gematria, 888 = Jesus

Now, Jesus is said to equal "The Son[/Sun]"

The biblical story of Jesus, in my (and many others) opinion, is a very clever metaphorical analogy of astronomical observance.

I'm not saying Jesus didn't exist, nor that he didn't heal people... Maybe he did, maybe he didn't....I remain open minded.

Jesus dying on a cross and resurrecting 3 days later is astrologically explained as follows:

Biblically, 3 Kings followed the "Star In the East," in order to find The Son (of God).

Jesus, born to the virgin Mary in Bethlehem . . . dies on a cross, resurrects 3 days later, and ascends into heaven;

Astrologically, the Star in the east is SIRIUS—the brightest star in the sky.

3 Kings are the brightest 3 stars in Orion's Belt. . . . Orion's belt was known to the ancients as "The Three Kings."

On the 24th of December, Sirius aligns with these 3 stars, and point to the location of the sunrise on Dec 25th. This is why the 3 Kings 'follow' the star in the east, to locate the *sunrise* (birth of the Sun).

The virgin Mary is the constellation VIRGO...Latin for virgin. The ancient glyph for Virgo is the altered "M." Hence, MARY, in other cultures is MYRRA, MAYA. . . . Virgo is also referred to as 'THE HOUSE OF BREAD;' thus, representation of Virgo is a virgin holding a sheath of wheat.

Likewise, BETHLEHEM literally translates to HOUSE OF BREAD...(the constellation)

This corresponds with August & September, the time of harvest.

From Summer solstice to winter solstice the days get shorter. From the northern hemisphere, the Sun appears to move south. Days are shorter and colder...symbolising (to the ancients) the process of death. . . . Death of The Sun.

Dec 22nd the sun is at it's lowest point. 22nd to 24th the sun stops moving south (for 3 days)... (winter solstice)

During this 3 day pause, the Sun resides in the vicinity of the SOUTHERN CROSS constellation.

On the 25th the sun moves 1 degree North...foreshadowing longer days, warmth and spring (symbolising LIFE).

So...the Sun...stops moving for 3 days under the southern cross constellation.

Only to be 'resurrected/born again' (moving North)...

And 'there you have it.' This is why you might say, "Jesus = THE SUN."

444 = THE SUN. 444 Hz on my guitar, using the Solfeggio, is E, or "Mi," as in "Do Re 'MI' Fa So La Ti Do." The Mi, some say, stands for "MIracle."

444 = Jesus = Miracles?......how fitting :-)

444 is a harmonic of 528 (universal frequency)..which is C

An octave starts with C..end with C.....Alpha and Omega?

444 (Jesus, The Sun, healing & miracles) resonates with 528 (Universal Energy, Alpha and Omega, 'GOD').

Thus, my interpretation that "You cannot reach God but through me," is like you cannot reach 528 but though 444.

John 4:44 provides more appropriate counsel: "And He (Jesus) said, 'A prophet is not honoured in his own country.'"

By the way 444 is also the number given to *John The Baptist*. Hence why I used this biblical reference....

Think about it , a prophet is not honoured in his own country, 1 John 4:44

What happened to the Solfeggio scale, to 528, to LOVE? . . . It was replaced. . . . It was not honoured.

Jesus (444 Hz?) was not honoured. God has not been honoured. . .

Finally, Jesus was betrayed by Judas, who was payed off by the church [controlled by the Illuminati]. (This could also be referencing The Vatican and/or the religion-controllers' New World Order.)

In this context, 444Hz was betrayed by the anti-christ that is related to "the mark of the beast, '666'".

Now try this experiment. Divide 444 by 666. It gives you .66666666, repeating decimal rational number. BUT if you then simply press the equal sign again, something very strange happens. You might get 0 .001001001001. . . .

You also get ."001" when you perform the same sequential operation on 528 / 666. [You first get 7927~ (to infinity), and then .001 when you press the equal sign again.]

This discussion suggests the Illuminai's use of this musical-mathematical hidden truth pertaining to 528, 444, religions, and corporate entities that use these newly discovered secret codes.

Dr. Horowitz: "MI6," as mentioned in my previous lectures and writings, stands for 528 and "MIracle 6," or Her Majesty's Secret Service, the "British Gestapo."

S Zipata: In other words, if you divide LOVE (528 or 444) by 666—the "mark of the beast"—you get into secret codes exposing the top of the Illuminati, through their most favored secret agent, "001."

Those who [control the music] control the minds of the people. The Nazi's advanced the International Standard of tuning precisely to create disharmony. With music and more, they have lead everyone away from the path of enlightenment.

I'm just speculating here, friends. I'm not calling this a concrete opinion...it is merely an idea that today I started looking into. I had weird dreams last night that I can't remember now. I meditated on the Jesus/Solfeggio connection last night before I went to sleep (listening to some 528 Hz relaxing music).

I woke up with the idea of doing a little digging. (I'm not claiming divine intervention here!)

I'd be VERY interested in hearing replies to this post. . . . It's the 1st time I've posted anything here or anywhere regarding the whole subject of Solfeggio (which I only recently found out about)...well, a week ago. . . .

I play the guitar for a living in Malawi (Africa). . . . I am from now on changing my tuning to A=444Hz.

I had a song I wrote in England a year prior. . . I can't sing very well on A=440. It's too high for me.

I knew 444 was Jesus in English Gematria....and I am a lover of 'coincidence'...

So I tried it....the song sounded great and I sang it (if I may say so myself) PERFECTLY. It resonated inside me. I had to sing a bit higher but somehow it worked wonders.

I also have a baby on the way (due November). I can't wait to bathe her/him in the glorious sounds of Solfeggio.

Anyone interested can contact me at: simonfgates@hotmail.com or "Simon Freddie Gates" on Facebook.

Check out this music festival....LAKE OF STARS MALAWI INTERNATIONAL MUSIC FESTIVAL. I sort of know the organizers, . . . and want to push for the inclusion of 444/528.. . . It's one of the fastest growing festivals in the world, on the beach of Africa's 3rd largest lake....Paradise! . . . WE NEED TO EXPAND this 528/H20 movement GLOBALLY :)

Another blogger replied in support, "The REAL return of the Christ is a mass Awakening—the Rapture—a spiritual uplift. This is the fulfillment of His ministry and LOVE mission."

Corrections and Miscellaneous 528 Support

Phill Polezoes: [Writing in the musician's 528 dialogue blog,] I'm new to all of this, but I have been into music, and how to help heal people and change lives through using it... 432 and 72 are tempos where 528 is frequency. So maybe the combination of both is the secret or at least worth exploring.

Dr. Horowitz: Indeed, combining the math of frequency and rhythm makes sense, given the revelations in this book.

Another blogger: I am an electronic music producer and I saw your video about the sacred frequencies and how to tune instruments into those frequencies with Michael Walton. I tried using Apple Logic, the sequencer that I use normally, to tune it with those frequencies.

I find few points in which I am not sure if I understood well your explanations.

1) to tune into 528 the C note (Do) it is necessary to master tune the keyboard at A=444Hz (+15%) and not as Michael Walton explaned in the video +12% or 443 that would give a C of 526.8 Hz

2) if you just master tune the keyboard either at +15% 444 Hz, or as Micheal said at +12% 443 Hz the other notes never will never fall into the other frequencies of the sacred circle.

3) to be able to use all frequencies of the sacred circle I tried to tune all the notes of the keyboard different:

F +5% = 174.1 Hz (174)
D +51% = 285.1 Hz (285)
G +18% = 396.1 Hz (396)
G# +7% = 417.1 Hz (417)
C +15% = 527.9 Hz (528)
D# +46% = 638.8 Hz (639)
F# + 3% = 741.1 Hz (741)
A - 56% = 852.1 Hz (852)
B - 44% = 962.9 Hz (963)

This allows you to use all the frequencies together when you are playing, but it is very complicated and only the Logic audio instruments will work.

I have an Access Virus TI Synthesizer, and only the master tune function is available and not the tuning of all the notes.

Did I do something wrong or missunderstood the instruction?

Dr. Horowitz: Well, you did the same thing wrong that Walton did when he started. And you appear to have corrected Michael Walton's synthesizer settings, so thanks. A=444Hz makes more sense than A=443.06. But the difference in test findings might have resulted from the fact that Walton used the

528 tuning fork struck at 1,000 feet above sea level, in a humid climate in Hawaii. That could have attenuated the sound signal, and caused the difference you are reporting.

The only problem is that you constructed the Perfect Circle of Sound scale that is quite interesting, like Walton did originally, but not melodic when played. We have been warning people about this. Again, the Perfect Circle of Sound is not melodic as a scale, yet evidence argues the nine tones are fundamental to universal construction as a musical-mathematical matrix.

In other words, God's music versus man's music may be melodically different. Like 528 and 741 do not sound well together, their dissonance is a part of nature. The choice is yours which one feels most comfortable to your ears, and heart.

Keep up the great work!

528 and the Speed of Light

Several bloggers deserve the world's thanks for revealing stunning relationships that had been missed by other researchers regarding the Solfeggio frequencies, and particularly 528. Raphael, Just Joolz, Tim Harada, and "Senior Member - Wiz Oz" posted a fascinating discussion delving deeply into the relationships 528 shares with the other Solfeggio numbers including "the complete 72 tone ordinal sequence" extrapolated from the Perfect Circle of Sound nine Solfeggio tones.

Figures 59 and 60 graph some of their findings viewed online at: http://forums.abrahadabra.com/showthread.php?2108-Sacred-Solfeggio-Frequencies/page34

Relevant to 528Hz, Figure 59 provides a diagram of the distances measured from the Earth to the Moon. Wiz Oz, writing from Australia, posted on 2-2-09:

"Note that the inscribed square is 31680 miles. I recognized that the figure was similar to the Solfa numbers. Here's the kicker: 528 x 60 = 31680. Bear in mind that 1 mile also = 5280ft. Then the 237600miles = 528 x 450.

"Light takes such a short time (0.000005 seconds, in fact) to travel one mile. To travel 31680miles, light takes 0.1584 seconds. Remember the previous post re: 417+528+639 =1584/3 = 528

"I'll repeat myself—I did not go looking for this," Oz concluded, "It found me and triggered something off intuitively. Here we now have direct geometric proof that the frequencies mentioned above have a relationship with our solar system

Fig. 59. Proof 528 is Instrumental to the Speed of Light

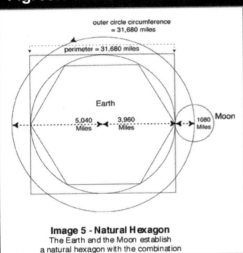

Image 5 - Natural Hexagon
The Earth and the Moon establish a natural hexagon with the combination

The Earth's mean diameter is 7,920 miles and its radius is 3,960 (scaled to Solfeggio "UT" 396). Moon diameter and radius is 2,160 and 1080 miles, respectively. The combined radii of the two bodies equals 5,040 miles.

A circle with radius of 5,040 has a circumference of 31,680 miles. "That length, 31,680 or 4 x 7920 miles, is equal to the perimeter of the square containing the circle of the earth."

Regarding 528 and the speed of light (scaled to Solfeggio "MI" 528), there are 5280 ft. per mile. Light travels 1 mile in 0.000005 seconds. To find how long it takes light to travel the "outer circle circumference" shown above as 31,680 miles, multiply 31680 x .000005 = .1584. Also, take Solfeggio 417+528+639 = 1584. Finally, consider that 528 is the mean number resulting from 1584/3 = 528. This proves 528 is definitively fundamental to: 1) the speed of light; 2) circles, squares, hexagons and other forms of sacred geometry; and 3) the universal constants pi, Phi, and the Fibonacci series. In other words, *without 528, the universe would not exist.*

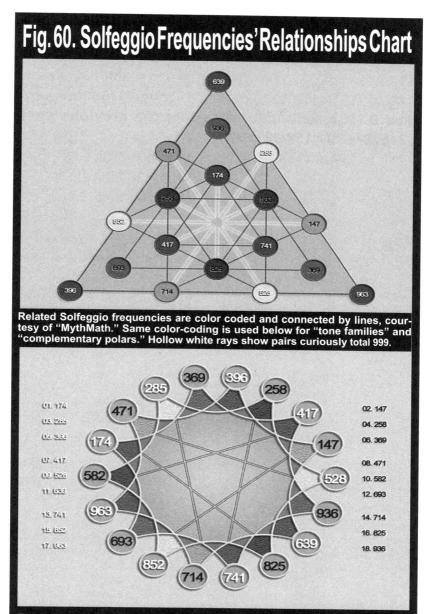

Fig. 60. Solfeggio Frequencies' Relationships Chart

Related Solfeggio frequencies are color coded and connected by lines, courtesy of "MythMath." Same color-coding is used below for "tone families" and "complementary polars." Hollow white rays show pairs curiously total 999.

01. 174
02. 147
03. 285
04. 258
05. 396
06. 369
07. 417
08. 471
09. 528
10. 582
11. 639
12. 693
13. 741
14. 714
15. 852
16. 825
17. 963
18. 936

The 3-tone 'families,' (i.e., "central triads") share colors. Complementary colors denoting polar-pairs, summing to 1110/2 = 555 = 15 = 6 (harmonic to 528/MIracle"6") are positioned diametrically opposite. Straight lines join pairs that sum to 999. Source: "MythMath" blogger (2-1-09), CLICK HERE for link to http://forums.abrahadabra.com.

i528Tunes.com: The World's First Music Transposition Service Spreading "528/LOVE"

The i528Tunes.com website exclusively transposes your CDs, mp3, aac, and mp4 files, into 528Hz frequency recordings in downloadable versions. (This site does not take orders for hardcopy CDs.)

The mission of i528Tunes.com is to EVOLve and heal our planet musically. 528Hz is revolutionizing the music industry and restoring humanity's original spirituality by playing and broadcasting the principle primordial frequency of creation "528/LOVE." By listening, performing, and recording in the "Key of LOVE" (528Hz), you too can engage this awesome transformation. And every time you do, it not only helps you, but like waves radiating out from a pebble thrown into a pond, your 528 musical energy reaches the farthest hearts.

Developing a Deeper Understanding

This book reveals why standard tuning (A=440Hz) is an unhealthy, spiritually-degrading, socially-repressive imposition.

Alternatively, 528Hz, the MIracle frequency" ("MI" of the original Solfeggio musical scale) is most preferred by nature and masterful musicians, especially for healing and the exponentially accelerating Spiritual Renaissance.

In this 528LOVERevolution, i528Tunes.com proudly serves three major functions, and operates exclusively by suggested donations:

1) TRANSPOSES your digital music files recorded in 440Hz into 528Hz;

2) DOWNLOADS music from our 528LOVE MUSIC LIBRARY by clicking the *genres* tab, and selecting your preferred folder(s), album(s) or track(s); and

3) UPLOADS music already recorded (or transposed) in A=444Hz or C=528Hz, to the LOVE528 MUSIC LIBRARY. This serves recording artists and their agents only, who receive 60% royalties on all donations made for their work(s). Artists (or their agents) "create albums" and select the appropriate *genres* folder into which their upload(s) go.

Information For Users

Many people prefer 528Hz tuning, saying that it makes music more natural and pleasant. On this website, you can compare the two mentioned ways to tune instruments.

The LOVE528 MUSIC LIBRARY grows by your donations of transposed music, and by registered artists' submissions. By using this music transposition website, users agree to donate their transposed music to the LOVE528 MUSIC LIBRARY to be shared with others by donation. You can download single tracks or albums.

Information For Artists

The best, most powerful, spiritually uplifting, and healing way to record music is tuned to (C5) 528Hz (A=444Hz) that is the heart of light and LOVE. If you are an artist performing in 528Hz or having an idea to convert your tunes to 528Hz – you are welcome to work with i528Tunes.com!

Registration as a musician is completely free!

About the author

Dr. Leonard G. Horowitz is an internationally known authority in the overlapping fields of public health, behavioral science, emerging diseases, and natural healing. Dr. Horowitz received his doctorate from Tufts University School of Dental Medicine in 1977. There, as a student and faculty member, he taught general and dental histology, and graduated with honors and a fellowship award in behavioral science at the  University of Rochester. He later earned a Master of Public Health degree from Harvard University focused on media persuasion technologies, and a Master of Arts degree in health education/counseling psychology from Beacon College, all before joining the research faculty at Harvard School of Dental Medicine to study psychosocial factors in oral health and disease prevention. For more than a quarter century he has directed the nonprofit educational corporation that evolved into Tetrahedron, LLC (http://www.tetrahedron.org).

Dr. Horowitz's earlier books include the American best-seller *Emerging Viruses: AIDS & Ebola—Nature, Accident or Intentional?* Now considered a medical classic, this publication earned Dr. Horowitz the "Author of the Year Award" from the World Natural Health Organization in 1999, the same year he released *Healing Codes for the Biological Apocalypse* which permanently expanded the field of musicology.

Dr. Horowitz's second best-seller was *Healing Celebra-*

tions: Miraculous Recoveries Through Ancient Scripture, Natural Medicine and Modern Science (2000). It provides practical information and advice for self healing.

In June, 2001, three months before the terrorist attacks of 9/11, Dr. Horowitz released the prophetically-titled critically-acclaimed book, *Death in the Air: Globalism, Terrorism and Toxic Warfare*. This book summarized the leading global industrialists' efforts to enslave humanity through toxicity and petrochemical/pharmaceutical malfeasance.

His 2004 book, *DNA: Pirates of the Sacred Spiral,* reviewed the science of electrogenetics that speaks to humanity's fundamental spirituality.

In 2006, Dr. Horowitz wrote another monumental book, *LOVE: The Real da Vinci CODE,* that presented the real da Vinci Code based on a decryption of the "Vitruvian Wo/Man" drawing. The circle in that most famous da Vinci image is The Perfect Circle of Sound™, according to Horowitz's research.

Dr. Horowitz is also an award-winning film-maker for having produced *PharmaWhores: The Showtime Sting of Penn & Teller*, and *In Lies We Trust: The CIA, Hollywood & Bioterrorism*, and *The LOVE CODE* DVD.

Aside from an active speaking schedule, Dr. Horowitz oversees the Creator's Rainbow Spa in "The Kingdom of Heaven" on the Big Island of Hawaii, where one of the world's most powerful natural healing resources—volcanically-heated steam—is being used for healing and helping to explain Divinity to humanity.

Resources

For more information about Dr. Horowitz visit his official website at http://www.drlenhorowitz.com.

Other Dr. Horowitz affiliated websites:

http://www.528Revolution.com
http://www.RevolutionTelevision.com
http://www.CureShoppe.com
http://www.Irife.net
http://www.HealthyWorldStore.com
http://www.HealthyWorldAffiliates.com
http://www.HealthyWorldSolutions.com
http://www.HealingCelebrations.com
http://www.MedicalVeritas.org
http://www.Tetrahedron.org
http://www.528Records.com
http://www.528Radio.com
http://www.i528Tunes.com
http://www.TheWaterResonator.com
http://www.OxySilver.com
http://www.LiquidDentist.net

Notes

Notes

Notes

Notes